Adventure Travel

Adventure
Travel

THRILLING GETAWAYS
FOR THE SPIRITED TRAVELER

FODOR'S TRAVEL PUBLICATIONS
New York • Toronto • London • Sydney • Auckland

www.fodors.com

Contents

KEY TO THIS BOOK

Adventure briefing Essential facts to help you get started.

Adventure calling A selection of the best destinations worldwide for each adventure activity. Where appropriate, the destinations have been given a difficulty rating (∅ – ∅∅∅). An explanantion of these ratings can be found on the relevant pages.

Adventure rating Each adventure activity is graded from ∅ to ∅∅∅∅∅ on five criteria – how daring it is, how eco-friendly, how expensive, how much expertise is required and how fit you need to be.

A taste of adventure First-hand account of an actual adventure.

EcoFile Tips on how to make your adventure more environmentally and culturally responsible.

Essential gear Must-pack items for each adventure.

Ethical travel dilemma Case study of a responsible travel issue.

FactFile Travel briefing for each 'A taste of adventure' feature.

Feature Information on related topics, from photography to space travel.

A world of adventure

Do something different. Escape the everyday. That's the essence of adventure travel – whether you set your sights on the summit of Everest or spend an hour or two wafting about in a hot-air balloon.

Once the exclusive realm of scientists, explorers or the seriously wealthy, adventure travel is now within reach of anyone. From rafting the rollercoaster rapids below Victoria Falls to husky sledding across the Greenland ice cap, never before have so many destinations and activities been available. In just four or five decades, the world has been transformed into a giant adventure playground. Not only has modern air travel shrunk the planet, but tour operators have developed the knowledge and expertise to take you to the back of beyond – and back again.

That's not to say, of course, that there aren't still plenty of 'prizes' for those with a more independent and pioneering spirit. Extreme surfers continue their quest for the elusive and mighty '100ft wave'; climbers challenge the world's most demanding rock faces freestyle (without ropes or safety equipment); kayakers and rafters look to the Congo and other rivers yet to be paddled from source to mouth, while a new

Top 15 adventure heroes

1. **Sir David Attenborough** (1926–present) Inspired millions to marvel at Earth.
2. **Ibn Battuta** (1304–68) Amazingly widely travelled Muslim geographer.
3. **Christopher Columbus** (1451–1506) Opened Europe's way to the Americas.
4. **Captain James Cook** (1728–79) Heroic explorer, navigator and surveyor.
5. **Charles Darwin** (1809–82) Undoubtedly the greatest wildlife explorer ever.
6. **Sir Ranulph Fiennes** (1944–present) Adventurer extraordinaire.
7. **Steve Fossett** (1944–2007) Long-distance solo balloonist and sailor.
8. **Yuri Gagarin** (1934–68) First man in space, blasting off on 12 April 1961.
9. **Sir Edmund Hillary** (1919–2008) Mountaineer, explorer and humanitarian.
10. **David Livingstone** (1813–73) Legendary missionary and explorer.
11. **Dame Ellen MacArthur** (1976–present) Solo long-distance yachtswoman.
12. **Fridtjof Nansen** (1861–1930) Pioneer of polar exploration.
13. **Michael Palin** (1943–present) Ever popular Python turned TV traveller.
14. **Sir Ernest Shackleton** (1874–1922) Heroic Antarctic explorer.
15. **Xuanzang** (602–44) Buddhist pilgrim and pioneer of travel writing.

Magical moment: a dhow off the coast of Zanzibar at dawn

Dettifoss Waterfall in Iceland is the most powerful in Europe at maximum flow

Adventure milestones

1872 Jules Verne's *Around the World in 80 Days* is published.

1884 Karl Elsener develops the Swiss Army Knife.

1897 Prospectors stampede to Alaska at the start of the Klondike Gold Rush.

1901 Annie Taylor makes the first successful barrel descent of Niagara Falls.

1911 Roald Amundsen becomes the first person to reach the South Pole.

1943 Jacques-Yves Cousteau invents the self-contained underwater breathing apparatus (SCUBA).

1947 Thor Heyerdahl sails the *Kon Tiki* across the Pacific.

1953 Edmund Hillary and Tenzing Norgay conquer Everest.

1965 Jimmy Roberts founds Mountain Travel, Nepal's first trekking company.

1969 OARS pioneer rafting trips through the Grand Canyon.

1977 The 'Breezer', the world's first modern mountain bike, is built.

1977 Bungee is born when members of the Oxford University Dangerous Sports Club leap off the Clifton Suspension Bridge near Bristol.

1985 Joe Simpson and Simon Yates 'touch the void' climbing in the Andes.

1997 Boerge Ousland becomes the first to cross Antarctica unsupported.

2001 Denis Tito pays US$20 million to become the first space tourist.

2002 Steve Fossett becomes the first to balloon solo around the world.

2003 Ranulph Fiennes and Mike Stroud complete seven marathons in seven days on seven continents.

2004 Pete Cabrinha surfs a 22m-high (72ft) wave in Hawaii – the tallest ever ridden.

Find perfect sand dunes in Sossusvlei, Namibia

generation of adventure tourists save their dollars and train for zero-gravity in the run-up to commercial sub-orbital space flights.

Bucketloads of adrenaline or money, however, are no longer pre-requisites for adventure travel. The industry has diversified to such an extent that it caters to everyone, from safety-minded families and backpackers to shark-diving fanatics and amateur polar explorers. These are ordinary people doing extraordinary things – stepping outside their comfort zones to realize personal dreams and ambitions, or simply for the sheer fun and fascination of adventure travel.

You don't have to embark on an expedition to conquer an 8,000m (26,000ft) peak or ride a camel across the Sahara – an equally satisfy-ing goal might involve tracking down a particular species of wildlife, meeting new cultures or experiencing a familiar world wonder using an unusual means of transport. There's nothing like an adrenaline buzz to shake off the drudge of day-to-day life, but sometimes it's the subtle aspects of a trip – the profound effect of wilderness, the close com-panionship of teamwork – that creates the most poignant memories.

Adventure bound

Counting down the days to departure, dusting off old equipment, buying new gear, fine-tuning your itinerary, endless hours poring over brochures, maps and guidebooks…it's all part of the anticipation and attention to detail that makes planning an adventure so important and enjoyable. Careful preparation won't necessarily guarantee that things always run smoothly, but it will certainly make you better equipped to deal with a crisis.

Yosemite National Park in California is a hiker's paradise

Varied terrain awaits you on your travels

You can make life easier for yourself by joining an organized trip, but even if you decide to go solo, you will find that today's comprehensive sources of information and equipment go a long way towards helping you realize your goals. And if you do ever find yourself wallowing in logistics, spare a thought for whoever organized Lord Randolph Churchill's safari in 1892. In addition to seven wagons and a staff of over 30, Churchill advanced into the bush laden with 20 tonnes of supplies, including a piano and a generous quantity of eau-de-cologne. Burke and Wills, meanwhile, set off across Australia in 1860 with over 14 tonnes of supplies, including a bathtub and an oak table with matching chairs.

Ultimately, however, the challenge for modern-day adventurers is how to ensure their forays have as little environmental and cultural impact as possible. Only by rooting itself in responsible travel ethics will adventure tourism become sustainable and safeguard the extraordinary places that travellers value so highly. That's why this book places such an emphasis on eco-friendly and socially aware travel. It's just as important as getting the right equipment or deciding where to go.

Adventure races

Marathons Several endurance-running events take place in the Sahara Desert, including the 100km del Sahara, Marathon des Sables and Sahara Marathon. The Coastal Challenge is a six-day, 225–250km (140- to155-mile) expedition run through the rainforests and mountains of Costa Rica, while the Tour du Mont-Blanc involves a demanding 163km (101-mile) circuit of the massif, with a total elevation gain of 9,400m (30,800ft).

Dog sledding The iconic Iditarod covers over 1,850km (1,150 miles) from Anchorage to Nome on the Bering Sea coast, each team of 12–16 dogs taking up to 17 days to complete the gruelling course across mountain ranges, frozen rivers and tundra. The Yukon Quest traces historic gold rush and mail delivery dog-sledding routes, with competitors mushing husky teams 1,600km (995 miles) between Fairbanks and Whitehorse.

Multi-sport Competitors in the New Zealand Coast to Coast cross South Island from Kumara Beach on the Tasman Sea to Sumner Beach on the Pacific Ocean, cycling 140km (87 miles), running 36km (22 miles), including 33km (21 miles) across the Southern Alps, and kayaking 67km (42 miles) through the Waimakariri Gorge.

Essentials

Contents

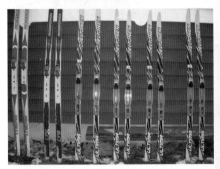

Main picture: Wolfberg Cracks, South Africa. Left, from top: Heating soup, Finland; canoe packed for expedition, Florida; cross-country skis; inflatable kayak

Travel logistics

It pays to start planning your adventure well before you set your departure date. As well as deciding where to go and what to do, there are numerous other factors that need to be considered.

STEP 1: THE WISH LIST

Careful planning is the key to a successful, safe and enjoyable trip. You not only need to give adequate thought to logistics like training, finances and equipment, but also assess what sort of trip best suits you. Start by asking yourself the following two key questions:

What adventure activities are you interested in? Perhaps you're a keen walker at home and have always aspired to tackling one of the world's great treks. A passion for a particular activity is a natural starting point for planning an adventure holiday. Then again, you might be keen to try something completely different that involves learning a new skill. Once you've compiled a shortlist of must-do activities, give some thought to what else you may want to do, whether it's a few days flopping on a beach or some city sightseeing.

Where do you want to go? The 'Adventure calling' sections in this book highlight some of the choicest places on earth for each adventure activity. Deciding on an iconic destination like the Red Sea or Great Barrier Reef might be an easy choice for dedicated divers. Or does the success of your adventure partly depend on how far off the beaten track you get? Alternatively, you might want to start the decision-making process with a shortlist of places you've always wanted to visit and then explore what adventure activities are available in each. Use the table on page 19 for an at-a-glance guide to the world's adventure hotspots. Finally, don't forget to check whether a travel advisory has been issued by your government, warning against visiting an unsafe country. In the US log on to www.travel.state.gov/travel, while UK citizens should visit www.fco.gov.uk/travel.

STEP 2: THE REALITY CHECK

Once you've addressed the two questions above and compiled an adventure wish list, it's time to start applying logistics to weed out the trips that are non-feasible.

Are you experienced enough? Give careful consideration to the difficulty ratings given in this book. A surprising number of adventures

Adventure activities on offer at Lake Bohinj, Slovenia

are suitable for complete beginners, while others require prior experience. Talk to operators, or people who have already been, to find out more about what's involved. Don't put yourself in a position where limited experience can jeopardize your enjoyment or safety on a trip.

When is the best time to go? Prime seasons are indicated for each of the adventure ideas in this book (see also pages 20–1). Check the websites of tourist boards or weather information services for additional information on climatic factors that could make or break your trip. You may have to compromise between the best season and when you are available to travel, though some destinations may be non-starters if you are unable to visit at a crucial time – sea-kayaking in the High Arctic, for example, has quite a brief window of opportunity.

How long do you want to be away? Trying to shoehorn an adventure into too few days is not only impractical, stressful and fairly pointless, but it can also be potentially dangerous. Find out what the minimum time required is, including travel, training and, if necessary, acclimatization. Then add extra days to allow for delays or emergencies.

How much do you want to spend? Budget is likely to reap the most casualties on your wish list. That dream trip overlanding through Asia might become prohibitively expensive once you've added up the hidden costs, like visas, non-inclusive activities and daily expenses. Simply getting to some far-flung places can seriously eat into your budget, while technical activities may involve training or specialized equipment – both of which need to be factored in. Many adventure destinations have a range of options when it comes to budget. Take Namibia's Skeleton Coast, for example. At the top end of the scale you could book a fly-in safari, zipping along the entire Namibian seaboard in a chartered Cessna, dropping in on a succession of private tented

Penguins eye up a cruise ship, Tierra del Fuego

camps. Or, for a fraction of the cost, you could experience the desolate beauty of the place on an overland expedition where you pitch your own tent and help cook the meals.

STEP 3: THE NITTY GRITTY

By now you should have decided on an adventure trip that is not only manageable in terms of finance and timing, but also offers the right challenge in the right place. Now it's time to start tackling the paper-work and practicalities.

Independent versus tour Deciding whether to join an organized group adventure or plan everything independently should already have been considered when deciding your overall budget. As well as cutting costs, going solo can offer the freedom to travel at your own pace and make responsible travel decisions, such as staying in locally owned accommodation and hiring local guides. However, be sure to check whether an organized tour doesn't, in fact, offer better value once you've taken into account the discounts that operators can pass on to their clients from block bookings. Remember, too, that access to certain locations, such as Antarctica, is virtually impossible on your own. Even more fundamental is the issue of safety. Attempting any of the activities in this book single-handed is potentially life threatening. On an organized trip your group leader should have enough first-aid experience (and appropriate kit) to deal with most emergencies.

Official documents Make sure that your passport will be in date for at least six months beyond your period of travel and apply well in advance for any visas that you might need. You may also be required to show vaccination certificates, particularly if you are travelling from a yellow fever zone (see pages 48–9). Make sure you have travel insurance and check that it will cover the activities you'll be doing. Some adventure operators may ask to see a medical certificate from your doctor.

Money matters Traveller's cheques are the safest way to carry money, but it's also a good idea to take some cash in either local currency or US dollars. A credit card is also useful for security deposits, cash advances at ATMs or in emergency situations when you might need to replace stolen gear or purchase an air ticket at short notice.

Getting there Although international flights are usually included as part of a tour package, some operators offer 'land only' rates, leaving you to make your own travel arrangements. Searching online for bargain flights is one option, but you could also consider travelling by train, overland truck or ferry to make the journey part of your overall adventure (and reduce your CO_2 footprint in the process).

Training and fitness It's vital that you include a training and fitness regime on your countdown-to-departure calendar. See pages 44–5 for pre-trip fitness tips tailored to various activities. For some adventures you may need to undertake pre-departure training to develop special-ist skills such as scuba-diving, while others may require experience of wilderness survival or first aid – see page 242 for details of courses.

WHAT ADVENTURE WHERE?

Use the table on the right to cross-reference each of the 24 major adventure
activities covered in this book to the countries where they are most readily available.

KEY TO SYMBOLS
■ Hotspot for this adventure activity
■ Adventure activity available
□ Adventure activity limited or not available

Clouds swirl below Mt Aspiring, New Zealand

Year planner

Weather patterns are likely to have the strongest bearing on when you decide to set off on your adventure, but other factors to consider include wildlife spectacles and festivals.

COLOUR KEY
Seasons
Wildlife
Festivals

	Jan	Feb	Mar	Apr	May	Jun	Jul	Aug	Sep	Oct	Nov	Dec
AMERICA												
Driest period, British Columbia & SE Alaska					■	■	■	■	■			
Best time to visit Canyonlands, Southwest				■	■	■			■	■	■	
Prime trekking season, Rocky Mountains						■	■	■	■	■		
Best time to visit Florida	■	■	■	■							■	■
Best time to visit Hawaii	■	■	■								■	■
Best time for whale-watching, Atlantic coast							■	■	■	■		
Best time to see polar bears, Churchill, Canada										■	■	■
Caribou migration, Northern Alaska, USA							■	■	■			
Orcas migrate in-shore, Johnstone Strait, Canada					■	■	■	■	■			
Calgary Stampede, Alberta, Canada							■					
Red Earth Festival, Oklahoma, USA						■						
Groundhog Day, Pennsylvania, USA		■										
LATIN AMERICA & CARIBBEAN												
Coolest, least humid period, Mexico	■	■										■
Hurricane season, Caribbean						■	■	■	■	■	■	
Dry season, Central America	■	■	■	■								■
Prime trekking season, Ecuador & Peru						■	■	■	■			
Prime season, Patagonia, Chile & Argentina	■	■	■	■							■	■
Warmest water for snorkelling with sealions, Galápagos	■	■	■	■								
Whale-, seal- and penguin-watching, Antarctica	■	■										■
Grey whale migration, Baja California, Mexico	■	■	■	■								
Prime time for birdwatching in the Pantanal, Brazil							■	■	■			
Rio Carnival, Brazil		■										
Chichén Itzá, Mexico			■									
Inti Raymi, Cuzco, Peru						■						
EUROPE												
Winter activity season, Lapland	■	■	■	■							■	■
Best time to see Northern Lights	■	■	■								■	■
24-hour daylight, northern Scandinavia						■	■	■				
Warm, least crowded period, Mediterranean					■	■			■	■		
Prime trekking season, Alps						■	■	■	■			
Prime sea-kayaking seasons, Adriatic						■	■		■	■		

	Jan	Feb	Mar	Apr	May	Jun	Jul	Aug	Sep	Oct	Nov	Dec
Bird migration through southern Spain		■	■	■					■	■	■	
Best time for whale-watching, Iceland			■	■	■	■	■	■	■			
Prime time for bear-watching, Poland				■	■	■	■	■				
Venice Carnival, Italy		■										
St Patrick's Festival, Ireland			■									
Greek Orthodox Easter, Greece				■								
Coolest period in North Africa	■	■	■	■	■					■	■	■
Dry season in East Africa	■	■	■				■	■	■	■		
Dry season in Zambezi Valley, Zambia						■	■	■	■	■		
Coolest period in Madagascar						■	■	■	■	■		
Cyclone season, Indian Ocean	■	■	■									■
Flowering season, Namaqualand								■	■	■	■	
Prime time for gorilla-watching, Uganda & Rwanda						■	■					
Wildebeest migration, Kenya & Tanzania						■	■	■	■	■		
Southern right whales migrate to South Africa	■	■	■								■	■
Hermanus Whale Festival, South Africa									■			
Timkat, Ethiopia	■											
Ku-omboka, Barotseland, Zambia			■									
Coolest period in Middle East	■	■	■	■						■	■	■
Coolest, driest period in India	■	■									■	■
Monsoon seasons, India						■	■			■	■	
Prime trekking season, Himalaya	■	■	■	■						■	■	
Rains affect west coast Malay Peninsula					■	■				■	■	
Rains affect east coast Malay Peninsula											■	■
Green turtle nesting season, Malaysia					■	■	■	■	■			
Prime season for tiger spotting, India	■	■	■	■	■							
Prime birdwatching season, Rajasthan, India	■	■								■	■	■
Pushkar Camel Fair, India											■	
Naadam, Ulan Baataar, Mongolia							■					
Holi, India & Nepal			■									
Best time to visit southern half of Australia	■	■	■	■							■	■
Best time to visit tropical north, Australia						■	■	■	■	■		
Coolest period in the outback, Australia						■	■	■	■	■		
Best time to visit South Island, New Zealand	■	■	■	■						■	■	■
Best time to visit North Island, New Zealand	■	■	■	■	■			■				
Prime birdwatching season, Kakadu, Australia						■	■	■	■			
Flowering season, Southwestern Australia								■	■	■	■	
Whale sharks migrate to Ningaloo Reef, Australia			■	■	■	■						
Humpback whales migrate along Queensland coast									■	■	■	■
Sydney Festival, Australia	■											
Henley on Todd Regatta, Alice Springs, Australia									■			
Heiva I, Tahiti, French Polynesia							■					

Classic adventures

Iconic places, inspiring journeys – these three classic adventures have historical legacies riddled with tragedy, yet rich in triumph.

Climbing Everest

On 29 May 1953, New Zealander Edmund Hillary and Sherpa Tenzing Norgay from Nepal became the first people to stand on top of the world. Some 29 years earlier, George Mallory and Andrew Irvine made an attempt on the summit of Everest from which they never returned. Whether they actually reached the top is still a matter of debate. Ascents of the world's tallest mountain have often been shrouded in controversy – particularly during 1996, Everest's single most deadly year. Jon Krakauer's book *Into Thin Air* vividly showed how unpredictable weather, miscalculated risks and a commercial mentality focussed on client satisfaction claimed the lives of 12 climbers.

Sailing around the world

Ferdinand Magellan led the first circumnavigation of the globe. Of the five ships and 237 men that left Spain in 1522, only one vessel and 18 survivors limped home three years later (the great navigator himself having been killed in the Philippines). In 1898, American Joshua Slocum became the first person to sail around the world solo – his three-year voyage eclipsed in 1967 by Sir Francis Chichester who took just 226 days, only stopping in Sydney for repairs. Two years later, fellow Briton Robin Knox-Johnston achieved the first non-stop navigation. The 312-day milestone has been whittled away ever since, with the most recent record-breaking solo voyages by Ellen MacArthur (71 days, 2005) and Francis Joyon (57 days, 2008). Setting out from Brest in his 29m (95ft) IDEC trimaran, Joyon's route took him past the Cape of Good Hope, southern Australia and Cape Horn. His secret for success? According to observers, Joyon chose an excellent window of weather and made very few errors. His yacht was also lighter than usual, having wind turbines and solar panels, rather than electrical generators, to power automatic piloting and communication equipment.

5 more ultimate adventures

1. Flying to the moon (see page 154)
2. Crossing the Sahara (see page 132)
3. Traversing the Silk Road (see page 132)
4. Riding the Trans Siberian railway
5. Navigating the Northwest Passage

Trekking to the Poles

On 14 December 1911 Norwegian Roald Amundsen and his party became the first people to reach the South Pole (see page 109), a month ahead of Robert Scott's expedition that was to end so tragically. Ernest Shackleton's 1914 Imperial Trans-Antarctic Expedition was also ill-fated, with the British explorer's ship, *Endurance*, becoming trapped and finally crushed in pack ice. Despite the US Amundsen-Scott South Pole Station being established and serviced by air since 1956, the South Pole has continued to lure overland explorers. In 1989, Arved Fuchs and Reinhold Messner made it to 90°S using only skis and wind power. The record for the fastest unsupported trek to the South Pole, meanwhile, was set in 2007 by Hannah McKeand, who took just 39 days to walk from Hercules Inlet. The conquest of the North Pole is normally credited to Robert Peary's 1909 expedition using sleds pulled by huskies. Subsequent attempts to reach 90°N have involved everything from hot-air balloons to nuclear submarines. As with the South Pole, it's now possible for tourists to embark on journeys to the North Pole with adventure tour operators.

Ellen MacArthur training off the French coast, 2005

Classic reads

Read these seven adventure classics for an adrenaline charged cocktail of surviving against the odds, battling the elements and exploring wild frontiers, from ocean to desert.

Annapurna by Maurice Herzog, 1952 (Pimlico, 1997)

Few books convey the compelling spirit of mountaineering better than Herzog's account of the first successful attempt to climb an 8,000m (26,240ft) peak. The French team had trouble even finding Annapurna. Nevertheless, Herzog and Louis Lachenal made it to the top – only for disaster to strike on the descent when an avalanche, lost gloves and frostbite took their toll.

Arabian Sands by Wilfred Thesiger, 1959 (Penguin, 2007)

The definitive account of desert exploration, this evocative book recounts Thesiger's mid-20th-century travels across the so-called Empty Quarter, living with the Bedouin and discovering – with respect and humility – the harsh reality of life in southern Arabia.

Kon-Tiki by Thor Heyerdahl, 1950 (Adventure Library, 1997)

With nothing more than a simple balsa-wood raft, Norwegian Thor Heyerdahl and his companions set sail from Peru toward Polynesia to test a theory that the South Pacific could have been settled from

12 more adventure classics

1. *A Short Walk in the Hindu Kush* by Eric Newby, 1958 (Lonely Planet, 2008)
2. *Around the World in 80 Days* by Michael Palin, 1989 (BBC, 2004)
3. *Dark Star Safari* by Paul Theroux, 2002 (Penguin, 2007)
4. *Gipsy Moth Circles the World* by Francis Chichester, 1967 (McGraw-Hill, 2003)
5. *In Trouble Again* by Redmond O'Hanlon, 1988 (Vintage, 1990)
6. *Passage to Juneau* by Jonathan Raban, 1999 (Vintage, 2000)
7. *Seven Years in Tibet* by Heinrich Harrer, 1953 (Flamingo, 1997)
8. *South from the Limpopo* by Devla Murphy, 1997 (Overlook, 2001)
9. *Terra Incognita* by Sara Wheeler, 1996 (Vintage, 1997)
10. *The Lost Heart of Asia* by Colin Thubron, 1994 (Vintage, 2007)
11. *The Snow Leopard* by Peter Matthiessen, 1978 (Penguin, 2001)
12. *West With the Night* by Beryl Markham, 1942 (North Point Press, 2001)

Shackleton's team pull a boat across the pack ice

the east. The debate still rages, but nothing can detract from this dramatically narrated tale.

South by Ernest Shackleton, 1919 (Penguin, 1999)
It's a well-known story – the *Endurance* breaking up in the grip of Antarctic ice, the incredible journey by open boat across the stormy seas of the Southern Ocean – but Shackleton's understated account still ranks as one of the most remarkable testaments to human endeavour ever written.

The Perfect Storm by Sebastian Junger, 1997 (HarperCollins, 1999)
A high-pressure system from the Great Lakes, storm-force winds in the North Atlantic and the brooding remnants of a hurricane – it all adds up to the 'perfect storm' of 1991, told here through the lives of a small New England fishing community. Junger's impressive, yet sensitive narrative skillfully evokes the elemental power of the storm and the sense of fear, desperation and bravery of those caught up in it.

Through the Dark Continent by Henry Stanley, 1878 (Dover Publications, 1988)
A few years after finding Livingstone in 1871, Stanley embarked on his most adventurous trip, tracing the length of the River Congo. Well over a century later, another *Telegraph* journalist, Tim Butcher, followed in Stanley's footsteps. Though equally enthralling, Butcher's contemporary account – *Blood River: A Journey to Africa's Broken Heart* (Vintage, 2008) – is pervaded by the horrors of modern-day, war-ravaged Congo.

Touching the Void by Joe Simpson, 1985 (Vintage Classics, 2008)
When things go terribly wrong during a descent of Siula Grande in the Peruvian Andes, Joe Simpson's climbing partner, Simon Yates, is forced to do the unthinkable. He cuts the rope between them. Incredibly, Simpson not only survives the fall, but crawls down the mountain, dragging his broken leg through crevasses and across glaciers to reach base camp. Survival stories don't come any more gripping than this.

Choosing an operator

Joining a guided adventure with like-minded individuals means you can share the fun and achievements, while leaving logistics to your tour operator. But how do you choose a reliable and responsible outfitter?

Track record, quality of equipment and guide training, as well as environmental and cultural ethics are all important considerations when selecting an adventure tour operator. Before making a reservation, use the following checklist to help you decide whether a company comes up to scratch.

Business matters
- How long has the tour operator been in business? Companies with several years of experience will have a certain amount of reliability.
- Is the company affiliated to a professional association which provides a quality charter and financial security? In the UK, for example, the Association of Independent Tour Operators (www.aito.co.uk) provides high standards of consumer protection should one of its members go out of business. Similarly, the US Tour Operators Association (www.ustoa.com) requires that its members carry at least $1 million in professional liability insurance and $1 million in traveller assistance insurance.

Group size and guides
- How large is the group? Small groups are unobtrusive and have less impact on the environment.
- Is the ratio of guides to tourists acceptable – particularly for technical or potentially dangerous activities, where one-to-one training may be required?
- What are the guides' responsibilities? Will you be expected to help with pitching tents or cooking food?

Schedules and safety
- Are enough days allocated to adventure activities or is too much time spent travelling between too many locations?
- Is the timing right? Cut-price deals might coincide with off-seasons.
- What safety procedures are in place? Are trip leaders suitably trained and equipped to deal with medical emergencies?

What's included?
- What exactly is included in the rate? Does your package include everything from transport and accommodation to national park entry fees and the services of a professional guide?
- Do you need to allow for any special equipment or training in your budget?

Responsible travel
- Does the operator have a written policy regarding local culture and the environment? Members of AITO (see opposite) are awarded a two- or three-star rating if they take measures to:
  - Protect the Environment (flora, fauna and landscapes)
  - Respect local cultures (traditions, religions and built heritage)
  - Benefit local communities, both economically and socially
  - Conserve natural resources, from office to destination
  - Minimize pollution (noise, waste disposal and congestion)
- How does the operator measure its contribution to responsible travel? How many local people are employed? Which local charities are supported? How much produce is sourced locally?
- Can the operator provide ideas on how you might get involved with local projects in a worthwhile and rewarding way?
- Is information and advice available on local customs and how to minimize environmental impact?

Travel group exploring Svalbard

Essential gear

Getting fitted out for your adventure can be an expensive and bewildering experience. Having the right gear, though, is crucial for your safety and enjoyment, so start looking early and research your needs thoroughly.

CLOTHING

Choosing the most suitable clothing is largely a balance between finding a fabric that offers insulation from the cold, yet allows your body to shed heat and moisture. Different fabrics have different properties. Cotton clothing, for example, is breathable, hardwearing and absorbs moisture, but can be heavy, cold and uncomfortable when wet. Fleece garments have good insulating and wicking properties (moving moisture away from the skin), but they are not usually windproof or easily compacted, while synthetic breathable fabrics allow sweat to evaporate while keeping rain and wind at bay – although dirt may clog their pores causing condensation to develop inside. The best clothing solution is a multi-layered approach, where several items of clothing offer a practical means of trapping warm air next to your body while being easily added or removed to control your temperature.

Core layer Close-fitting but not too tight, the core layer goes next to your skin and should have good wicking properties. A vest or long-sleeved thermal top/long-johns are good choices.

Second layer A long-sleeved shirt provides sun protection (especially at the back of the neck), but you can roll up the sleeves to keep cool. Choose a zipped polo neck for when it's colder. Trousers should be loose fitting.

Third layer A lightweight fleece jacket or woollen pullover is ideal – although you may just want to keep it handy in a backpack for rest stops, when your body may rapidly cool.

Outer layer Choose a waterproof and windproof jacket in a breathable fabric, with a hood and zip vents under the armpits to prevent overheating. You may also need waterproof over-trousers.

FOOTWEAR

When choosing footwear, consider the terrain and climate you will be encountering, and remember to wear in new boots to prevent blisters.

Trainers Although they are comfortable and lightweight, most trainers don't offer much in the way of ankle support, grip or durability.

ADVENTURE TRAVEL PACKING CHECKLIST

- Underwear
- Thermal top/bottom
- Cotton T-shirts
- Long-sleeved shirts
- Fleece jacket
- Long trousers
- Shorts
- Waterproof jacket
- Poncho
- Waterproof trousers
- Swimwear
- Belt
- Gloves/woollen hat
- Wide-brimmed sun hat
- Bandana
- Nightwear

- Walking boots/shoes
- Walking socks
- Spare bootlaces
- All-terrain sandals
- Gaiters
- Trekking poles
- Blister pack

- Backpack/kitbag
- Daysack
- Waist bag/pouch
- Stuff bags/drybags
- Security lock
- Cotton money belt
- Backpack rain cover

- Tent
- Sleeping bag
- Sleeping bag liner
- Compact pillow
- Foam sleeping mat
- Mosquito net
- Hammock
- Torch/flashlight
- Spare batteries/bulbs
- Candles and lighter
- Garbage bags

- Compass
- Maps
- Travel guidebooks
- Pocket dictionary
- Wristwatch
- Whistle
- Penknife/multi-tool
- 10m (33ft) length of cord
- Travel alarm clock
- Sewing kit
- World travel adaptor
- Shortwave radio

- 1-litre water bottle
- Bladder bottle
- Water purifier kit

- Plate, bowl and mug
- Knife, fork and spoon
- Dishcloth
- Compact stove
- Fuel bottle
- Mess tins or saucepan
- Snacks/dried foods
- Vitamins
- Resealable bags
- Food storage bottles

- Washbag
- Travel wash
- Clothes line/pegs
- Universal sink plug
- Travel towel

- Biodegradable soap and shampoo
- Drywash
- Toothbrush and toothpaste
- Steel mirror
- Razor and shaving foam/oil
- Fold-down washbowl
- Sanitary protection
- Wet wipes
- Toilet paper
- Foot powder
- Insect repellent
- Sun protection cream
- Lip balm
- Moisturizing lotion
- Sunglasses
- Earplugs

- Document pouch
- Passport and visas
- Vaccination certificates
- Travel tickets
- Travellers' cheques, cash and credit card
- Driver's licence
- Passport photos
- Photocopies of paperwork
- Travel insurance details
- Notebook/pencil

- Camera
- Battery recharger
- Memory cards/film
- Binoculars
- Mobile phone
- GPS

- Personal first-aid kit
- Anti-malarial tablets
- Sterile injection kit
- Survival kit

Replenishing your water supplies from natural sources where possible means you have less to carry

Walking safari in the Semliki Valley, Uganda

They're fine for rafting or sea-kayaking, however, when you want something quick drying that has adequate grip for slippery rocks.

Sandals All types of sandals keep feet cool in hot climates, but more technical designs feature good grips, neoprene-padded straps, anti-bacterial footbeds and air-cushioned soles.

Fabric boots For light walking on firm paths, fabric boots offer good ankle support and grip. Although less durable and waterproof than leather boots, they dry quickly and are much quicker to break in. Being lightweight they are also less likely to cause strain or fatigue.

Leather boots Hard-wearing and water resistant (particularly if regularly reproofed), leather boots have sturdy soles and padded ankle supports for rough, rocky terrain and extended treks.

Specialist boots See pages 34–7 for jungle boots, desert boots and snow boots.

Socks Hiking socks have thick soles for padding and insulation. For warm-weather treks, choose socks that have thin uppers to minimize sweating. For cold conditions, wear an additional pair of thin inner socks in a breathable fabric to wick moisture away from the feet.

Gaiters An extra layer of protection for wet conditions, gaiters prevent water and mud from getting inside your boots and also help to keep trousers dry. Snow gaiters, meanwhile, keep snow from entering the tops of boots.

SLEEPING GEAR

Don't underestimate the importance of a comfortable, warm sleeping bag – your life may depend on it in a survival situation. Getting a good night's sleep is crucial on any adventure trip, so make sure your sleeping bag's rating (defined by 1–4+ seasons or a temperature gradient) more than adequately reflects the climatic conditions you'll be experiencing.

Sleeping bags Sleeping bags trap air in their filling, which is warmed by your body heat. They are constructed in one of three ways: simple stitch-through bags are often the cheapest because warmth tends to escape through the stitching; box-wall bags keep the filling evenly distributed and often have a comfort rating of 2–3 seasons, while double-quilted bags have two layers of offset quilting, which minimizes cold spots, but increases weight and bulk. Down-filled sleeping bags are warm, lightweight and compact easily, while bags with synthetic fillings tend to be cheaper, heavier and bulkier. Other factors to consider include the design of the hood, foot and zip – each of which have a bearing on comfort and warmth.

Sleeping bag liners Use a cotton liner on its own in hot, humid climes, or as a liner to keep the inside of your sleeping bag clean. Silk liners provide added luxury and warmth, while thermal liners upgrade your bag by one season.

Sleeping mats Essential for protection from cold and hard ground, a typical self-inflating mat weighs around 500g (1lb), while simple foam

It's a jungle out there (or a desert, ice cap, mountain range…). You've packed the essentials, but here's a list of easily overlooked but nifty little extras that you should also find room for:

Bungee cords Unlimited potential (at a stretch) for rigging up a shelter or attaching items to your pack.

Karabiners Essential for climbers, but useful for anyone else who wants to clip a water bottle to their pack.

Gaffa tape Seriously sticky stuff for quick, strong, weather-resistant repairs.

Journal Non-essential, but your trip is certain to inspire you and, in any case, you'll enjoy reading it years later and marvelling at how you survived all those bug bites, blisters and irregular bowel movements.

mats are less than 200g (7oz). Don't forget a repair kit if you opt for the self-inflating type.

Pillows Choose from a compact pillow with its own stuff sack or an inflatable version. To save space, simply stuff a pillowcase with your fleece jacket.

CARRYING EQUIPMENT

Your style of travel will often dictate what type of luggage you need – a soft holdall for a flying safari, panniers for bicycle touring, drybags for sea-kayaking, backpacks for trekking and so on. Think carefully about what size bag you need. Will it be practical to carry when fully loaded? And will you need an additional daypack or belt bag to hold accessories?

Backpacks Top-loading backpacks with a capacity of 55–75 litres (3,350–4,570cu in) are ideal for carrying heavy loads on treks. An adjustable back system, padded waist belt and shoulder straps ensure comfort, stability and even weight distribution. Side and lid pockets provide easy access to essential items like water bottles, while a zipped internal divider separates the pack into two compartments. Other features to look out for include removable daypack, integral rain cover and external cords for holding a sleeping mat.

Climbing packs These slim-line packs are no wider than shoulder width to allow climbers to squeeze through narrow gaps.

Convertible backpacks See page 135.

Holdalls/kit bags Capable of swallowing a huge amount of gear, holdalls are made of heavy-duty fabric, reinforced with webbing. Some have grab handles at both ends, while others have shoulder straps or wheels.

Daypacks With a capacity of 15–35 litres (915–2,135cu in), day-packs typically have a single compartment for daily essentials, such as water, snacks, camera and waterproofs. The best models have a ventilated back system, contoured shoulder harness, padded waist belt and integral rain cover.

Belt bags Useful for keeping small personal items close to hand.

Stuff bags Essential for compressing sleeping bags and other bulky items.

Drybags Vinyl or coated nylon bags with roll-up closure for a watertight seal.

Security pouches Made from cotton, silk or ripstop nylon, these unobtrusive but secure bags are designed to be comfortable worn next to the skin – either around your waist or neck. Essential accessories for your valuables.

It's all too tempting to be seduced by the latest gadgets in your local adventure equipment store, but make sure you have these essential accessories before adding unnecessary extras to your backpack and bank statement.

Compass Indispensable for when your life may depend on orienteering accuracy. Some expedition-style wrist watches have built-in compasses.

Penknife/multi-tool A toolbox in your pocket, penknives and multi-tools have everything from blades and screwdrivers to bottle openers and scissors.

Torch/flashlight For hands-free illumination while trekking, setting up camp and so on, a head torch (lamp) makes life easier than a traditional flashlight. Choose a model with an adjustable beam and longlife light-emitting diodes (LEDs).

Water bottle Available as a daypack-toting 'bladder' with an attached drinking hose or as a more traditional screw-top container.

Repair kits As well as a sewing kit for patching up clothing, backpacks and so on, make sure you have maintenance kits for tents, camping stoves and self-inflating sleeping mats.

Health and safety essentials See pages 47 and 50–1 for first-aid kit, survival kit, water purification equipment, plus measures to protect against the sun and biting insects.

A break from the rucksacks, Everest Base Camp

Braving the elements

From muggy tropical rainforests to wind-scoured ice caps, it's vital that you are properly equipped for any environmental extremes you might encounter during your adventure trip.

Impressive trees along the Hoh River Trail, Olympic National Park, USA

JUNGLE

With high temperatures and humidity, muddy tracks, river crossings, frequent thunderstorms, ensnaring vegetation, biting insects and potentially fatal diseases, jungles pose some of the most challenging conditions for adventure travellers.

Essential gear

- Cotton long trousers and long-sleeved shirts stay damp and keep you cool. Pre-treat clothing (and mosquito nets and hammock) with permethrin to deter biting insects and keep a spare set of clothes in a drybag.
- Ponchos are less clammy than jackets and can also be opened out to use as a shelter or groundsheet.
- Jungle boots have quick-drying, breathable canvas uppers, anti-clogging soles and high-lacing sides to keep leeches out.
- Treat socks with DEET or buy leech-proof ones.
- A bandana can be used as a scarf or sweat rag.
- Choose a pack with ventilated back system, rain cover and water reservoir.
- Head torch, whistle, compass and knife are essential jungle survival tools.
- Treat cuts regularly with antiseptic and dry dressings; dust feet with talc to prevent fungal infections.
- Insect repellent and head net help to deter biting insects. Check whether you need to take a course of anti-malarials.

Ultimate adventure: Manu, Peru

Why? This vast chunk of Amazonian rainforest probably has more species of plants and animals than anywhere else on earth, including 1,000 different birds and 13 varieties of monkey.

How? Fly in or take the two- to three-day overland journey from Cusco, crossing the Andes and delving into cloudforest en route. Once in Manu explore the jungle on foot and by canoe, staying in simple but comfortable lodges.

When? February–October.

DESERT

Fierce sun and heat are not the only factors you need to contend with in desert conditions. Temperatures can plummet during the night, while harsh winds exacerbate dehydration and kick up dust. Most desert adventures, however, are vehicle- or animal-supported, providing some level of protection from the elements.

Essential gear

- Clothing should be breathable and loose fitting with built-in SPF. Choose a long-sleeved shirt with underarm zip vents for keeping cool. Trousers should be hardwearing to protect against thorny scrub.
- For added protection against sun and dust, wear a wide-brimmed sun hat, plus sunglasses with UV protection and side shields. Cotton gloves prevent sunburn if you're horseriding or driving.
- A windproof jacket and warm sleeping bag are essential for nights.
- Desert boots have breathable canvas or suede uppers, as well as high sides and strong soles to protect against rocks and thorns.
- Sandals are fine for airing feet around camp during the evenings, but not during the day, when the tops of your feet could easily burn.
- Carry a daypack with built-in water reservoir, plus two extra bottles.
- Sandflies and mosquitoes may be a problem around waterholes, so remember to pack insect repellent.
- A compass and whistle could be life-savers if you get lost.
- When water is scarce, maintain hygiene levels by cleaning your hands using an antibacterial drywash.
- Make sure your first-aid kit contains rehydration and sunburn treatment, skin moisturizer, lip balm and eyewash.

Desert driving in Dubai

Ultimate adventure: Skeleton Coast, Namibia

Why? Littered with the remains of ships and whales, this vibrant fusion of desert and ocean lures visitors into a spectacular realm of vast dune fields, crowded seal and seabird colonies and the poignant legacy of the San Bushmen.
How? Venture out on short forays from the coastal towns of Swakopmund and Ludertiz or join an organized safari, camping along the coast's stark, yet beautiful, hinterland.
When? Year-round.

MOUNTAINS

Taking your time to properly acclimatize is the best way to avoid altitude sickness. Make sure you are also well-equipped to deal with other common mountain-related problems, such as blisters, dehydration, exhaustion, muscle sprains, stomach upsets and getting lost.

Essential gear

• Trekking or mountaineering is hot work, but you cool down rapidly during rest breaks, so layered clothing is the best solution.

• Your choice of footwear (see pages 28–31) depends on climate, altitude and terrain, as well as the type of activity you'll be doing. With a plastic shell and thermal inner boot, snow boots are designed to insulate feet and hold them rigid while using crampons over ice or snow.

• A backpack with adjustable back system is essential. What size you opt for depends largely on whether you are trekking independently or with porters on an organized trip.

• Choose a warm, lightweight sleeping bag and don't forget to take a survival bag in case of an emergency.

• Must-haves for independent trekkers, a compass, map and whistle are also important on group trips should you get separated.

• Trekking poles help take the strain off your knees during descents.

• All mountain activities use plenty of energy and fluid, so it's crucial to keep drinking (6–10 litres per day depending on the climate) and eating high-energy snacks. Keep water bottles handy or wear a pack with a built-in drinking reservoir.

• Protect yourself from the intense radiation at high altitude by covering up and wearing good-quality sunglasses with side shields or wrap-around design.

• Bolster your first-aid kit with rehydration powders, support bandages, blister patches and foot powder.

Damaraland, Namibia

Ultimate adventure: Pamirs, Tajikistan

Why? A tangled knot of peaks, glaciers and wind-scoured plateaux, the Pamirs are one of the world's least visited mountain ranges – an austere land sparsely inhabited by Tajik tribespeople and a refuge for the snow leopard.

How? Don't expect lodges. Apart from scant trails and a few shepherd huts that's it. Make sure you're well equipped for some challenging trekking.

When? July–September.

POLAR

Wind chill is your worst enemy – take clothing that you know will block those icy drafts. If you are heading south, always choose an operator that is a member of the International Association of Antarctic Tour Operators (IAATO, www.iaato.org) that sets a stringent code of conduct to minimize environmental impact.

Essential gear

- Windproof and waterproof jacket and trousers should be roomy enough for plenty of layers underneath. Choose garments that have taped seams.
- Core and mid-layers should consist of thermal underwear, warm pullovers and a fleece jacket.
- Wear a pair of thin socks beneath thick wool outer socks. Keep hands snug with insulated inner gloves and thick waterproof mitts.
- Minimize heat loss through your head by wearing a windproof hat with ear flaps. A warm scarf will keep out draughts.
- Wellington boots are a good idea on cruises when shore excursions may involve paddling through shallow water. Where trekking is involved, waterproof walking boots and snow gaiters are a good option.
- Protect your eyes from glare with wrap-around sunglasses and apply plenty of sun screen to face and lips (minimum SPF 30).
- Don't forget seasickness pills and binoculars, plus a waterproof case and extra batteries for cameras (they power down rapidly in extreme cold).
- For serious polar expeditions, additional gear should include mid-thigh length down parka with secure hood, down sleeping bag (rated to –40°C/°F) with generous hood and easy closure system, knee-high winter boots (rated to –60°C/–76°F) and tinted ski goggles.

King penguins with chicks

Ultimate adventure: Antarctica

Why? It's a wilderness the size of a continent with sublime scenery and wonderful wildlife.

How? The port of Ushuaia in Tierra del Fuego is the embarkation point for most Antarctic expeditions. Itineraries vary from ten-day cruises taking in the Antarctic Peninsula and South Shetland Islands to trips lasting three weeks or more that visit more far-flung places like South Georgia and the Ross Sea.

When? November–February.

Responsible travel

Throughout this book EcoFiles outline ways of minimizing environmental impact for each activity. Use the following checklist to help ensure that all aspects of your adventure holiday are environmentally and culturally responsible.

Before you go
- Plan a route that minimizes carbon emissions. Where possible, opt for train travel (www.seat61.com is an excellent worldwide resource).
- For unavoidable flights, offset carbon emissions (see pages 228–9).
- Choose an adventure tour operator with a proven track record in responsible travel (see pages 26–7).
- Ask your tour operator if there are any local schools, charities or orphanages that you can include on your itinerary and whether it would be appropriate to take along some useful gifts or supplies. Check out www.stuffyourrucksack.com for additional information.
- Keep packaging to a minimum, especially if you are visiting countries with limited waste disposal and recycling facilities.
- Pack eco-friendly products, such as biodegradable soap and clothing made from ethical as well as recycled or renewable sources.
- Familiarize yourself with local cultures, customs and dress codes, and learn a few words of the local language.

While you're there
- Where possible, use public transport, hire a bike or walk to reduce pollution and carbon emissions.
- Water is a precious commodity in many countries, so use it wisely. Treating your own water avoids the need to buy bottled water, which can contribute to the build-up of litter. Balance this, however, against the fact that drink sales may support local livelihoods. Remember to use eco-friendly products when washing near streams or rivers – people downstream may rely on the same source of water for their drinking supply.
- Always buy local produce in preference to imported goods and, if possible, hire local guides – you'll get a good insight into local culture and they will earn an income.
- Never buy souvenirs made from endangered species. See www.cites.org for details.

- Avoid disturbing wildlife, damaging habitats or interfering with natural behaviour by feeding wild animals.
- Leave shells, plants and ancient artifacts exactly where you find them.
- Although it may be customary to haggle in markets, always pay a fair price.
- Respect cultures, traditions and religious sites by complying with customs and dress codes. If in doubt, ask a local rather than assuming you know best.
- Always ask permission before taking photographs of people.
- Don't hand out sweets or money. Encouraging begging, especially in children, undermines parental authority and self-respect. Consider making a donation to a local charity or school instead.
- As well as ensuring that you take away all of your own litter, consider picking up garbage left by others, or joining a local beach or trail clean-up.

A scene unchanged for centuries – meadow flowers, Morocco

When you get back
- Give feedback to your tour operator on how they can further reduce their environmental impact and increase benefits to local communities.
- Honour any promises you've made to send photographs to local people.
- Support humanitarian or conservation organizations that work towards resolving any issues you may have encountered on holiday.

Camping in the wild

Suitably equipped with the right equipment and bush skills,
setting up camp in the wilderness can be both liberating and
comfortable. It's also a privilege that you can help to maintain
for others by leaving little or no trace.

CAMPING EQUIPMENT

Tent Decide how many people (plus their kit) your tent needs to
accommodate, where and when you are planning to use it and how
you intend to carry it. Traditional ridge tents are simple to erect and
can withstand bad weather in a range of environments. Entrances at

Boardwalk camping in the Everglades, Florida

both ends provide flexibility, although the metal poles can make them heavy to carry. With flexible plastic poles, hoop tents and tunnel tents are lighter in weight and have less cramped interiors, but they do need to be firmly pegged and may lose their shape (or worse) in high winds. Lightweight and easy to pitch, geodesic dome tents have interlocking poles that provide a sturdy and stable option, even in strong winds – but they can be expensive.

Stove Start by considering what type of fuel may be available at your destination. Gas stoves are easy to operate, but butane or propane cylinders may be hard to come by. A multifuel stove, on the other hand, can burn on white gas, paraffin or aviation fuel, but requires careful priming and maintenance. Other options include non-pressurized stoves, which run on methylated spirit, and solid fuel stoves, which burn alcohol jelly. Whichever stove you choose, always remember to use it in a well-ventilated place and to store fuel in clearly labelled and leak-proof bottles.

Cooking utensils Take the bare minimum unless you are travelling with a group or have the luxury of vehicle or animal support. One-person essentials include cutlery, plastic mug, wooden spoon and a lightweight aluminium cooking pot with a lid that doubles as a bowl.

Sleeping gear See page 31.

Camping EcoFile

- If possible, use an existing campsite.
- Contact landowners for area restrictions and permit requirements.
- Try to pitch your tent on non-vegetated areas, or at the very least, avoid particularly sensitive habitats such as meadows and wetlands.
- When selecting a campsite, avoid disturbing wildlife or livestock, and avoid areas where access would cause unnecessary erosion.
- Make sure your camp is located well away from game trails and waterholes.
- Avoid damaging historical, archaeological and palaeontological sites.
- Do not dig trenches around your tent unless flash flooding is a real threat.
- For cooking use a camp stove. If you need to build a fire, use only fallen timber. Allow the fire to burn down to a fine ash, which can be raked out and disposed of. Aim to leave no trace of your fire.
- If toilets, portable latrines or composting toilets are not available, dig latrines at least 50m (55 yards) from water sources, trails and campsites. Cover the hole with natural materials and either burn or take away your toilet paper.
- Wash clothing and cooking items well away from water sources and scatter grey water so that it filters through soil. If you must wash in streams, rivers or lakes, use biodegradable, phosphate-free soap.
- Take away all rubbish and unused food, plus litter left by others.
- Keep noise to a minimum, especially during the early morning and evening.

Adventure food

What you eat will depend on the style of your adventure. Self-sufficient trekkers may have to rely on lightweight freeze-dried foods, while vehicle-supported expeditions often have the luxury of refrigerated fresh produce.

Engaging in a strenuous outdoor activity like trekking, sea-kayaking, scuba-diving or horse-riding consumes a lot of energy – around 3,500kcal a day for an average man, or up to 5,000kcal if your body is also burning energy to keep warm in a cold environment.

What to eat

Bread, pasta, rice and beans are all rich in complex carbohydrates, which break down slowly during digestion to provide a sustained source of energy. Fruits are a good source of sugary carbohydrate, providing a quick energy fix and an important source of vitamins. Protein-based foods also provide energy, although pulses and beans may require soaking before cooking, and meat, fish, eggs and dairy products may be difficult to transport or keep fresh. High-fat foods, like nuts, milk and cheese, provide the most concentrated source of energy. Remember that drinking is just as important as a well-balanced food intake – maintaining good body-fluid levels not only wards off dehydration but also aids digestion and metabolism. Aim to drink 4–5 litres (1–1.3 gallons) a day – and double this if you are travelling in hot countries or taking part in strenuous activities.

Local foods

One of the great pleasures of adventure travel is sampling local dishes, but you need to take stringent precautions against eating contaminated or undercooked food. If you are in any doubt about hygiene standards, stick to canned or powdered milk rather than fresh milk and avoid ice cream, ice in drinks and soft cheeses. When buying fresh fish or meat cook it on the day it is bought. Wash vegetables and salad in purified water and choose fruit that you can peel.

Portable foods

Light to carry and quick to cook, pasta makes a filling meal that can easily be embellished with herbs, spices, fresh garlic and other easy-to-carry flavourings. Porridge, muesli, soup and instant dessert mixes are

Pre-packed wilderness food is easy to prepare

other essential basics for a portable larder. Dried fruits keep the weight
down, while a few luxury items like chocolate, boiled sweets, cereal
bars and trail mix provide an energy boost on the move and will
prevent blood-sugar levels dipping between meals. It's also a good idea
to take a multi-vitamin supplement for when fruit is in short supply.
Freeze-dried foods are available in a wide range of 'ready meals',
such as chicken curry, vegetable hotpot and fruit porridge. Simply
open the pouch, add boiling water, stir and leave to stand for a few
minutes. When eating any dried foods, however, it's important to
use ample cooking water, otherwise you may become dehydrated
and constipated.

Wild foods

Harvesting and eating wild food requires experience and care, and
you would be well advised to attend a course in wilderness survival
techniques before attempting to live off the land. Freshly caught fish –
gutted and then baked over an open fire – is simple and delicious, but
you need to ensure that mussels and other shellfish are from a safe
source. Avoid mushrooms unless you are totally certain they are edible.

Getting fit

Begin a daily fitness programme at least a month before
your trip. It will not only build strength and stamina for
the activities ahead, but will also help to protect you
against injury and illness.

Regular gentle exercise improves the efficiency of your heart and
lungs, keeps your muscles well toned and boosts endurance, agility
and co-ordination. For most adventure trips, however, you will need
to build on this basic level of fitness by planning a programme that
develops strength and stamina where it's needed most. If you
have any health concerns, consult your doctor before beginning a
fitness programme.

How fit are you?
Check your fitness by performing a step test. This involves stepping on
and off an exercise bench about 30cm (12in) high, maintaining a steady
'walking' rhythm for three minutes before stopping and taking your
pulse. Once you've established this useful benchmark you can monitor
improvements in your fitness by regularly checking your post-exercise
heart rate.

Stretching and breathing
Before and after any exercise session spend ten minutes or so stretching and loosening up to minimize the risk of muscle or joint injury.
Start with your neck and work downwards, holding each stretch
position for several seconds to flex (in turn) muscles in your shoulders,
back, arms, waist and legs. Limber up before exercise by taking a brisk
walk or short jog. Learning some breathing exercises is also a good
way to improve your endurance and resist fatigue.

Strength and stamina
Many of the adventure activities in this book require specific fitness
training to develop certain muscle groups and boost stamina. Such
exercise, however, should be built on a solid platform of all-round
cardio-vascular and muscular fitness. Swimming and cycling are both
excellent for general aerobic exercise and toning muscles with little risk
of strain or injury. If you prefer running, make sure you wear suitable
footwear to protect yourself from impact injuries.

Ultimately, of course, you need to exercise in a way that matches your adventure activity as closely as possible. For trekking or mountaineering, get used to carrying a backpack on walks near home, gradually building up the distance covered, the weight of your pack and the roughness of the terrain. Rock climbers can hone their strength and agility on practice walls at local gyms. Mountain bikers and scuba-divers should also find it straightforward to bolster their endurance by training locally. However, for more unusual activities, such as sea-kayaking or husky sledding, you may need to resort to the gym and concentrate on the muscle groups that you will be using most.

Mental fitness

Tackling an adventure with a positive mental attitude is a crucial part of overall fitness, and it stems largely from confidence in your physical ability, travel-planning, equipment and safety training. Knowing that you could cope in an emergency helps to eradicate anxiety, while personal commitment and determination will help you realize your goals. Never become so overambitious or obsessed with targets, however, that you start compromising safety.

It all feels worthwhile when you reach the summit

Staying healthy

Adventure travel, by its very nature, involves an element of risk. However, by carefully researching the potential health and safety hazards you will be better equipped to deal with emergencies.

RISK ASSESSMENT

Carrying out a risk assessment should go hand in hand with the very earliest stages of planning your adventure. These are some of the questions you should ask yourself:

- Are you experienced enough? If not, will training be provided?
- Are you satisfied that the tour operator maintains high safety standards?
- Do you have the right clothing and gear?
- Are you physically and mentally prepared?
- Do you need any vaccinations?
- Have you researched potential natural hazards?
- Do you need to take a course in first-aid or wilderness survival?

You should know how to administer basic first-aid (for minor bites, stings etc) or stabilize someone who is seriously injured (with toxic shock or severe wound, for example) while you summon medical help.

NATURAL HAZARDS

Extreme weather Find out what temperatures, humidity, wind, rainfall or snowfall you can expect at your destination and plan accordingly – either by changing your dates of travel or taking clothing and equipment that will withstand the elements. Severe weather can trigger a wide range of potentially lethal events, from lightning and sandstorms to bushfires and extreme windchill.

Land and sea hazards Fast-flowing rivers, offshore rip-currents, quicksand, avalanche zones, glacier crevasses – be aware of the potential danger posed by these natural hazards and how to cope with them or, better still, how to avoid them.

Dangerous animals and plants Most wild animals avoid human contact and will only attack you if they feel threatened. There are exceptions – crocodiles, for example, are opportunistic ambush predators quite capable of taking people who approach within range, while mosquitoes transmit potentially fatal diseases. As far as plants and fungi are concerned, remember to leave well alone anything you even vaguely suspect is poisonous. It's vital that you understand what's out there and know how to avoid it or deal with an unforeseen encounter.

PERSONAL FIRST-AID KIT

Several outdoor gear suppliers produce first-aid kits tailored for different uses. For example, Nomad Travel (www.nomadtravel.co.uk) has everything from a Travel Survival Kit, suitable for minor day-to-day treatments when you are within 24 hours of medical facilities, to an Independent Medical Kit for longer travels in remote areas. If you are compiling your own first-aid kit, make sure it contains the following:

- Scissors
- Tweezers
- Thermometer
- Surgical gloves
- Antiseptic wipes
- Gauze swabs
- Assorted plasters (Band-Aids)
- Roll of adhesive strip
- Surgical tape
- Wound dressings
- Triangular bandage
- Crêpe bandage
- Cotton wool
- Cotton buds (swabs)

- Safety pins
- Scalpel blades
- Antiseptic cream
- Anti-fungal cream
- Calamine lotion
- Painkillers *
- Throat lozenges *
- Indigestion pills *
- Diarrhoea pills *
- Rehydration sachets
- 5ml spoon
- Tiger balm
- Eyewash
- Antihistamines *
- Iodine tincture

- Insect bite relief
- Prescription medicine *
- Motion sickness remedies *
- Blister pads
- Dental kit ***

Sterile kit **

- 2ml, 5ml, 10ml syringes
- Sterile needles
- Intravenous cannula (tube)
- Pre-injection swabs
- Certificate of verification

Key

These items may only be available after consultation with your doctor or pharmacist.
** Sterile equipment should be used only by a medical professional.*
*** Designed for temporary treatment of loose fillings, dislodged caps or teeth, toothache and broken teeth.*

Notes

- Always keep your first-aid kit in your hand luggage.
- Keep empty packaging to remind you of what you need to replace.

PERSONAL SURVIVAL KIT

- Fishing line, hooks and sinkers
- Scalpel and wire saw
- Length of sturdy cord
- Safety pins and sewing kit
- Rehydration sachets
- Sterile wipes

- Plasters (Band-Aids) and bandage
- Painkillers
- Potassium permanganate
- Water sterilizing tablets
- Plastic bag for holding water

- Compass and whistle
- Waterproof matches
- Flint and steel
- Tealight candles
- Notepaper and pencil
- Survival blanket/ bivvy bag
- Tin opener

DISEASES

Most travel entails either recommended or compulsory vaccinations, and it's important that you begin a programme of immunization at least six weeks prior to departure.

Disease	Symptoms	Causes
Cholera	Nausea, diarrhoea, vomiting, cramps and dehydration.	Bacterial infection from contaminated water and food.
Diptheria/ tetanus/ polio	Diptheria: sore throat, swollen neck, skin ulcers. Tetanus: fever, muscle spasms, difficulty with swallowing. Polio: fever, sore throat, nausea, headache and, in extreme cases, paralysis.	Diptheria: bacterial infection spread through close contact. Tetanus: bacterial infection from spores entering wounds. Polio: viral infection from contaminated food or drink.
Hepatitis A	Chills, fever, loss of appetitive, nausea, lethargy, jaundice, dark urine, pale faeces.	Viral liver disease from faecally contaminated food and drinking water.
Hepatitis B	Nausea, vomiting, jaundice, pale urine. Infected people may not develop symptoms.	Viral infection transmitted through sexual contact or contact with contaminated blood, needles etc.
HIV	No specific symptoms.	Viral infection that can lead to AIDS. Transmitted through sexual contact or contact with contaminated blood, needles etc.
Japanese encephalitis	Severe flu-like symptoms, including headache, stiff neck, confusion and eventually coma. Fatal in 30 per cent of untreated cases.	Viral disease from nighttime-biting mosquitoes in areas of Indian subcontinent and Southeast Asia.
Malaria	Fever, chills, shivering, headache, lethargy. In worst cases, a life-threatening coma can develop within 24 hours of first symptoms developing.	Parasitic disease transmitted by mosquito bite.
Rabies	Fever, headache, aggression, loss of appetite, thirst, inability to drink, tingling around wound, paralysis.	Viral disease transmitted through the bite of an infected mammal. Usually fatal once symptoms develop.
Tick-borne encephalitis	Fever, headache, nausea, followed by confusion, coma and paralysis.	Viral disease spread by infected tick bites. Occurs from Central Europe to Russia and Japan during summer months.
Typhoid	Headache, fever, delirium, lethargy, abdominal pain, constipation.	Bacterial infection from faecally contaminated water and food. Highest risk area is the Indian subcontinent.
Yellow fever	Severe flu-like symptoms, jaundice.	Viral disease spread by daytime-biting mosquitoes in parts of Africa and Central and South America.

Notes
• Other diseases spread by biting insects include dengue fever (mosquito), river blindness (blackfly), leishmaniasis (sandfly) and sleeping sickness (tsetse fly).
• Check the latest government health reports for outbreaks of avian flu and meningitis and follow recommended preventative measures.

Prevention (see also page 50)	Vaccine
Treat drinking water, avoid undercooked food.	Recommended for high-risk areas.
Diptheria: avoid contact with carriers. Tetanus: Clean all wounds thoroughly. Polio: treat drinking water, avoid undercooked food.	Combined vaccine; part of childhood immunization programme with booster every ten years for travel.
Treat drinking water, avoid undercooked food, maintain high levels of hygiene.	Vaccination plus booster provides immunity for 20 years or more.
Carry a sterile kit, avoid unprotected sex.	Recommended for people spending long periods in endemic areas.
Carry sterile needles, avoid unprotected sex.	Currently no vaccine or cure, although anti-viral drugs can delay the progress of the disease.
Take precautions against being bitten. Avoid rice fields at night, where this type of mosquito is known to breed.	Recommended for stays of one month or more in rural areas. A course of three vaccines should be started six weeks before travel.
Take precautions against being bitten. Seek professional advice on the best course of anti-malarial tablets for your destination – note that this only reduces the risk of malaria. Seek urgent medical attention if you develop a temperature of 38°C (100°F) or more after entering a risk area.	None currently available. Medication is effective if given early enough. Self-treatment kits are available for those travelling for long periods in remote locations.
Never approach or handle animals you don't know. Clean and sterilize wounds thoroughly. Seek vaccination without delay.	Recommended for travellers who are more than 24 hours away from medical facilities. One-month course of vaccines.
Avoid tick-infested areas. Wear long trousers treated with repellent. Check for ticks and remove carefully to ensure mouthparts do not remain embedded in the skin. Apply antiseptic cream.	Recommended for those who may be visiting infected areas (that is, forests and farmland) for long periods.
Treat drinking water, avoid undercooked food. Antibiotics provide effective treatment.	Provides around 80 per cent protection for three years. Available as combined vaccine with hepatitis A. Recommended for travellers visiting areas with poor hygiene.
Take precautions against being bitten.	Certificate of vaccination is a mandatory entry requirement for certain countries. Immunization is effective for ten years.

BASIC PREVENTATIVE MEASURES

Safe drinking water Boiling water for five minutes is the best way to ensure it's safe for drinking. However, you can also obtain clean water by using a purifying pump containing filters impregnated with sterilizing chemicals such as iodine, chlorine and silver. Remember to carry spare filters. Avoid ice and ice cream made from uncertain sources.

Insect bite prevention Wear long-sleeved shirts and long trousers treated with 100 per cent DEET. Use bedding and mosquito nets pretreated with permethrin. Apply repellents to exposed skin, particularly between dusk and dawn, when many mosquitoes are active. Wear a head net if swarms are likely. Use plug-in devices, sprays, burning coils or citronella candles to keep your room free of insects.

The king cobra is the world's longest venomous snake

BASIC FIRST-AID

Altitude sickness Caused by ascending mountains over 3,000m (9,800ft) too quickly, symptoms range from headache and nausea to life-threatening pulmonary or cerebral oedema. Always allocate sufficient days for acclimatization, climb slowly and drink plenty of fluids. The best cure is to descend as quickly as possibly. If symptoms persist, seek urgent medical help.

Bites Flush wound with clean water and soap, apply sterile dressing (adding pressure to stop blood flow if necessary) and bandage. In the event of a venomous snakebite treat the casualty for shock (see right), bandage the area

The ABC of resuscitation

Airway Check patient's mouth and remove any obstruction. Tilt head back by lifting chin and pressing gently on forehead.

Breathing Place your cheek next to patient's mouth and nose for up to 10 seconds to detect breathing. Watch for movement of chest.

Circulation Check the patient's pulse.

• If pulse and breathing are found, put patient in recovery position.

• If the patient is not breathing, begin cardiopulmonary resuscitation (CPR). The British Red Cross recommends 30 chest compressions, at a rate of 100 per minute, to a depth of 4–5cm (1.5–2in), followed by two rescue breaths of 1 second each, ensuring the airway is open and mouth sealed. Then repeat this sequence, starting with the chest compressions. Do not apply pressure over the ribs or the bottom of the breastbone.

and keep it below heart level. Do not apply a tourniquet, cut
the wound or try to suck out the venom. Get to a hospital as soon
as possible.

Bleeding Clean and dress even minor cuts to avoid infection. Use
sterile tweezers to remove small foreign bodies, like thorns, but never
attempt to dislodge large or deeply embedded objects. For severe
external bleeding, perform ABC if necessary (see box), press a clean
dressing to the wound and apply pressure to stop blood flow. Bandage
firmly but not too tightly. Monitor patient until professional help arrives.

Blisters Clean affected area and apply padding. Do not burst.

Burns Flood the burn with cold water for ten minutes, then cover
with non-adhesive dressing and bandage. Do not apply creams.

Diarrhoea Encourage the patient to drink plenty of fluids, including
rehydration solutions, to ward off dehydration.

Fractures Immobilize the fracture and the joints above and below
with a sling, splint or padding. Treat for shock and monitor patient until
help arrives.

Frostbite First, treat for symptoms of hypothermia (see below).
Remove gloves or socks and boots carefully. Warm affected areas in
your lap or under your armpits. Alternatively, place in luke-warm water.
Do not rub.

Heat exhaustion Recognize the symptoms: headache, dizziness,
nausea, cramps and rapid breathing. Lay casualty in a cool, shady place
with feet raised. Administer sips of weak saline solution (one teaspoon
of salt per litre of water).

Heatstroke A potentially fatal condition where the body temperature
soars to over 40°C (104°F). Symptoms include headache, dizziness, hot
and flushed skin, rapid pulse and delirium, followed by unconsciousness.
Reduce the body temperature as quickly as possible, covering the
casualty in cold soaked clothing. Monitor the patient carefully in case
resuscitation is required. Contact emergency services.

Hypothermia A dangerous condition caused when the body
temperature drops to below 35°C (95°F). Hypothermia victims should
be wrapped in warm dry clothing and helped into a sleeping bag
or survival blanket. Offer a warm drink and be ready to resuscitate
if necessary.

Shock A reduction of blood flow around the body can lead to
organ failure and death. Treat shock by lying the victim down with legs
raised above head level. Loosen clothing, monitor pulse and breathing
and offer reassurance. Keep the patient warm with a sleeping bag until
medical help arrives.

Stings Remove bee stings, wash affected area and apply sting relief
cream. Check whether patient is susceptible to anaphylactic shock.

Sunburn Always protect your skin by wearing a hat, sunglasses and
long-sleeved clothing and regularly apply high-factor suncream and lip
balm. Treat sunburn by laying a cold soaked cloth over affected area.
Apply calamine lotion or after-sun cream.

Action

Contents

Main picture: Climbing Aconcagua, the highest mountain in the Americas. Left, from top: Camel safari to Petra, Jordan; quad-biking; surfing in Queensland, Australia; hot-air ballooning over the Serengeti

Land

In a world where adventure travellers seek ever more daring and high-tech challenges, it's reassuring – though not altogether surprising – to discover that good old-fashioned trekking is as popular as ever. The original adventure holiday, trekking is a term derived from an old Boer word describing their long, arduous journeys into South Africa's hinterland during the 1830s. Nowadays, of course, you can trek almost anywhere in the world, from Cornwall to Kilimanjaro, desert to jungle. You can get a taster of life on the trail with day-hikes like New Zealand's Tongariro Alpine Crossing, or you can embark on more epic affairs like the six-month Appalachian Trail. Even in the depths of winter, cross-country skiing provides the adventure traveller with the means to roam and explore. Those with higher ideals can take a step up into the rarefied (and far more technical) world of mountaineering or rock climbing, while more down-to-earth types will find endless adventure opportunities in the world's cave systems.

Top left: Along the Inca Trail. Bottom left: Climbing 'El Cap', Yosemite. Right: Clearwater Cave, Mulu National Park

Contents

> **Key**
>
> The numbers/letters in circles on this page correspond to the locations marked on the map on pages 56–7.

Land: World Map

ARCTIC
OCEAN

ROCKY MOUNTAINS

Vancouver

Winnipeg

Quebec

New York

San Francisco

Washington
DC

Los Angeles

Dallas

SIERRA MADRE

NORTH
ATLANTIC
OCEAN

Dublin

Barcel
Madrid

Marrakesh

Hawaiian
Islands

Mexico City

PACIFIC
OCEAN

Bogotá

BRAZILIAN HIGHLANDS

Lima

Brasilia

ANDES

São Paulo

Santiago

Buenos
Aires

SOUTH
ATLANTIC
OCEAN

St Petersburg

Moscow

SAYAN MOUNTAINS

Ulaanbaatar

GOBI DESERT

Beijing

Istanbul ③

Baghdad

Tehran

Tokyo

⑯

Cairo

Karachi

②④

Delhi

②③

②⑤ HIMALAYA

②②

②①

PACIFIC OCEAN

R A

Khartoum

Mumbai

Hong Kong

②⓪

Bangkok

⑲

Nairobi

inshasa

①⑧

⑤

INDIAN OCEAN

②⑥

Cairns

Harare

Great Barrier Reef

Johannesburg

④

④

⑧

GREAT DIVIDING RANGE

Perth

Sydney

Auckland

②⑦

Canberra

⑦

⑤

②⑧

③⓪

⑤

②⑨

Trekking

Few adventures are more liberating, satisfying or straightforward than trekking. Venture onto one of the world's great hiking trails and you immediately feel a strong sense of freedom and purpose. The dilemma is deciding where to go.

Naturally, Mt Everest looms large in the minds of many trekkers. But while the hallowed trail to Base Camp still ranks as one of the world's ultimate hiking adventures, there are plenty of equally exciting alternatives to explore – not only in the Himalaya, but in just about every mountain range and wild place

> The forest had drawn a green veil around us; a silent shroud of moss and leaves strung between soaring trunks of Sitka spruce.

you care to set foot in. Treks can last for anything from a day up to several months. Many follow long-established trading routes or ancient pilgrimage trails, while others probe remote tracts of wilderness. On Peru's Inca Trail (see pages 72–5), you can step out in search of the fabled Lost City of Machu Picchu, while Australia's Larapinta Trail (see pages 76–7) takes you on a spiritual stroll through the Dreamtime. Some routes are well trodden and can be tackled by the relatively inexperienced; others require a pioneering spirit, careful preparation and a whole support team of guides and porters. Wherever you choose to roam, however, the intrinsic pleasure of trekking lies in its ability to reset your daily routine to a slower and simpler rhythm, helping you to tune into the local environment, its culture, people and wildlife.

ADVENTURE**RATING**

Daring:	⍟⍟
Eco-friendly:	⍟⍟⍟⍟
Expensive:	⍟⍟
Physical:	⍟
Technical:	⍟⍟⍟

The stunning turquoise water of Lake Gokyo, Nepal

ADVENTURE CALLING
The world at your feet

Although there are numerous trekking locations around the world, your wish list will be whittled down by factors such as budget, experience, season and time. Chances are, however, it will always feature some of the following classic treks.

KEY TO SYMBOLS

Ø **Easy:** Although you may be walking for five or six hours a day, these treks are at low altitude and are suitable for anyone of reasonable fitness.
ØØ **Moderate:** Good fitness required for up to seven hours walking a day, sometimes at altitude, but usually on good paths and tracks.
ØØØ **Challenging:** Remote trails, difficult terrain and long walking days, often at high altitude, but a superb challenge for regular hillwalkers.

NORTH AMERICA
South Kaibab Trail, USA *ØØ*
www.nps.gov/grca
Best time to go: Late spring and early autumn
The Grand Canyon is extraordinary enough when viewed from the rim, but it's only when you hike into its depths that the immense scale and special atmosphere of this natural wonder can be fully appreciated. The South Kaibab Trail descends through a series of steep switchbacks from the South Rim, passing the aptly named Ooo-Ahh Point before reaching Cedar Ridge – a sensible 5km (3-mile) round-trip target for a day hike. Overnight hikers can push on to Phantom Ranch, beside the Colorado River in the base of the canyon. Do not attempt to hike from the rim to the river and back in one day, especially during summer. Plan on taking twice as long to hike up as it took to hike down, and carry plenty of water.

Appalachian Trail, USA *ØØ*
www.appalachiantrail.org
Best time to go: March–September
Allow six months (and five million steps) to hike the entire 3,500km (2,175-mile) Appalachian Trail, from Springer Mountain in Georgia to Katahdin, Maine.

Kalalau Trail, Hawaii *ØØ*
www.kalalautrail.com
Best time to go: Year-round; June–July is driest
Hawaii's premier trek, the 18km (11-mile) Kalalau Trail clings to lushly forested cliffs and valleys

on Kauai's magnificent Na Pali Coast. Stunning views aside, the ultimate goal is a secluded sandy beach where most walkers camp two nights before hiking out again.

John Muir Trail, USA ∅∅
www.pcta.org
Best time to go: July–September
From the granite domes and ostrich-plume waterfalls of Yosemite to the 4,418m (14,491ft) summit of Mt Whitney, this 340km (211-mile) trail (part of the 4,265km/2,650-mile Pacific Crest Trail) celebrates the best of California's High Sierra.

Chilkoot Trail, USA and Canada ∅∅
www.nps.gov/klgo
Best time to go: Mid-June to September
Follow in the footsteps of eager prospectors in the 1890s Klondike Gold Rush on this 53km (33-mile) trail from Dyea (near Skagway) in Alaska deep into the heart of the Canadian Yukon.

West Coast Trail, Canada ∅∅∅
www.pc.gc.ca
Best time to go: May–September
Originally used to rescue shipwreck survivors on Vancouver Island's notorious 'Graveyard of the Pacific' coast, this 76km (47-mile) trail links a wild succession of sandy beaches, rugged cliffs and ancient virgin rainforest. Allow five to seven days and make sure you're completely clued up on tides, weather and bears before you set off.

SOUTH AMERICA
Torres del Paine Circuit, Chile ∅∅ – ∅∅∅
www.torresdelpaine.com
Best time to go: October–March
The ultimate Patagonian hike, the 115km (71-mile) Torres del Paine Circuit loops around the surreal, sawtooth peaks of the Paine massif. Even with pack-horses to carry your baggage, you should reckon on eight days of demanding hiking, camping beside glacial lakes and scaling the 1,241m (4,070ft) John Garner Pass in the most remote part of the range.

Huayhuash Circuit, Peru ∅∅∅
www.peru.info
Best time to go: May–October

See the Grand Canyon close up on the South Kaibab Trail

ACTION 61

Allow at least 11 days for this epic circuit of the towering, ice-fluted Huayhuash massif. With a support crew of Quechua Indians, you scale a succession of passes before reaching a high-point of 5,200m (17,00ft) if you include the optional ascent of Cerro Jyamy. Views of Andean giants like Huascaran (6,768m/22,199ft) and Yerupaja (6,634m/21,759ft) are the crowning glories of this challenging trek, but you also get a chance to visit the base camp of Siula Grande where Joe Simpson 'touched the void'.

Roraima, Venezuela 🌿🌿
www.think-venezuela.net
Best time to go: December–March
Trek into Arthur Conan Doyle's Lost World on this fascinating hike which scales the 2,810m-high

End of the line: Robin Hood's Bay on England's northeast coast

(9,217ft) table mountain of Roraima. There are no dinosaurs on top, but you will find an otherworldly landscape of bizarre rock formations and plants and animals found nowhere else. Allow two days to explore the summit.

Camino Real, Panama ∅∅ – ∅∅∅
www.visitpanama.com
Best time to go: January–May
Dating from the 1500s, when mules laden with Inca gold trudged along a cobblestone path from the Pacific to the Caribbean to meet galleons bound for Spain, the 80km (50-mile) Camino Real has been reclaimed by the jungle. Be prepared for five days of tough, often muddy, hiking, wading along rivers and venturing into remote rainforest where sightings of jaguar are not unheard of.

EUROPE
South West Coast Path, England ∅
www.southwestcoastpath.com
Best time to go: Year-round
One of Britain's finest long-distance routes, this 1,014km (630-mile), eight-week ramble follows the crinkle-cut coastline of Dorset, Devon and Cornwall, delving into sheltered estuaries and sleepy fishing villages and striding out along surf-strafed beaches and cliffs.

Coast to Coast, England ∅ – ∅∅
www.coast2coast.co.uk
Best time to go: Year-round
A fitting legacy to legendary fell-walker Alfred Wainwright, this 306km (190-mile) trail links the

Irish Sea to the North Sea, passing through three national parks on its route between St Bees in Cumbria and Robin Hood's Bay in North Yorkshire.

Tour du Mont Blanc, France, Italy & Switzerland ∅∅∅
www.leshouches.com
www.aiat-monte-bianco.com
Best time to go: July to mid-September
Cower beneath the imposing hulk of the Mont Blanc massif on this 170km (105-mile) circuit, which takes seven to ten days and reaches a highpoint of 2,665m (8,741ft) at Col des Fours.

GR10, France ∅∅ – ∅∅∅
www.gr-infos.com
Best time to go: Spring and autumn
Dabble your toes in the Atlantic, then put on your boots for an 800km (500-mile), seven-week jaunt across the French Pyrenees to paddle in the Mediterranean.

GR20, Corsica ∅∅∅
www.visit-corsica.com
Best time to go: Late June and early September
One of Europe's toughest trails, the 190km (118-mile), 13-day GR20 weaves beneath rocky pinnacles and pink granite peaks between Bavella and Calenzana, with an optional hike to the summit of Paglia Orba (2,525m/8,282ft).

Lycian Way, Turkey ∅ – ∅∅
www.lycianway.com
Best time to go: February to mid-July, September to mid-November

You will need a month to complete the 509km (316-mile) Lycian Way along Turkey's south coast (from Fethiye to Antalya). Alternatively, dip in for a taste of its pine forests, Mediterranean coastline and ancient ruins.

AFRICA
Toubkal Circuit, Morocco ∅∅
www.visitmorocco.org
Best time to go: Spring or autumn
Undulating between valley and pass, this 88km (55-mile) trail immerses walkers in the dramatic scenery and Berber culture of the Atlas Mountains. There's also an opportunity to climb Djebel Toubkal (4,167m/ 13,668ft), from where there are far-reaching views towards the Sahara.

Kilimanjaro, Tanzania ∅∅ – ∅∅∅
www.tanzaniatouristboard.com
Best time to go: January–February, September–October
Six well-maintained trails lead to Kilimanjaro's Ulhuru Peak (5,896m/19,339ft) and although none require mountaineering skills, trekking to the Roof of Africa is physically demanding and can only be attempted in an organized group led by a registered guide. Around half of those who set out to climb 'Kili' turn back before they reach the top. The popular 64km (40-mile) Marangu Route links three overnight huts and requires at least five days for both the ascent and descent. The more demanding Machame route involves camping and is one of the most scenic options, particularly if you descend on the Mweka Route. The seven-day Rongai Route, meanwhile, follows a remote and relatively untrekked trail on the mountain's northern flank.

Rwenzori Mountains, Uganda ∅∅∅
www.uwa.or.ug
Best time to go: November–March
For trekkers, the highpoint of the Rwenzoris (or Mountains of the Moon) is usually Elena Hut at 4,540m (14,890ft). To reach it you must tackle cloying bogs and dense stands of giant bamboo in some of Africa's most demanding mountain wilderness. To venture further on the glaciated peaks of Mt Stanley (5,190m/17.025ft) requires crampons, an ice axe and technical skill.

Simien Mountains, Ethiopia ∅∅
www.tourismethiopia.org
Best time to go: October–May
With stomach-swooping escarpments, broad river valleys and towering mountain plateaux, the Simien Mountains have some of Africa's most dramatic scenery. Allow around ten days for a classic trek taking in the Geech Abyss and 4,543m (14,901ft) summit of Ras Dashen.

ASIA
Everest Base Camp, Nepal ∅∅
www.welcomenepal.com
Best time to go: October–May
After flying into Lukla, follow in the footsteps of Hillary and Tenzing to the Sherpa capital of Namche Bazaar and beyond to the upper reaches of the Khumbu Valley, where the trekkers' summit

The trek up Kilimanjaro is very demanding

of 5,600m (18,370ft) Kala Patar provides a head-spinning panorama of Himalayan giants, including Mt Everest (8,850m/29,000ft). If your legs and lungs are up for it, walk the extra few kilometres across the jumbled moraine of the Khumbu Glacier to reach Everest Base Camp. With at least three weeks to spare, add on a side trip to the Gokyo Valley – another superb vantage point for Everest.

Annapurna Circuit, Nepal ∅∅

www.welcomenepal.com

Best time to go: October–May

The 190km (118-mile) Annapurna Circuit has been trodden by pilgrims and traders for centuries. A trek of contrasts, it threads through farmland, forest, desert and tundra, offering spectacular views of no fewer than 12 peaks above 7,000m (23,000ft), including Dhaulagiri and Annapurna. But none of this comes easy. In addition to scaling

the 5,416m (16,764ft) Thorung La, one section of the trail gains 430m (1,410ft) in altitude over 3,000 gruelling steps – akin to scaling Chicago's Sears Tower. Allow 16–21 days for the Circuit, staying in villages en route.

Markha Valley, India ∅∅∅

www.ladakh-tourism.com

Best time to go: June–October

The finest short trek in Ladakh, this eight-day trail enters the realm of the snow leopard in a remote and little-changed corner of the Himalaya.

Concordia, Pakistan ∅∅∅

www.tourism.gov.pk

Best time to go: June–September

Prepare to be dazzled by the 'Throne Room of the Mountain Gods' on this 14-day Karakoram trek beneath the mighty peaks of K2 (8,611m/28,244ft), Broad Peak (8,047m/26,394ft) and Gasherbrum IV (7,925m/25,994ft).

ACTION 65

Majestic peaks along the Annapurna Circuit

Mt Kailash, Tibet ⍉⍉

Best time to go: May–October

According to Tibetan Buddhists, a circuit of Mt Kailash (6,714m/ 22,021ft) cleanses your life of sins. Walk 108 times around this sacred mountain (a 52km/32-mile route) and devotees believe you will achieve nirvana.

Kokoda Trail, Papua New Guinea ⍉⍉

www.kokodatrail.com.au

Best time to go: May–September

The site of bitter fighting between Australian and Japanese forces during World War II, the 96km (60-mile) Kokoda Trail links the north and south coast of Papua New Guinea across jungle-clad mountains. Expect slippery trails, high temperatures and humidity – and a warm welcome from Koiari and Orokaiva villagers.

AUSTRALASIA

Great Ocean Walk, Australia ⍉

www.greatoceanwalk.com.au

Best time to go: December–February

Australia's newest trek, the 100km (62-mile) Great Ocean Walk hugs the Victoria coastline, delving into fern gullies and undulating between soaring cliffs and empty beaches before reaching the Twelve Apostles – a regiment of giant sea stacks marching into the Southern Ocean.

Overland Track, Australia ⍉⍉

www.overlandtrack.com.au

Best time to go: November–April

Keep your eyes open for wombats, wallabies and Tasmanian Devils as you hike this 65km (40-mile) trail through the heart of world heritage wilderness. The seven-day Overland Track links Cradle Mountain and Lake St Clair with an optional excursion to climb Mt Ossa (1,617m/ 5,304ft). Accommodation is in huts – but you need to book well in advance for this popular trek.

Milford Track, New Zealand ⍉ – ⍉⍉

www.newzealand.com

Best time to go: November–April

This classic Kiwi tramp promises a quintessential Fiordland experience (wet, wild and wonderful) as you hike 54km (34 miles) from Lake Manapouri, through Tolkeinesque forests, to the shores of Milford Sound.

Tongariro Alpine Crossing, New Zealand ⍉⍉

www.newzealand.com

Best time to go: Year-round

Often hailed as New Zealand's finest day walk, this 17km (11-mile) North Island tramp grapples with the lunar terrain of Tongariro and Ngauruhoe – a pair of volcanoes in World Heritage-listed Tongariro National Park. As well as trekking through a variety of habitats, from alpine scrub to tussock grassland and lush podocarp forest, you will see jade-coloured lakes, sulphur-encrusted rocks and hissing fumaroles. Optional sidetrips include an ascent of Ngauruhoe from Mangatepopo Saddle or a bid for the top of Tongariro from Red Crater. If you have time, extend the tramp to four days to include the entire 61km (38-mile) Tongariro Northern Circuit.

ADVENTURE BRIEFING
Best foot forward

Setting off on your trekking adventure might seem as simple as putting one foot in front of the other. However, even if you opt for a fully supported guided trek, there are several important factors you need to consider before hitting the trail.

Getting on the right track

You've decided where to go, you've sussed out the prime trekking season and allowed enough time (with a few contingency days) to safely tackle the hike. What next? Some decisions, such as where to sleep, how far to walk each day and whether or not to hike solo or as part of a group, depend largely on your destination. For example, many

Admiring the view on the Larapinta Trail, Australia

people trek Nepal's Annapurna Circuit on their own, staying in lodges or teahouses and planning each day as it comes. This independent approach, however, is extremely inadvisable in more remote areas – and may even be ruled out entirely on treks like the Inca Trail and Kilimanjaro, where guides are compulsory. Even if you yearn for peace and solitude, don't underestimate the added value of a knowledgeable guide – or the support of fellow trekkers and porters during an emergency. At the very least you should always remember to obtain relevant permits well in advance and notify authorities of your plans. Research your route carefully, taking into account the ups and downs, maximum altitude and type of terrain. Build in acclimatization days and allow extra time for rest stops or simply to appreciate particularly beautiful sections of the trail.

Beginners and children

Trekking is one of the most accessible adventure activities, with everything from day hikes for beginners to non-technical summit attempts for the more experienced. Even parents with young children needn't be restricted, thanks to the lightweight backpack-style carriers now available. In some locations, such as the Atlas Mountains, mules can be used to carry flagging children.

What to wear

A layered system of clothing (see page 28) provides adaptability during a typical trekking day, when you might be setting off during the chill of pre-dawn and either sweating it out by midday or coping with freezing winds on a high pass. Try to keep base- and mid-layer clothing as dry as possible to avoid becoming chilled. A breathable waterproof jacket and trousers are essential, although you may prefer a poncho for

ECO**FILE**

- Pack biodegradable soap and toilet paper, long-lasting lithium batteries and plastic rubbish-collecting bags.
- Take away non-biodegradable items and use a water filter instead of buying bottled water.
- Save fuel at lodges by ordering the same food at the same time.
- Wear extra clothing to keep warm rather than huddling around a camp fire.
- Only indulge in a hot shower if water is heated by solar power or non-wood stoves.
- If no toilet facilities are available, make sure you are at least 30m (32 yards) from any water source.
- Keep to trails to avoid erosion and damage to vegetation.
- Always ask permission before photographing somebody.
- Make a donation to local schools rather than handing out money and sweets.
- Support local conservation groups, such as the Annapurna Conservation Area Project in Nepal.

ESSENTIAL**GEAR**

• Map • **Compass** • Whistle • **Knife** First-aid kit • **Waterproof coat** • Spare clothes • **Head torch** • Matches • **Sunhat** • Sunblock • **Sunglasses (with side shields)** • Water purification • **High-energy snacks** • Repair kit containing spare bootlaces, needle and thread etc • **Trekking poles for shock-absorption going downhill and extra power going uphill**

Adequate water and suncream are essential when hiking in hot climes, like Morocco

added circulation on jungle treks where humidity is high. A hat, gloves and scarf are also crucial. You might also want to pack a pair of gaiters, while lightweight walking sandals are useful for river crossings or for 'airing' your feet around camp. Generally speaking, however, footwear should consist of waterproof walking boots and wool-based socks with thick soles for padding and insulation. In cold conditions, wear an additional pair of inner socks made from a breathable fabric that wicks moisture away from the feet. For extreme environments, such as deserts or tropical rainforests, boots are available with specialist features such as increased breath-ability, soles that resist mud-clogging and lace-up systems that help keep leeches out.

What to carry

What you end up carrying depends on the style of trek. Venture solo into the wilderness and you will need everything on your back, from camping and cooking equipment to clothes, food and survival gear. With a team of guides and porters, on the other hand, you will just need to carry day-to-day essentials, such as a water bottle (plus some means of water purification), trail snacks, water-proofs, warm clothing and a personal first-aid kit. Ideally, this should all fit into a 35–45-litre (2,135–2,745cu in) daypack with a padded, well-ventilated back system. Some daypacks even have internal water pouches attached to a flexible hose that you can drink from on the go. Waist belts are also a good idea for storing items that you need frequent access to, such as a camera, binoculars, sunblock, sunglasses, map and compass.

How to stay healthy

As well as getting you fit, a pre-trek regime of walking, wearing a fully laden backpack, will not only ensure that your hiking boots are well worn in, but will also help reduce the risk of muscle strain, fatigue and blisters on your actual trek. Irrespective of fitness, altitude sickness can occur above 2,400m (7,800ft) – see page 50. Other potential dangers for trekkers range from exhaustion and dehydration to heat stroke and hyperthermia. Check that your first-aid kit contains blister patches, rehydration sachets and spare sunblock. Trekking is hot, sweaty work, so aim to drink at least 5 litres (1.3 gallons) of fluid a day (more in hot climates). Adaptable clothing (see page 69) is crucial to protect against the elements, while a carefully planned and realistic walking schedule (taking account of difficult terrain, altitude and the level of experience in your trekking group) helps to prevent exhaustion and accidents. Remember to stop before you look – you can easily twist an ankle (or worse) on uneven terrain. If you hear porters or pack animals coming downhill towards you, always step to the side furthest from the edge.

How to trek...

Uphill: Lean forwards, ensuring your feet are placed flat on the ground before pushing upwards.

Downhill: Lean backwards slightly and take short steps using your trekking pole to relieve strain on the knees.

On steep ascents: Use the so-called 'rest step', dropping your heel and momentarily pausing as you straighten your leg with each step. This shifts weight onto your skeleton, giving muscles a rest.

Across scree slopes: Climb sideways using a trekking pole for support; descend by taking hopping strides.

Across boulder fields: Detour if possible, otherwise move slowly, testing each boulder before committing your full weight.

Across marshy ground: Test the ground ahead with your trekking pole and, if possible, stick to firm patches of grass.

Across rivers: Face the direction of the current and wade across sideways, using your trekking pole both as a support and to probe for holes or rocks.

How to stay footloose and fancy-free

- Ensure toenails are cut short and straight to prevent them from tearing or bruising the ends of your toes.
- Try to wash your feet daily to reduce the build-up of microbes that flourish in sweaty conditions.
- After drying your feet, leave them to air and spend a few minutes massaging the balls and heels with your thumbs.
- Rub antifungal foot powder in between your toes to prevent athlete's foot.

The road to ruins

The record time for the Inca Trail marathon is a little under four hours – but don't treat your trek as a race. Give yourself time and space to enjoy the scenery and ruins of the ultimate Andean pilgrimage.

'The main aim of the Spanish Conquest,' explained our guide, Ruben, 'was to take the soul out of the people; make them forget their culture.' He gestured towards the stone terraces of Llaqtapata, an Inca ruin draped across a hillside below us like tidemarks on a beach. 'That's why Machu Picchu is so special – the Spaniards never found it. The Inca Trail was a state secret. They made it very hard to find, let alone follow. Even commoners weren't allowed to use it.'

We, on the other hand, were being treated like Inca nobility. Having set out from the trailhead next to the milky blue Urubamba River, our group of seven arrived in the village of Huayllabamba to find Sixto, our head porter, waiting for us with a tray of hot, wet towels. Our top-of-the-range tents had already been pitched for us and there was a separate dining tent with a table set for dinner.

Not, of course, that any amount of campsite pampering could conceal the fact that the Inca Trail is actually quite a demanding trek. Scaling the 4,200m (13,800ft) Warmiwañusqa (Dead Woman Pass) on

Spectacular scenery along the Inca Trail

Aerial view over the ruins of Machu Picchu

A taste of adventure

Descending is easier with a sturdy stick

day two, for example, involved a relentless five-hour plod and a vertical gain of 1,200m (4,000ft).

The pass marks the point at which the original surface of the Inca Trail began. Until then we had been walking on rough, dusty tracks – now it was all paved slabs of white granite, meticulously jointed to form a knee-jarring stairway all the way to our second campsite in the Pacamayo Valley.

The following day, we reached Sayacmarca, an exquisite Inca ruin that seemed to have metamorphosed from the bedrock like a cluster of crystals. 'The Incas always worked with nature – never against it', Ruben enthused.

There was thick mist at 5am the next morning. Ruben made us linger over breakfast, so the trail was deserted when we set off on our final stretch of the Inca Trail. I found myself walking slowly, half savouring the last few kilometres – the forest waking, mountain peaks ghosting in and out of view – and half fearing that if I went too fast I might run into a queue of trekkers and shatter the quiet air of expectation.

As the sun emerged, white and pallid in the thinning mist, I climbed a stone stairway and abruptly found myself walking between the stone buttresses of Intipunku, the fabled Sun Gate. There was the murmur of voices – not too many, not too loud – as I stepped forward and braced myself for a first glimpse of Machu Picchu – its terraces barely clinging to a ridge above the Urubamba canyon; the shark-fin peak of Wayñapicchu rising behind the citadel and the whole scene enveloped by the smoky outline of the Vilcanota Mountains.

As the first buses disgorged day-trippers into the ancient streets of the Lost City it suddenly struck me that, for all the spiritual beauty and inspiring architecture of Machu Picchu, they were only going to see part of the story – the dramatic finale, if you like, that accompanies the individual movements of a long, engrossing symphony. During the last four days we'd witnessed the entire masterpiece, from the breathless highs to the grumbling lows – and every Inca-paved step in between.

ECO**FILE**

- To prevent erosion of Inca paving, rubber tips are mandatory for trekking poles. Alternatively, buy local bamboo ones at the start of the trek.
- Don't be tempted to take short cuts; the vegetation at high altitude may take years to recover from careless trampling.
- Take away your rubbish and use boiled/treated water instead of buying bottled water.

FACT**FILE**

Inca Trail, Peru ∅∅
Distance: 43km (27 miles)
Allow: 4–5 days
Start & finish: Most treks begin at Kilometre 82, which, after a 3.5-hour drive from Cusco, is as far as buses can go. Kilometre 88, further down the Urubamba Valley, is only accessible by rail (www.perurail.com). The Inca Trail ends at Machu Picchu, from where you can catch a bus down to Aguas Calientes, where trains depart for Cusco.
When to go: Although the dry season is officially May–October, be prepared for rain at any time of the year. Temperatures range from 0–28°C (32–82°F). The trail is closed each February for maintenance. The November–April rainy season makes paths muddy and slippery, while permits for the July–August high season are booked well in advance.
Need to know: You can only trek the Inca Trail with a registered agency (which will provide a package of permits, guide, porters, camping gear, food, transport to and from trailheads etc) or with a licensed local guide (where you organize everything, carry your own gear, cook for yourself and so on).
Next step: Log on to www.peru.info, the official website for travel in Peru.
Operators: There are numerous trekking agencies in Cusco, including Inka Natura Travel (www.inkanatura.com).

Dream walk

They were once mighty peaks, but 300 million years of erosion have reduced the West MacDonnell Ranges to a stately procession of rust-coloured hills and deep gorges – the wild, yet spiritual, setting for Australia's Larapinta Trail.

Cockatoos fussed overhead as we crossed the dry sandy bed of the Todd River at the start of our week-long trek. Alice Spring's Telegraph Station, built in 1872, stood on its far bank – a monument to the first Europeans who ventured there. Beyond the cluster of buildings the path became more rugged. It sloughed off the last traces of settlement and slipped back into the Dreamtime – the mysterious Aboriginal creation when totemic ancestors roamed Australia, forging its landscape. Caterpillar Dreaming was just one of the spiritual tracks or 'songlines' that we touched on during our first day's walk. The Dreamtime paths of the Arrernte Aborigines are deeply entwined in cultural complexity and secrecy. By contrast, our route would be clearly waymarked.

At Wallaby Gap, a wilderness campsite 17km (11 miles) from Alice Springs, we were met by the 4WD vehicle that would transport our camping gear to each overnight stop. 'These are your swags', explained

The narrow walls of Standley Chasm

our guide, kicking bulky canvas bivouacs off the Land Cruiser's roof. 'It's how we do things out here'. Swags saved the hassle of erecting tents and, as I discovered later that night, they had the added bonus of allowing unsurpassed stargazing. Venus was still a bright pinprick in the east when the camp stirred to life the following morning. By the time the rising sun had inflamed the feathery leaves of the mulga trees, we were back on the trail.

Although technically a desert, the MacDonnell Ranges support over 250 species of plants. Many were deeply rooted in Aboriginal bushlore. Bark from the gnarled old corkwoods, for example, could be burnt and ground to produce a soothing powder for sores, while sap from the sticky hopbush was effective against toothache. This 'pick-your-own pharmacy' was part of a bush superstore that offered juicy witchety grubs and nectar, as well as poisons and spear shafts. All that was missing were the Arrernte people themselves. Their hunter-gatherer lifestyle faded soon after the arrival of European settlers.

At Jay Creek, dingoes passed through our camp some time before dawn. We followed their tracks later that morning, boulder-hopping along a dry creekbed to Fish Hole – a sacred Aboriginal waterhole nestling like quicksilver in a narrow canyon. Permanent water is a rarity in the MacDonnell Ranges. Flash floods have left a legacy of gorges, but even the most determined torrents are eventually quenched by the Simpson Desert to the southeast. This is a place, wrote Banjo Patterson, 'where the creeks run dry or ten feet high'.

The landscape on that day's hike seemed equally extreme. From wading through hillsides of spinifex grass, their unruly tufts of flowering spikes combed by the wind, we later found ourselves striding along a knife-edge ridge where wedge-tailed eagles pirouetted on thermals. We delved into the 'lost world' of a ravine choked with rare cycad palms and clambered amongst the flood-torn limbs of trees lodged in Standley Chasm.

Continuing west by vehicle, we picked up the trail at Ormiston Gorge, where myths of the Dreamtime flow strongly through the contorted strata of ancient, crumbling cliffs.

How out of touch we would have seemed to the Arrernte people, who had learned to mould their lives to the West MacDonnell's natural rhythms of drought, flood and bushfire. Instead of Dreaming tracks, we followed blue arrows on marker posts and relied on a vehicle to carry our supplies.

As we reached the 1,380m (4,256ft) summit of Mt Sonder on the final day, the rest of the West MacDonnell Ranges lay crumpled below us, like monstrous vertebrae half-consumed by the desert. The Larapinta Trail had taken us on a privileged journey through a complex and delicate environment – a part of the outback I had never dreamed existed.

ECO**FILE**

- Respect sacred Aboriginal sites.
- Keep to trails to avoid erosion.
- Take away all garbage.
- Minimize the risk of bushfires.

FACT**FILE**

Larapinta Trail, Australia ∅∅
Distance: 223km (139 miles)
Allow: 12–16 days for a typical trek sampling most highlights, or 20 days to walk the entire trail.
Start & finish: Alice Springs Telegraph Station to Mt Sonder.
When to go: You'll bake in summer; try May–August for cooler daytime temperatures, but chilly nights.
Need to know: Campsites and water sources are well spaced along the trail. You can swim in some gorges.
Next step: Download trek notes and maps from Northern Territory Parks & Wildlife Commission (www.nt.gov.au/nreta/parks/walks/larapinta).
Operators: Trek Larapinta (www.treklarapinta.com.au); World Expeditions (www.worldexpeditions.com).

Should I hire a porter?

Fair employment or flagrant exploitation? There's little doubt that trekking porters have one of the world's toughest jobs, but should you feel guilty about hiring them or view it as a vital contribution to local livelihoods?

Backs bent under crushing loads, feet clad in flip-flops and little more than a plastic bag to provide protection from the rain – such is the stark contrast between the plight of local porters and daypack-toting tourists that some trekkers insist on carrying their own gear. On the face of it, this seems like a noble and justified decision. Each year, porters suffer from more illnesses and injuries than trekkers and, in the event of a porter dying, his dependents have no government social security.

Having said that, however, porters contribute significantly to local employment and livelihoods, and may well earn more hefting loads for tourists (or supplies for lodge owners) than they would working as farmers or traders. Porters on the Inca Trail, for example, receive around 100 sols ($33) per trek – plus tips – and most do two a week. A local farmer, on the other hand, might earn only 50 sols a month. Just as important, though, is the fact that conditions for Inca Trail porters have been improved over recent years with, for example, maximum loads reduced to 25kg (55 lb). The role of porters will always be

Porter ready for action

one of sweat and toil, but that doesn't mean that they should be denied basic rights to appropriate clothing, equipment, shelter, food and medical care. As their employers (either directly by hiring porters themselves, or indirectly by booking through a trekking agency), tourists have a responsibility to ensure that these rights are met before becoming too obsessed with their own trekking goals.

What clothing and equipment should porters have?

Porters are human. They suffer from exposure to cold, rain, snow and glaring sunshine just as trekkers do. It's therefore paramount that they should have adequate clothing, including a windproof jacket, walking boots, thick socks, gloves, hat and sunglasses. Make sure they are also kitted out with a blanket or sleeping bag and have a dedicated shelter in which to spend nights. Cooking equipment, fuel and food are also essential.

What should I do if one of my porters falls ill?

Porters should receive the same standard of medical care as trekkers. Ill or injured porters should never be simply paid off. Instead the trek leader should ensure that the sick porter is accompanied to a medical centre and that sufficient funds are provided to cover treatment.

What else can I do to ensure appropriate porter welfare?

On organized trips, quiz your trekking agency (preferably before you book) on their porter welfare policy. Ask them if they follow guidelines set out by the International Porter Protection Group (www.ippg.net) – a voluntary organization that works to improve the conditions of mountain porters in the tourism industry worldwide. In addition, check that maximum loads (25–30kg/55–66 lb per porter) are not exceeded, that minimum wages are met and that porters receive the full tip intended for them.

Porters are often heavily laden

Rock climbing & ice climbing

Two of the most challenging and potentially dangerous adventure activities, rock climbing and ice climbing not only demand strength and endurance, but also a high level of technical competence and thorough training. Not for the faint-hearted!

> **KEY TO SYMBOLS**
>
> Ø **Easy**
> ØØ **Moderate**
> ØØØ **Challenging**

ADVENTURE CALLING

El Capitan, USA ØØ – ØØØ
www.nps.gov/yose
Best time to go: Spring and autumn
Probably the most revered chunk of granite in the rock-climbing world, 'El Cap' looms 1,095m (3,593ft) above the Merced River at the entrance to California's Yosemite Valley. There are many routes up the sheer face, all of them difficult; allow five days for the 31-pitch ascent of the Nose.

Hell's Gate, Kenya Ø – ØØØ
www.mck.or.ke
Best time to go: July–March
Only a two-hour drive from Nairobi, the dramatic cliffs of Hell's Gate offer excellent rock climbing opportunities for all abilities, from easy routes on East Rib to the more challenging 37m-high (121ft) Groove on Fischer's Tower.

Waterval Boven, South Africa Ø – ØØØ
www.climbing.co.za
Best time to go: Year-round
Nestled in the Drakensberg Mountains on the fringe of the Mpumalanga escarpment, Waterval Boven is the gateway to South Africa's finest rock climbing, with more than 600 routes.

Mt Arapiles, Australia Ø – ØØØ
www.arapiles.net
Best time to go: Spring and autumn
Looming 369m (1,210ft) above the Wimmera plains in western Victoria, the quartzite monolith of Mt Arapiles offers more than 2,500 climbing possibilities, from beginner routes at Declaration Crag and the Organ Pipes to the famous overhanging roof at Kachoong. Arapiles also has arguably the world's hardest climb – 'Punks in the Gym' on The Pharos, a large pillar of rock isolated from the main mountain.

Wharepapa South, New Zealand Ø – ØØ
www.climb.co.nz
Best time to go: Year-round

Scaling the vertiginous El Capitan, Yosemite

Climbing is a technical sport that demands a high degree of fitness

Keystone Canyon, USA ⬚⬚⬚
www.valdezalaska.org
Best time to go: Winter
A short distance from the Alaskan town of Valdez, frozen waterfalls along this 5km-long (3-mile) gorge provide some of the best multipitch ice climbing in the United States. As proof of its pedigree there is an annual Ice Climbing Festival in early March.

Agawa Canyon, Canada ⬚⬚ – ⬚⬚⬚
www.climbingcentral.com
Best time to go: January–April
Reached by the Algoma Central Railway 'Snow Train' from Sault Ste Marie, the Agawa Canyon on Lake Superior's northeast shore is just one of many ice climbing locations in Ontario. At least 70 routes (some more than 200m/650ft high) are available, with new climbs being added each season. One of the most spectacular (and popular) ice climbs in the canyon is the 80m-route (260ft) on the frozen Bridalveil Falls. The 50m (164ft) Flying Circus and 200m (650ft) Pins and Needles, meanwhile, are two of the most challenging.

Hvalfjördur, Iceland ⬚⬚ – ⬚⬚⬚
www.visiticeland.com
Best time to go: November–March
With dozens of routes of all grades, Múlafjall in Hvalfjördur (Whale Fjord) is Iceland's most popular ice climbing area. Most of the climbs are single pitch and there are several safe routes from which you can walk back down from the top.

One of New Zealand's most accessible and diverse rock-climbing areas, Wharepapa's spectacular ignimbrite rock formations on North Island boast more than 800 easily accessible routes. Wharepapa Crag has 180 bolted routes, many of which are suitable for beginner or intermediate climbers, while Froggatt Edge is a popular spot for bouldering.

ADVENTURE BRIEFING

There are several climbing styles, from bouldering (short technical climbs on jumbles of rock) to free climbing (scaling rock faces using only your hands and feet, with equipment for protection only) and ice climbing (using ice axes to tackle frozen waterfalls). Whatever aspect of the sport appeals, however, it is important to accept the element of risk involved and also to undergo formal training. Indoor climbing gyms are excellent places to learn basic techniques, moves and other skills such as rope-handling and tying climbing knots. You also need to become familiar with various items of climbing gear, while a specialized programme of fitness training will help develop strength where it matters most. There is more to climbing than pure muscle power, however. Balance, poise, vigilance and teamwork are equally important.

ECO**FILE**

- Minimize damage to rock faces by avoiding indiscriminate use of fixed equipment.
- Do not disturb vegetation, nesting birds or other wildlife.
- Avoid excessive use of chalk.
- Use slings to protect trees while belaying or abseiling.

ESSENTIAL**GEAR**

• **Helmet** • Lightweight boots with smooth rubber soles for maximum traction on dry rock • **Harness consisting of a waist belt and leg loops** • 50m-long (164ft), 9–11mm (0.35–0.43in) thick rope • **Belay device to help control and stop the rope attached to a climbing partner in the event of a fall** • Safety devices (wires, cams, slings and quickdraws) to secure climber to rock • **Carabiners for attaching rope to safety devices** • Chalk to improve handgrips • **First-aid kit and whistle**

ADVENTURE**RATING**

Daring:	⦾⦾⦾⦾⦾
Eco-friendly:	⦾⦾⦾⦾⦾
Expensive:	⦾⦾⦾⦾⦾
Expertise:	⦾⦾⦾⦾⦾
Fitness:	⦾⦾⦾⦾⦾

Caving

Squirming through narrow passageways deep underground may not be everyone's idea of fun, but there's no denying the adventurous allure of caving – and there are plenty of caves with enough headroom for those who prefer to be upright.

KEY TO SYMBOLS

Ø **Easy**
ØØ **Moderate**
ØØØ **Challenging**

ADVENTURE CALLING
Carlsbad Caverns, USA
Ø – ØØØ

www.nps.gov/cave

Best time to go: Year-round
A subterranean maze beneath the Chihuahuan Desert of New Mexico, Carlsbad Caverns National Park contains 113 caves. Some, like the 3.3ha (8.1-acre) Big Room, can be visited on a self-guided tour, while more challenging caves are only accessible on ranger-led expeditions. The Hall of the White Giant, for example, involves scaling ladders and crawling through tight passageways, while Spider Cave is recommended for anyone afraid of confined spaces.

Hidden Worlds Cenotes, Mexico Ø

www.hiddenworlds.com.mx
Best time to go: November–March

A series of flooded and sunlit caverns near Tulum on the Yucatan Peninsula, the Hidden Worlds Cenotes are best explored on guided swimming or snorkelling tours – unless, that is, you're a certified diver, in which case an 8m-deep (26ft) plunge into stunning Dream Gate Cenote beckons.

Škocjan Caves, Slovenia
Ø – ØØ

www.park-skocjanske-jame.si
Best time to go: Year-round
Top of Europe's underworld, the 5.8km-long (3.6-mile) Škocjan Caves (a UNESCO world heritage sight) can be easily explored on guided tours, which follow slippery but well-lit paths through caverns dripping with stalactites. The highlight is Müller Hall, where 100m-high (330ft) walls rear above the rapid-strewn Reka River. A narrow bridge 45m (147ft) above the cascades and whirlpools is the only way across – and if that doesn't faze you, experienced cavers can delve deeper into the passageways leading down to Dead Lake.

Cango Caves, South Africa
∅ – ∅∅

www.cangocaves.co.za

Best time to go: Year-round

A short way from Oudtshoorn in the Klein Karoo region of the Western Cape, the Cango Caves have easily accessible show caverns. Those in search of adventure can join a guided tour that descends several hundred steps to reach the Grand Hall and King Solomon's Mines before squeezing through the Tunnel of Love, which narrows at one point to just 30cm (12in). Next comes the Ice Chamber, the Coffin and the Ice Cream Parlour, followed by a final tight scramble through the Devil's Chimney.

Sarawak Chamber, Malaysia
∅∅∅

www.mulupark.com

Best time to go: March–September

Gunung Mulu National Park in Sabah, Borneo, is riddled with hundreds of kilometres of spectacular caves, including Deer Cave, the world's largest cave corridor and the site of an incredible exodus of up to three million bats each evening. For

ESSENTIAL**GEAR**

• **Helmet** • Headlamp (white LEDs are best), plus two back-up light sources • **Oversuit made of tough material** • Strong boots • **Gloves** • Knee and elbow pads

ADVENTURE**RATING**

Daring:	∅∅∅∅∅
Eco-friendly:	∅∅∅∅∅
Expensive:	∅∅∅∅∅
Expertise:	∅∅∅∅∅
Fitness:	∅∅∅∅∅

Well-placed lighting makes the most of the awesome formations in the Cango Caves

spelunkers, however, Mulu's holy grail is the Sarawak Chamber – a world-record-holding cavern that could comfortably accommodate St Peter's Basilica in the Vatican. To reach this inner-Earth 'black hole' you first need to prove to park officials that you have caving experience. Then it's a three-hour trek through the rainforest to the entrance of Good Luck Cave, followed by another three hours tracing a subterranean river and scrambling over a steep boulder slope to reach the black void at the mouth of the chamber.

More great caving adventures

- Descend into the 111m-deep (364ft) abyss of **Gaping Gill** in the Yorkshire Dales.
- Float on an inner tube through New Zealand's **Waitomo Caves**, where glow worms light the way.

ADVENTURE BRIEFING

Nothing beats getting out there (or rather down there) with experienced cavers to learn effective and safe spelunking techniques. Before you go underground, however, it is vital to be properly kitted out. As well as obvious items like a helmet and headlamp, pack some spare warm clothing and energy snacks in case you get wet, cold, lost – or all three.

Subterranean navigation is one of the most important skills to master for caving. Always go with

an experienced leader who has visited the cave before and try to get into the habit of looking back frequently so you can recognize the passageway on your return. Caving is very rarely just a 'walk in the dark'. The terrain underground is, at best, uneven and there may be times when you are forced to belly-crawl through narrow clefts or brace yourself against the walls of a fissure to climb upwards. Taking things to even greater extremes, you can scuba-dive through flooded cave chambers or even base-jump into giant sinkholes with a parachute strapped to your back. In these cases, claustrophobia or a fear of bats are going to be the least of your worries.

ECO**FILE**

- Avoid touching cave formations – many are fragile or easily spoiled by mud from your hands or gloves.
- Keep to established trails.
- If you need to mark your route, never write or scratch on cave walls. Instead use pieces of brightly coloured reflective tape that can be removed on your way out.
- Do not leave food, garbage or human waste in a cave – remember that many lie at the headwaters of rivers.
- Many caves are home to endangered species, so take care not to disturb bat roosts or other highly specialized habitats.

Vast tunnel in Mulu National Park, Borneo

Cross-country skiing

There's no better way to appreciate the beauty and silence of a winter wilderness at your own pace than with a pair of cross-country skis strapped to your feet. Technique and clothing are important, as is a good level of overall fitness.

KEY TO SYMBOLS

Ø **Easy**
ØØ **Moderate**
ØØØ **Challenging**

ADVENTURE CALLING

From Ushuaia in Tierra del Fuego to Hokkaido in Japan, cross-country skiers will find a range of locations and grades to suit all abilities. Major cross-country ski centres, such as those listed here, usually have areas where beginners can practise their snowploughs and poling action, while certain classic trails, like the 140km (87-mile) Haute Route between Chamonix and Zermatt in the European Alps, are best left to ski touring enthusiasts.

Jackson Ski Touring, USA
Ø – ØØØ
www.jacksonxc.com
Best time to go: December–March
Jackson in New Hampshire has myriad opportunities for cross-country enthusiasts. Beginners can start with the flat 8km (5-mile) Ellis River Trail. For those steadier on their skis, the Betty Whitney Trail offers wonderful views of the White Mountains, while the Wildcat Valley Trail provides a backcountry tour through pristine forest.

Mont-Sainte-Anne, Canada
Ø – ØØØ
www.mont-sainte-anne.com
Best time to go: December–March

The Alpine Haute Route

Close to Quebec City, Mont-Sainte-Anne has more than 220km (137 miles) of cross-country skiing trails, from short, flat and well-groomed tracks to longer backcountry routes for advanced skiers.

Geilo, Norway Ø – ØØØ
www.geilo.no

Best time to go: December–April
This excellent all-round ski village in the wild moorland region of the Hardanger Plateau in western Norway has a 220km (137-mile) cross-country network with tracks up to 20km (12 miles) long.

Ylläs, Finland Ø – ØØØ
www.yllas.fi

Best time to go: December–April
Western Lapland's premier cross-country skiing destination has 330km (205 miles) of trails, as well as numerous other winter activities such as snowshoeing, dog sledding and ice fishing.

ADVENTURE BRIEFING
Cross-country skiing can be as easy or as hard as you want it to be. At one extreme you can slip-slide about, pausing at frequent intervals, while at the other you can push your body into cardiovascular overdrive covering several kilometres an hour. Whatever your level of experience, however, it's more enjoyable if you get fit first. It's also hot work, so even in sub-zero temperatures you will be grateful for clothing layers that can be shed.

Try to perfect a smooth sliding style in which you glide across the snow, feet side by side and your poles (lightly gripped) providing a rhythmic punting action. Two additional techniques that will prove useful are the uphill herringbone-step and the downhill snowplough in which you skid the skis sideways, digging the edges into the snow to help you slow down or turn.

ECO**FILE**
- Avoid walking or snowshoeing on cross-country ski tracks – it ruins the trail.
- Take away all litter.
- Do not harass wildlife which may already be struggling to cope with winter conditions.

ESSENTIAL**GEAR**
• Cross-country skis – either 'waxable' or 'waxless' with a grip pattern moulded to the base • **Shoulder-height poles** • Integrated boots/bindings • **Long thermal underwear that wicks moisture away from your skin** • Wind- and waterproof outer layer • **Warm hat** • Thin gloves and overmitts • **Sunglasses or snow goggles** • Small pack for water bottle, snacks and fleece jacket to keep warm during breaks

ADVENTURE**RATING**

Daring:	Ø ØØØØ
Eco-friendly:	ØØØØØ
Expensive:	ØØ ØØØ
Expertise:	ØØ ØØØ
Fitness:	ØØØØ Ø

Mountaineering

Once the preserve of the elite few, mountaineering is becoming increasingly popular – especially for experienced hikers determined to set their sights higher and conquer some of the world's less technical, so-called 'trekking peaks'.

KEY TO SYMBOLS

Ø **Easy**
ØØ **Moderate**
ØØØ **Challenging**

ADVENTURE CALLING

Mont Blanc, France ØØ – ØØØ
www.montblancguides.com
Best time to go: June–September
At 4,808m (15,770ft), Western Europe's highest mountain dominates the French Alps and offers summiteers unsurpassed views over the Eiger, Matterhorn and Monte Rosa, among other peaks. Climbing Mont Blanc is not technically difficult, but you need to be fit and acclimatized – climb the Petite Fourche (3,520m/11,546ft) and the Aiguille du Tour (3,542m/11,618ft) beforehand.

Monte Rosa, Switzerland
ØØ – ØØØ
www.myswitzerland.com
Best time to go: June–September
High above Zermatt, the 4,633m (15,196ft) Dufourspitze of the Monte Rosa massif is usually tackled after practice climbs on the Breithorn (4,164m/13,658ft) and Pollux (4,082m/13,389ft).

Mt Ararat, Turkey ØØ
www.kackarmountains.com
Best time to go: June–September

ECOFILE

See also Trekking EcoFile on page 69
- Carry all garbage off the mountain.
- Drinking water is usually obtained from melted snow, so take precautions to avoid contamination by human waste.
- Always follow your team leader's instructions to minimize risk of erosion or personal injury.

Allow four days for the approach trek from Dogubeyazit, after which it's a straight climb across snow slopes to Mt Ararat's 5,165m (16,941ft) summit.

Lobuche East, Nepal ∅∅∅

www.visitnepal.com

Best time to go: April–May or September–November

Of the 18 peaks open to trekkers in Nepal, 6,119m (20,070ft) Lobuche East is one of the most popular and challenging. It is best tackled as part of an extended expedition, on which you can also climb Mera Peak (6,476m/ 21,241ft) and Imja Tse/Island Peak (6,189m/20,300ft).

Aoraki/Mt Cook, New Zealand ∅∅∅

www.doc.govt.nz

Best time to go: November– early January

The Linda Glacier route is the quickest and least technical for reaching the summit of 3,754m (12,313ft) Aoraki. Be prepared for a tough climb, including a 1,500m (4,920ft) ascent from the Grand Plateau Hut.

ADVENTURE BRIEFING

Joining an organized expedition gives you logistical and technical support, and also ensures there will always be someone to help in an emergency. Even so, thorough preparation is crucial. Find out as much about the route as possible and begin fitness training (including trekking and climbing with a backpack) months in advance.

On the climb itself, it's imperative that you know when to turn back – lives are lost when climbers push themselves too far. Mountaineering is exhausting and dehydrating, so you need to keep energy and fluid levels as high as possible. Food should be easy to carry and prepare – remember that at high altitude water boils at a lower temperature so food takes longer to cook.

ESSENTIAL**GEAR**

• **Double-layer plastic climbing boots** • Ice axe and crampons • **Alpine climbing harness** • Carabiners, ascender and belay devices • **Trekking poles** • Technical clothing, including thermal base layer, fleece jacket and down parka • **Gaiters, wool socks, liner socks** • Liner gloves, fleece gloves, expedition mitts • **Baseball cap, balaclava, wool hat, bandanas, neoprene face mask** • Glacier glasses/snow goggles • **Climbing backpack** • Expedition sleeping bag, sleeping pad, tent, stove, cup, spoon, bowl • **Two tubes each of sunblock and lip screen (chapstick)** • Water bottles, pee bottle, waste compactor bags • **Personal first-aid kit** • Rope (at least two 50m/164ft, 9–11mm/ 0.35–0.43in water repellent rope per two people) • **Head torch (lamp), repair kit, GPS system, snow shovel, whistle, knife, toilet paper**

ADVENTURE**RATING**

Daring:	∅∅∅∅∅
Eco-friendly:	∅∅∅∅∅
Expensive:	∅∅∅∅∅
Expertise:	∅∅∅∅∅
Fitness:	∅∅∅∅∅

The Seven Summits

The Seven Summits challenge – conquering the highest peak on each continent – is a breathless task that also puts the squeeze on your wallet with climbing permits for Everest alone starting at around US$10,000 per person.

First attained in 1885 by Dick Bass, the Seven Summits role of honour listed around 200 names by the end of 2007. There is some debate, however, as to how the Seven Summits are interpreted. While some climbers quite correctly cite Kosciuszko (2,228m/7,308ft) as the highest peak in Australia, others take a wider view of Oceania and elect Papua New Guinea's far more challenging Puncak Jaya, also known as the Carstensz Pyramid (4,884m/16,020ft). Further controversy appears in Europe, where Mt Elbrus (5,642m/18,506ft) in the Caucasus competes with Mont Blanc (*see* page 90) for the title of highest summit. Elsewhere, things are more clear-cut. Aconcagua (6,962m/22,835ft) reigns supreme in South America, while North America's undisputed king of mountains is Denali (6,194m/20,316ft) – the native Athabascan name for Mt McKinley. Antarctica's ice cap is pierced by the 4,900m (16,072ft) Vinson Massif, while Kilimanjaro (*see* page 64) towers over the Tanzanian savannah. That just leaves Everest – 8,848m (29,021ft) and still rising at a rate of about 25mm (1in) a year.

Reality check

Although conquering Kosciuszko requires no more than a chairlift ride and a 6km (4-mile) stroll, reaching the summit of Everest, or any of the other Seven Summits for that matter, confronts climbers with considerable expense, physical hardship and potentially lethal dangers. On Kilimanjaro the main threat (and too often a killer) is altitude sickness, with trekkers pushing themselves to the 5,895m (19,336ft) summit in three or four days with inadequate acclimatization time built into their schedule. Elbrus has the added threat of unpredictable and often ferocious weather, while climbers on Aconcagua, Denali and Vinson must also contend with punishing cold. Perhaps the most technical of the Seven Summits, the Carstensz Pyramid requires rock-climbing skills in a remote and sometimes politically unstable region. Everest, of course, has more than its fair share of mountaineering risks – from altitude sickness, extreme cold and severe weather to the perilous terrain of the Khumbu Icefall.

Meeting the challenge

Don't attempt to scale the financial mountain of funding a Seven Summits challenge until you're confident about tackling the physical and mental barriers. Start by climbing on lower peaks, enrolling on courses to develop your mountaineering skills. Multiple-week camping trips will help you get a feel for life on an extended expedition, as well as putting clothing and gear through its paces.

One of the most accessible of the Seven Summits, Aconcagua makes for a strenuous but non-technical climb (best between December and February) where you can gauge your reaction to altitude. Allow at least two weeks for the approach trek, acclimatization and summit attempts. Next, test your endurance to cold on Denali – best climbed following the West Buttress route between mid-April and mid-July. Remember that even with these formidable summits in the bag, Everest is far from a forgone conclusion. Most climbers edge into the rarefied atmosphere of 8,000m-plus (26,240ft) peaks by attempting less technical mountains like Cho Oyu (8,201m/26,900ft) on the Nepal-Tibet border.

High achieving

A typical week-long mountaineering course will increase your technical knowledge and skills in the following:

- Using crampons and ice axe
- Glacier travel and crevasse rescue
- Wilderness navigation
- Rope and belay techniques
- Self arrest and rappelling
- Safe climbing
- Critical decision-making
- Coping with adverse weather

Mt Everest: still the ultimate challenge

Animal

There is something about an 'animal-powered' adventure that evokes the pioneering spirit of travel. Hannibal marched his elephants across the Alps, Roald Amundsen mushed huskies to the South Pole, Lawrence of Arabia used camels to explore the arid wastes of Wadi Rum and, of course, John Wayne rode his stallion into countless Wild West sunsets. But you don't have to be a fearless explorer or even a real-life cowboy to embark on an adventure with a four-legged friend. Horses, huskies, camels and elephants provide a world of opportunities for venturing into the wilderness, whatever your level of experience. They open up remote and rugged places with a lightness of touch that is well beyond an all-terrain vehicle. You cannot fail to bond with your devoted charges as you gain an intimate insight into their care and behaviour. Perhaps the most privileged and humbling aspect of an animal adventure, however, is the natural silence that accompanies your wanderings – just the sound of footsteps, a dog panting, an elephant's stomach rumbling…

Top: Riding along the beach. Bottom left: Elephant-back safari. Bottom right: Camel at Petra

Contents

> **Key**
> The numbers/letters in circles on this page correspond to the locations marked on the map on pages 96–7.

Animal: World Map

St Petersburg

Moscow

SAYAN MOUNTAINS
Ulaanbaatar 7
GOBI
DESERT

Istanbul

Baghdad   Tehran   Beijing

Cairo   Karachi   HIMALAYA   Tokyo
                         Delhi 10   9
A   7 7   8   PACIFIC
Khartoum   Mumbai   OCEAN

                                   Bangkok 12
                                           13   Hong Kong

                            11

         Nairobi

                INDIAN
                OCEAN
            5
  1   Cairns
B 6 5   Great Barrier Reef
  3 6 5   GREAT DIVIDING RANGE
  4 Johannesburg
  2   6
                              Perth   Sydney
                                   Canberra   Auckland

A

holm 4

5

A

Horse riding

Whether you're an apprehensive first-timer or fancy yourself as a bit of a Lone Ranger, a horse-riding adventure can take you on an exhilarating canter through some of the world's most spectacular locations.

It's the intimacy and responsiveness of horse riding that sets it apart from other forms of animal-based travel. Elephants have their mahouts, camels have their drivers and huskies often seem to have their own frenetic agenda. Horse and rider, however, quickly learn to develop a mutual respect and awareness –

> " Heaven for horse riders, the Cardrona Valley is a beautiful spot in the Southern Alps with hillsides of wind-combed tussock grass. "

a finely tuned and sensitive collaboration that's crucial for long days in the saddle roaming wild country.

The flip side to this, of course, is that a relaxed, confident riding style (especially over challenging terrain) isn't something a complete novice is going to master on day one of a week-long riding expedition. Prior experience is necessary for many equine adventures, but that doesn't mean you need to be a regular rider at home. Ranch-based riding holidays, with their excellent training facilities, are particularly well suited to beginners. You'll quickly pick up the basics and develop the techniques required for more demanding trail rides. Before you know it, you will be saddling up for those wild-spirited gallops across the foothills of the Rockies or the plains of Patagonia.

ADVENTURE**RATING**	
Daring:	⌀⌀⌀⌀⌀
Eco-friendly:	⌀⌀⌀⌀⌀
Expensive:	⌀⌀⌀⌀⌀
Physical:	⌀⌀⌀⌀⌀
Technical:	⌀⌀⌀⌀⌀

Crossing obstacles is easier on horseback

ADVENTURE CALLING

The world from a saddle

Many equine adventures are deeply rooted in local culture and tradition, allowing you to ride out with nomadic herders in Mongolia, gauchos in Argentina or ranchers in Arizona.

KEY TO SYMBOLS
∅ **Easy:** Suitable for novices confident of controlling a well-behaved horse, mounting, dismounting and sustaining short periods of trot and canter.
∅∅ **Moderate:** Intermediate riders able to trot, canter and gallop, and comfortable with spending several hours in the saddle at a time.
∅∅∅ **Challenging:** Experienced riders capable of controlling spirited horses in challenging environments.

Arizona, USA ∅ – ∅∅∅
www.arizonaguide.com
Best time to go: May–September
The natural choice for wannabe cowboys, Arizona is right in the thick of the Wild West. Grab a Stetson and a pair of wrangler jeans and mount up western-style, driving cattle, roping and branding – or simply enjoy lazy rides across the high plains. There are numerous ranches to choose from, including Tanque Verde (www.tvgr.com), an authentic Arizona 'dude ranch' offering walking rides for beginners and canters across the cactus-studded Sonoran Desert for the more experienced.

Chilcotin Mountains, Canada ∅ – ∅∅∅
www.chilcotinholidays.com
Best time to go: Spring–early autumn
A horse-powered wilderness adventure for able riders, trekking into British Columbia's Chilcotin Mountains on sure-footed Cayuse horses is the ultimate North American safari. Travelling nomad-style, you'll follow game trails, ford rivers and camp near streams teeming with trout, and may spot bighorn sheep, mule deer, moose, wolf and grizzly bear on your way. If that sounds too adventurous, stay at a guest ranch, where you can hone your riding skills while getting a taste of the great outdoors.

Patagonia, Argentina ∅∅ – ∅∅∅
www.argentinaturistica.com
Best time to go: November–March
Experience gaucho life at a working *estancia* like Huechahue (www.huechahue.com) where confident riders can help herd

Safaris on horseback allow you to get closer to the wildlife you encounter

cattle across the windswept plains of Patagonia. Advanced riders will revel in the wide-open spaces, galloping with gauchos and trying their hand at lassoing. There are also opportunities for multi-day pack rides, venturing deep into Lanin National Park.

Iceland ∅∅ – ∅∅∅
www.ishestar.is
Best time to go: September–October
Iceland's dramatic scenery is best explored on a pure-bred Icelandic horse. If you come in the autumn, you can take part in an ancient tradition where horses are rounded up to be brought down from highland summer pastures to farms in the north.

Nyika Plateau, Malawi ∅ – ∅∅∅
www.nyika.com/chelinda
Best time to go: Year-round
Limited to a maximum of eight riders, horseback safaris from Mbawala Stables, near Chelinda Camp, follow elephant trails across the rolling hills and escarpments of the Nyika Plateau where you may well find yourself trotting alongside herds of eland, roan and zebra.

Make like the Magnificent Seven: Estancia Huechahue, Patagonia

Mashatu Game Reserve, Botswana ⵰⵰ – ⵰⵰⵰

www.lvhsafaris.co.za

Best time to go: Year-round

Often overshadowed by the Okavango Delta (where there is also excellent riding from camps like Macatoo and Kujwana), Limpopo Valley Horse Safaris offers exciting horseback safaris in Mashatu Game Reserve in eastern Botswana. Expect plenty of ditches and logs to jump, and if that doesn't get your pulse racing, the regular encounters with elephant, lion and giraffe certainly will.

Mongolia ⵰⵰ – ⵰⵰⵰

www.mongoliatourism.gov.mn

Best time to go: June–October

Vast, rolling grasslands, larch forests and mountains form the dramatic setting for horseback journeys across the Mongolian steppes – a wild, invigorating land where horses play a pivotal role in nomadic life. Covering around 25km (16 miles) a day, most rides include a visit to the ancient capital of Karakorum and the beautiful Orkhan Valley, spending at least some nights in traditional ger (Mongolian tent) camps.

ADVENTURE BRIEFING

Best hoof forward

Horse-riding adventures are available for all abilities, but don't run away with the idea that you'll go from beginner to bronco-busting cowboy during a week's stay at a ranch.

How to choose the right trip

Horse-riding holidays are either centre-based, where you stay at a ranch or lodge and set off on day rides, or mobile, where you explore a wider area and stay in a succession of camps. The former approach not only suits novice riders (who can practise their technique in a safe environment or have a day off if they're feeling stiff or tired), but it also works well for groups or families with non-riders, who can then take advantage of other lodge-based activities, such as swimming or fishing. A working ranch can also be an excellent option for more advanced riders – particularly if they time their visit to coincide with cattle drives.

Horseback safaris in Africa involve trail rides linked by accommodation that ranges from basic mobile camps with long drop toilets and bucket showers to luxury camps and lodges with en suite bathrooms. Life is less pampered on a pack ride where you'll venture (usually at a walk) into remote locations with packhorses carrying your luggage, camping gear and food.

Touring the Sierra Nevada, Spain, on native Andalucian horses

What to wear

To ensure the best comfort and fit, always take your own riding hat. Full-length riding boots are impractical since you may often be walking beside your horse across rough terrain. A better option is a good pair of boots designed for riding and walking that you can combine with a pair of full- or half-leg chaps to protect your jodhpurs or jeans. Boots should always have a heel, particularly for western-style riding, where the stirrups are often wide and smooth. Remember that you may be exposed to sun for long periods during horseback rides, so be sure to pack long-sleeved shirts, sunblock and sunglasses. A riding helmet cover with a brim will help keep the sun and rain off your face and neck. Riders who are unused to long days in the saddle may find comfort in padded cycling shorts, while other useful extras include riding gloves and a waist pouch in which to keep trail snacks and other personal items handy.

Safety and fitness

All reputable horse-riding operators will take care in matching rider to mount, and will also assess your ability in a ring before unleashing you on the trail. Many also offer a range of facilities, from lessons for complete beginners to gallops over rough ground for fit and experienced riders. Whatever your skill level, however, it is important to remember that horses can be unpredictable and easily startled. Hard hats and adequate insurance are strongly recommended.

ECO**FILE**

- Avoid taking horses into fragile natural areas vulnerable to trampling and grazing.
- Take care when crossing streams and rivers not to damage banks; choose firm, stony crossings wherever possible.
- Before entering conservation areas, make sure that horse feed is free of weed seeds.
- Wash horses at least 50m (55 yards) from watercourses and water them downstream from where campers obtain their water.
- Use tree protectors on nightlines to prevent trees from being damaged.
- Take away all rubbish from camp-sites and scatter horse manure to speed up decomposition.

ESSENTIAL**GEAR**

• **Riding helmet** • Boots • **Chaps** • Jodhpurs • **Jeans** • Sun protection • **Layered clothing to protect against cold** • Riding gloves • **Padded cycling shorts** • Waist pouch • **Water bottle** • Insect repellent • **Trail snacks** • Lightweight binoculars • **Camera**

Should wilderness be sacred?

Wilderness may be blandly written off in dictionaries as a 'wild uncultivated area' (more 'unkempt allotment' than Mongolian steppe), but it will always be one of travel's 'tingly' words, guaranteed to titillate the weariest of globetrotters.

Wilderness is the promise of remoteness, the challenge of a new frontier, the privilege of glimpsing wildlife that knows no boundaries and of scanning a wide, unblemished horizon. More than anything, however, wilderness is somewhere devoid of people.

And therein lies our dilemma. Purists would argue that wilderness areas should, by their very nature, be inviolate. No one would advocate mass tourism to the world's last wild frontiers, but even the most eco-sensitive, small-scale tours leave human impressions – whether it's something as transient as footprints or a shattered silence.

But there is no denying the lure of wilderness. People will always crave the pristine beauty, spiritual renewal and sense of escape that accompanies a journey somewhere totally removed from the noise, pollution and clutter of everyday life. And, ironic as it may seem, one of the best ways to preserve wilderness is to give people direct experience of it. Only then can they develop the empathy and enthusiasm that's so vital for ensuring its future.

Left: Lush jungle, Sabah, Malaysian Borneo. Right: Everglades National Park

Wilderness? I didn't think there was any left.

It's true that humans have laid claim to the most far-flung places on earth, mapped each one from space and wrought a great deal of environmental havoc, but large swathes of wilderness do still exist. Every continent has wild places brimming with opportunities for the adventurous traveller.

Call me a wimp, but I'm no Ranulph Fiennes. Rope burns and frostbite are not my idea of a holiday.

No one is suggesting you set off solo across the Arctic wastes. There are plenty of adventure tour operators that specialize in taking small groups into wilderness areas and bringing them out again, fingers and toes intact. Safety is their paramount concern. Just make sure you choose a reputable company that employs expert local guides, uses the best equipment and practises environmentally responsible tourism.

Will I have to carry my own backpack, eat rehydrated meals and sleep in one of those coffin-shaped tents?

No. On some trips you can stay in luxury wilderness lodges that carefully blend with their surroundings – it's a matter of taste and budget. Having said that, however, everyone should at least once in their lives set off into the wilds with everything they need carried on their back (or strapped to a horse, or stowed in a kayak etc). There is something wonderfully liberating about travelling light through a wilderness. Your

daily rhythm quickly synchronizes with natural cues, such as the passage of the sun, the rise and fall of tides and the movement of wildlife.

Leave only footprints, take only pictures. Is that really realistic?

It has to be. In fact, in some places you could argue that even footprints aren't acceptable. For example, the fragile tundra of some Arctic islands rapidly becomes pockmarked by even a small cruiseship landing party, while some deserts have a similarly fragile crust. Any activity that potentially jeopardizes the wilderness value of a region should be avoided. Needless to say, it doesn't require much thought to take away all your refuse, stick to trails to minimize erosion and avoid contaminating water sources with waste.

Dog sledding

Huskies have mostly one thing on their minds – to run: few adventures can match the sheer elation of mushing through a polar wilderness with a team of these exuberant canines.

As your sled sweeps through a winter-gilded landscape of silent forests and frozen lakes, all you can hear is the panting of your team of dogs and the tinkle of their collar chains. Drooping long, pink tongues, they occasionally snatch mouthfuls of thirst-quenching snow from the trailside or prick their ears when they catch scent of nearby wildlife. But nothing it seems will ever stop them running. Controlling a team of huskies takes practice and a bit of nerve. Like in any winter sport,

> From the cacophony of barks rose a single, piercing howl. Other huskies took up the cry, filling our ears with that mesmerizing 'call of the wild'.

you may well find yourself taking an occasional tumble, but any hardship is more than compensated for by the privilege of bonding with your dogs. With their thick coats and well-padded feet, huskies are perfectly adapted to life in polar regions, but you still need to take on their day-to-day care, including feeding, checking for sore paws and so on.

In 1911, Norwegian explorer Roald Amundsen used sled dogs to help him become the first person to reach the South Pole (some suggest that Amundsen's expertise with Greenland huskies helped him to beat Scott to the post). Nowadays, dog-sledding adventures range from extreme challenges like the 1,600km (1,000-mile) Yukon Quest or trans-Alaskan Iditarod race (see page 11) to hour-long tasters where you can ride in a sled with an experienced handler in control.

ADVENTURE**RATING**		
Daring:		🐾🐾🐾
Eco-friendly:		🐾🐾🐾🐾🐾
Expense:		🐾🐾🐾
Expertise:		🐾🐾
Fitness:		🐾🐾

Dog sledding in Swedish Lapland

ADVENTURE CALLING
The lure of the north

Developed thousands of years ago by the Inuit, dog sledding is a common way to travel around Greenland during winter and spring. Other prime locations include Swedish Lapland (see page 114) and the arctic fringes of North America.

> ### KEY TO SYMBOLS
> Ø **Easy:** Easily accessible locations offering short 'taster' sessions in dog sledding.
> ØØ **Moderate:** Remote locations where it's possible to join overnight husky sledding tours, usually staying in comfortable cabins.
> ØØØ **Challenging:** Wilderness areas where sledding expeditions may involve long days mushing.

The route to Bonneville Lakes, Yukon

Ely, Minnesota, USA Ø – ØØ
www.ely.org
Best time to go: December–March

Located in the beautiful Boundary Waters Wilderness, Ely is the self-proclaimed 'Sled Dog Capitol of the US'. Operators such as Wintergreen Dogsled Lodge, White Wolf Dog Sled Trips and White Wilderness Dog Sled Adventures offer everything from half-day tours to mushing adventures lasting a week or more and staying in snug lodges or yurts. You can also combine dog sledding with other winter activities like ice fishing, snowshoeing and wolf tracking.

Yukon, Canada Ø – ØØ
www.travelyukon.com
Best time to go: December–March

Several kennels offer dog-sledding adventures in the mountains and forests of the Yukon, including Muktuk Adventures, where Yukon Quest Champion Frank Turner runs half-day, full-day and week-long tours, as well as a six-day Rookie Ranch option for beginners. You could also try Kingmik Dog Sled Tours and Cathers Wilderness Adventures.

Greenland ∅∅ – ∅∅∅
www.greenland.com
Best time to go: February–April
Although most dog sledding in Greenland takes places above the Arctic Circle, the southeastern district of Ammassalik is one of the most popular destinations for tourists. Spreading over 1.5 million square kilometres (580,000sq miles) of wilderness – including the world's largest national park – it is a rugged, sparsely populated region sandwiched between the polar sea ice and Greenlandic ice cap. The main centre of Tasiilaq offers dog-sled training courses, completing which will qualify you for an official licence. Alternatively, join dog-sledding tours exploring Ammassalik's frozen fjords and mountain valleys. On the west coast, Sisimiut and Kangerlussuaq are the two most southerly towns offering dog-sled trips during winter and spring, while the Lyngmark Glacier on Disko Island extends mushing possibilities into the summer months.

Varanger Peninsula, Norway ∅∅ – ∅∅∅
www.varanger.com
Best time to go: December–April
Clinging to the edge of Europe, the Arctic outpost of the Varanger Peninsula juts into the Barents Sea, providing an adventurous opportunity for dog-sledding expeditions from the fishing port of Vestre Jakobselv.

Karelia, Finland ∅ – ∅∅
www.visitfinland.com
Best time to go: December–March
Make tracks across frozen lakes and through the taiga forest of eastern Finland, driving your dog team between wilderness cabins and enjoying other local winter pastimes such as ice fishing and saunas. Flights from Helsinki connect to Joensuu, the region's main centre.

Time for a break

ADVENTURE BRIEFING
When mush comes to shove

Don't worry if the closest you've come to dog sledding is grappling with a trolley (cart) down the frozen foods section of the supermarket. With expert coaching you'll quickly get the hang of it – and don't forget the sleds do have brakes.

What to wear
Although there will be occasional uphills when your dogs need a helping scoot, you will spend much of the time balanced on the rear runners of your sled, moving only to shift weight from one to the other (to handle corners) or to apply the foot brake (a metal spiked affair between the runners). Warm, windproof clothing is therefore essential. As well as donning thermal underwear, fleece mid-layer and all-in-one polar suit, be sure to protect face, feet and hands from sub-zero temperatures and wind-chill.

How to mush
First, you will need to get used to the canine cacophony of dozens of huskies as they whip themselves into a frenzy of leaping, slavering,

Fitting the harness

wild-eyed excitement. Fitting their harnesses requires a firm hold and you should always ensure that your sled is securely anchored (either by a grappling hook stamped in icy ground or by a rope tied with a slipknot around a tree) before you place the dogs in their traces. The number of dogs in each team depends on your weight, experience and the type of terrain you will be covering. Usually, though, teams consist of between four and six dogs arranged in pairs. In Greenland, ten dogs are typically arranged in a fan-shape.

The moment of departure is super-charged with adrenaline. The huskies will be pulling strongly, so you need to time the moment well when you release the sled. Stand with one foot on a runner and the other stamped firmly on the brake. Untie the slipknot or pull up the anchor. The sled will lurch forward, so grab the handlebar with both hands and get your feet balanced on the runners as soon as possible.

Lean into corners, crouching to lower your centre of gravity. There's no need to shout continuously – a few calm and consistent commands will do. Nor is there any need to repeatedly use the brake. This tires the dogs very quickly. Use their names and work as part of the team, warning the dogs if you're about to apply the brake and helping them through soft snow by kick-pedalling the sled. Remember to keep your lead dogs a safe distance from the sled in front.

A common mistake with novice mushers is to tense up, gripping the handlebar so tightly that neck, shoulders and arms become rigid. Not only is this extremely fatiguing, but it also increases the chances of falling off, so try to adopt a relaxed stance, placing your trust in the huskies and moving with the dips and turns in the trail. Don't panic if you do fall, only to see your dogs bounding away without you. Your tour leader will be able to restrain any 'driverless' sleds.

Mini-mushers

Young children can ride in the sled, but make sure they are very well wrapped up – including goggles to protect their eyes from bits of ice kicked up by the huskies. Remember that some huskies look like they've stepped straight from the local wolf pack and can be frightening to kids.

ECOFILE

- Although huskies are hardy animals capable of sleeping out in blizzards and pulling heavy loads, you should check that dog welfare is given priority by your operator.
- Dog sledding is an environmentally friendly means of transport, but the pristine nature of arctic environments means you should take extra care not to leave litter.
- Keep to traditional routes and trails.
- Book with operators that employ local guides and support indigenous cultures.
- Take care to ensure that dog waste does not contaminate local water sources (even if frozen at the time).

ESSENTIAL GEAR

- Polar suit • **Boots** • Layered thermal clothing • **Thick woollen socks and thin liner socks** • Warm gloves or mitts and thin liner gloves
- **Warm hat that protects your ears**
- Scarf or balaclava • **Ski goggles**
- Sunblock • **Lip salve**

Call of the Arctic wild

Husky fur is as thick as a sheep's fleece. It has to be when you are mushing a team of dogs through the frigid wilderness of Swedish Lapland, 200km (125 miles) north of the Arctic Circle

'This is Sara' explained our guide, Niclas, struggling with a writhing, silver-grey beast with enormous pointed ears. 'She's a little crazy.'

'Hello girl,' I crooned in my best doggy voice, but Sara was beside herself with excitement. She paused briefly to swipe a drooling tongue across my face, rolled her mismatched eyes (one blue, one brown), then let out a delirious whining yelp as she wriggled in my grasp. Eventually I managed to cajole her and three other squirming dogs into harnesses and clip them to the running-line attached to the front of my sled. Niclas sprinted to his own team and waved a hand above his head – the signal to mush. Tugging the restraining anchor free, my own sled lurched forwards, stretching my arms to their limit.

'Stanger!' I shouted the Swedish command for 'slow', but my huskies were beyond listening. The sled careered through the forest, skipping off moguls in the trail like a speed-boat riding a choppy sea. I soon caught sight of the other teams threading, single-file, ahead of me. Miraculously, in those first frenzied moments of departure, no one took a tumble.

Without warning, we broke out of the woods into the white expanse of a frozen lake. On its far shore we reached the wooden cabin that was to be our base for the next few days. While we stoked the sauna, the huskies curled up in the snow, seemingly oblivious to the penetrating cold of nightfall.

The following morning, we woke to a howling chorus. Stiff-shouldered from the previous day's exertions, we donned polar suits and hobbled outside.

Niclas handed me a shovel and nodded at the frozen turds scattered amongst the huskies. Treating it as a kind of 'pre-mush' warm-up I spent several minutes chipping

FACT**FILE**

Kiruna, Swedish Lapland

When to go: The best period for embarking on a winter adventure from Kiruna, Sweden's northernmost town, is December to March when you may also see the northern lights.

Need to know: On a husky sledding trip, accommodation is usually in rustic wilderness cabins with bunk beds, basic washroom facilities, sauna and outside toilet. A popular option is to combine a few days dog sledding with an overnight stay in the Icehotel at Jukkasjarvi.

Next step: Fly from London Heathrow direct to Kiruna or via Stockholm.

Operators: Discover the World (www.arctic-experience.co.uk) has a specialist Lapland programme, which features three- or four-night husky sledding trips.

them into the trees. After feeding the dogs with hot meat soup, we collected water for ourselves from a nearby stream before retreating to the cabin for porridge and coffee. An hour later we were back on the trail, sweeping through a winter-gilded landscape of silent forests and frozen lakes. Twice we spotted reindeer browsing amongst the lichen-clad fir trees and Sara's huge ears pricked alert. But the trio had settled into a steady but exhilarating rhythm.

The next day, snow-laden clouds smudged the sun and by mid-morning we were sledding through the white void of a blizzard. Every sound, from the dogs' breathing to the rasp of the sled's runners, was muted by the snowstorm.

Sara heard them first – her ears flicking upright – but it took several seconds before I detected the grating whine of protesting engines. Moments later the skidoos burst into view, darting along the trail like a swarm of hornets. We stopped to let them pass, wincing in the acrid wake of their exhausts.

'Have you ever tried that?' I asked Niclas. There was a wry smile on his cold-reddened face. 'On a skidoo the first hour is like every other,' he replied. 'With huskies you just never know what's going to happen next – it's much more fun.'

Everyone nodded in agreement as Niclas and his team of dogs disappeared into the forest. Soon I was hurtling along the trail after him, revelling in the huskies' speed and blissfully unaware of the sharp turn looming ahead.

The upright posture can be tiring to maintain for novices

Elephant & camel riding

Travelling in the company of elephants or camels, whether riding on their backs or walking alongside them, is a thrilling experience – you'll learn about their daily habits, venture far off the beaten track and get close to wildlife.

ADVENTURE CALLING
Elephant safaris

It has to be the ultimate safari – roaming the bush on elephant back, regal as a maharajah, exploring trails and lagoons where even the most determined 4WD vehicle would flounder. Elephant-back safaris are popular in southern Africa, with Botswana's Abu Camp (see page 118) leading the herd in the luxury stakes. In Zambia, Thorntree Lodge near Livingstone operates elephant safaris where you can either ride in comfortable saddles or walk alongside them as an honorary member of the herd. In South Africa, options include Addo Elephant-Back Safaris, Pilanesberg Elephant-Back Safaris, the Elephant Sanctuary at Hartbeespoort Dam and Camp Jabulani in Kapama Private Game Reserve.

In India, elephant safaris tracking tiger, rhino and other wildlife are possible in several national parks, including Bandhavgarh, Corbett, Kanha and Kaziranga. Royal Chitwan National Park in Nepal is another good spot. Sri Lanka, Thailand and Cambodia's Mondulkiri Province offer further possibilities.

Camel safaris

North Africa and the Middle East are the obvious choices for camel trekking, with rides ranging from quick jaunts around the Pyramids in Egypt to longer forays in

Elephant safari in Botswana

Jordan's Wadi Rum. Overnight camel trips into the fringes of the Sahara are available at Erg Chebbi in Morocco and Siwa Oasis, Egypt. In northern Kenya, Lewa Wildlife Conservancy runs camel safaris lasting 3–14 days. Another arid region that's well suited to exploration by camel is the Australian outback – several operators run camel safaris along the Oodnadatta Track at Lake Eyre, South Australia, between April and October. For a different kind of adventure, head to India's Pushkar Camel Fair, where Thar Desert camel drivers and around 50,000 camels converge on the lakeside town each November.

ADVENTURE BRIEFING

Unless you're planning something truly epic, such as a full-blown camel expedition across the Gobi Desert, elephant and camel safaris are fairly soft adventures where you will be either based in comfortable lodges or, in the case of camping trips, have a support team looking after you. With a mahout or camel driver in control, all you need to do is get on and hang on. Of course, taking charge of your own camel or elephant is an entirely different matter – read Benedict Allen's *The Skeleton Coast* or Mark Shand's *Travels on my Elephant* for a reality check.

Most elephant and camel safaris provide an opportunity to walk alongside the animals (on some camel treks you'll spend much of the time on foot), so it is important to wear comfortable walking shoes. Sunglasses and a cotton bandana will protect your eyes, nose and mouth from dust kicked up by the animals.

ECO**FILE**

- Before booking, check that operators place priority on the welfare of their animals.
- Minimize erosion and overgrazing by ensuring that safaris are not concentrated in small individual areas.
- Avoid contamination of water sources.

ESSENTIAL**GEAR**

• **Walking shoes or boots** • Wide-brimmed sunhat • **Sunblock** • Sunglasses • **Bandana** • Binoculars and camera, both with sturdy straps • **Insect repellent** • Neutral-coloured clothes – particularly for wildlife-watching trips

ADVENTURE**RATING**

Daring:	⌀⌀⌀⌀⌀
Eco-friendly:	⌀⌀⌀⌀⌀
Expensive:	⌀⌀⌀⌀⌀
Expertise:	⌀⌀⌀⌀⌀
Fitness:	⌀⌀⌀⌀⌀

The ultimate safari

Trumpeting six sumptuous en suite tents overlooking a lagoon, Abu Camp is the pampered setting for elephant-back safaris in the spicy-sweet grasslands and cool waterways of Botswana's Okavango Delta.

The elephants stood patiently, like a row of solemn statues, their amber eyes framed by long lashes, each mouth a wrinkled smile. As Randall Moore, owner of Elephant Back Safaris, introduced me to each member of the herd, the moist tip of a trunk snaked into his hand then curled back into the elephant's mouth where his scent was tasted and recognized. The younger ones, bored with formalities, clowned about in the dust, grappling each other's trunks.

'OK, let's go ride some elephants!' With a flourish of his cigar, Randall brought order to the proceedings and began allocating elephants to guests. No more than 12 visitors are allowed at Abu Camp, Randall's luxurious safari base set in 200,000ha (495,000 acres) of prime Okavango. We edged forward, like children eager to be picked for a playground game.

I was expecting a five-ton elephant to be big, but the reality of stepping inside Cathy's shadow was overwhelming. Born in 1960 and brought back to Africa by Randall after spending her youth in a Canadian zoo, Cathy stood around 3m (10ft) at the shoulder, her legs solid as Roman pillars. Her flank swelled above me like an overfilled zeppelin, while enormous ears, like twin maps of Africa, slapped gently against her shoulders.

With a twinge of guilt, I watched her mahout order her to kneel on all fours so I could scramble into the padded seat

FACT**FILE**

Elephant Back Safaris, Okavango Delta, Botswana
When to go: Annual floods creep across the delta between May and September, with the wet season following from November to March. The winter months of June–August can be cold at night, while December and January are hot.
Need to know: Named after the herd's original matriarch who died in 2002, Abu Camp offers three-night elephant-back safaris with twice weekly departures on Saturday and Tuesday. A course of anti-malaria prophylactics is recommended.
Next step: Maun, the gateway to the Okavango Delta, is served by flights from Johannesburg, Windhoek, Gaborone and Cape Town. Light aircraft, with a personal luggage restriction of 10kg (22 lb), link Maun to Abu Camp.
Operators: Abu Camp (www.abucamp.com).

strapped to her back. 'Hold on, we're going up!' With a series of jerky movements, I was elevated into the woodland canopy. Then Cathy, as matriarch of the Abu Camp herd, led the other elephants, single file, into the herb-scented grasslands of the Okavango.

From the back of an elephant you can see more of Africa. You can feel the elephant's spine dip and flex and run your fingers across the wrinkled maze of its skin. You can hear the vacuum rush of air in its probing trunk, the deep, resonating rumble of its cavernous stomach and the rhythmic grinding of fist-sized molars.

The elephants walked at 5kph (3mph), a slow, but nonetheless ground-swallowing gait, 'pacing along as if they had an appointment at the end of the world', as Karen Blixen once put it. Their spongy soles deadened the sound of each gargantuan footfall – if desired, a large herd can move in virtual silence. But not if they're feeding. Cathy and the others noisily entered a tangle of mopane woodland, and began stripping leaves and splintering branches like a bush fire on the rampage.

So captivating was their behaviour that it was almost distracting when someone spotted the lioness. She was crouching at one side of a clearing, a forepaw raised, frozen in mid-stalk. Beyond a curtain of yellow grasses, a herd of zebra stood motionless, staring.

Randall signalled for us to stop and we pretended to be an uninterested herd of browsing elephants. Suddenly, there was a series of harsh barks and pandemonium broke out in a nearby copse. Baboons had spotted the lioness. The zebras wheeled in unison, kicking up a screen of dust as they galloped away.

'OK, let's go, Cathy.' Relieved to be on the move again, the elephant obediently rocked into motion. We reached the edge of a shallow lagoon and, with slow purposeful strides, Cathy waded in. Some of the other adults had already paused to drink, siphoning 8 litres (2 gallons) at a time through their pulsing hose-noses. As the youngsters splashed around, Cathy drooped her trunk to the surface and I heard a deep satisfied groan as she squirted a jet of water into her mouth.

ECO**FILE**

• Although game drives in 4WD vehicles are also available at Abu Camp, take advantage of mokoro (dugout canoe) and walking safaris, which, like the elephants, are gentler on the environment.

Elephants are ideal transport for exploring the Okavango Delta

Capturing the moment

Once you've decided what camera gear to take and how to protect it, the two key elements for successful adventure travel photography are storytelling and effective use of light.

The best adventure photography portfolios are the ones that tell a story. Plan and research a storyline before you set off and you will be rewarded with far more powerful, intimate and informative images than if you merely react spontaneously to each day. Learning to understand and anticipate the different qualities of light is also crucial, whether it's the rich colours, contrast and texture that accompany dawn and dusk, or the soft haze of an overcast day.

Cameras and lenses

Don't rush out and buy a new camera the day before you leave. The best camera to use is likely to be the one you've had for years; the one you know so well you can adjust any control without taking your eye from the viewfinder. It feels right in your hands and you're not afraid of getting it scratched.

The ideal camera outfit for adventure photography is one light enough not to be a burden. An SLR camera body and a couple of well-chosen lenses are comfortable to carry and provide optimum versatility. For those who want to carry minimal gear, digital compacts

Remember to ask permission before photographing people

are ideal for slipping in a pocket or a waist pouch. Choose one with a good-quality optical zoom lens and look for features such as rubber armour, water-resistance and a large, bright LCD screen.

For SLR users, zoom lenses are a flexible option for adventures where fast-changing situations call for rapid shifts in focal length. They also help to minimize lens changes – a boon for digital users who need to keep dust away from delicate sensors. An ideal combo for a typical trip would be a 28–70mm and 70–210mm zoom, although on specialized trips, such as rafting, an ultra-wide-angle 17–35mm zoom will cram in all the action from the confines of a dinghy.

Top 10 tips for adventure photography

- Never compromise a fragile habitat in pursuit of the perfect shot.
- Always ask before photographing people.
- Use a companion to add scale and drama to a shot.
- Check behind you before stepping back for that extra wide view.
- Make sure your photographic gear is insured.
- Try fast and slow shutter speeds to capture movement.
- Light is the key! Be bold and experiment.
- Try different viewpoints to emphasize drama.
- Do your homework and plan shots that tell a story.
- Don't let a speck of water or dust stop you taking pictures.

Bags and accessories

Don't skimp on the camera bag. Saving a few pounds may prove to be a false economy. There are several excellent ranges for adventure photography, including photo-backpacks, waist pouches and hybrid backpacks where you can store personal belongings above a dedicated camera compartment. An ideal bag should have comfortable shoulder straps and waist belt, ease of access, good-quality zips and seams as well as a slip-on waterproof cover. Steer clear of traditional shoulder bags – they're cumbersome and pull you off balance. Remember that cameras and water are not good partners; keep all gear in drybags or watertight camera cases if you're thinking of kayaking, sailing or rafting. Camera support is your next vital consideration. At the very least, pack a beanbag (for resting your lens on boulders, tree trunks etc) to help ensure sharp images. Ideally, though, use a lightweight carbon-fibre tripod and cable release to minimize camera shake.

Other essential accessories range from spare batteries and a recharging unit to a spare camera body and portable hard drive for backing up memory cards. To protect the front element of your lenses against scratches and dust, fit a UV or skylight filter to each one. Lens hoods provide additional protection, as well as cutting out flare. Finally, a maintenance kit should contain a jeweller's screwdriver, duct tape (for emergency repairs), lens-cleaning fluid and tissue, lint-free cloth, pencil eraser for cleaning battery contacts, cotton buds (swabs) for reaching tricky places), zip-lock plastic bags with silica desiccant sachets for absorbing moisture from rain- or wave-soaked gear, and digital sensor swabs and microfibre cleaning brush.

Vehicle

Distance is no object when you have a set of fat wheels and a long-range fuel tank beneath you. At least, that's how it seems when you embark on an overland adventure in an expedition truck or 4WD vehicle. Travelling in your own mobile, all-terrain life-support system is your ticket to getting well and truly off the beaten track for weeks, months or even years at a time. Equally liberating and free-spirited (and a great way to get fit), cycling trips help you mingle with locals in places where bicycles still rule the road. You can travel at your own pace and experience destinations more intimately, focussing on things that might otherwise pass in a blur. For riders who prefer throttle-pumping to pedal-pushing, quad bikes and snowmobiles offer adrenaline-charged forays across challenging terrain. And for the ultimate in vehicle-assisted adventure travel, look no further than a sub-orbital spaceflight – blasting off in 2010 from a spaceport near you.

Top left: Wheels aloft in New Zealand. Top right: Snowmobile, Finland. Bottom: Overland truck, Khiva, Uzbekistan.

Contents

> **Key**
> The numbers/letters in circles
> on this page correspond to the
> locations marked on the map
> on pages 124–5.

Vehicle: World Map

olm
St Petersburg
Moscow
SAYAN MOUNTAINS
Ulaanbaatar
GOBI DESERT
Istanbul
Beijing
Tehran
Tokyo
Baghdad
Cairo
A
Khartoum
Karachi Delhi
HIMALAYA
Mumbai
Hong Kong
Bangkok
Nairobi
PACIFIC OCEAN
nshasa
Harare
INDIAN OCEAN
Cairns
Great Barrier Reef
GREAT DIVIDING RANGE
Johannesburg
Perth
Sydney
Canberra
Auckland

Overland expeditions

A slow, bumpy, but environmentally friendly alternative to long-haul flights, overlanding can take you across entire continents – as long as you've got a few months to spare and don't mind sharing the experience with other like-minded travellers.

From Marco Polo's 13th-century journey along the Silk Road to the 1960s and 70s Hippy Trail from London to Kathmandu, overlanding has almost become a rite of passage as much as a great opportunity for an extended adventure. Whether you join an organized trip in a converted truck or plan your own 4WD expedition, there are almost limitless routes available. Classic overland journeys, such as Cairo to Cape Town, Istanbul to Xi'an and Alaska to Tierra del Fuego, provide the ultimate continental dot-to-dot, where you not only visit iconic landmarks, but also immerse yourself in the cultures, cuisines and quirks of the various countries through which you travel. That doesn't mean to say, however, that shorter overland journeys are any less satisfying. Many operators offer a 'pick and mix' approach, breaking a transcontinental itinerary into three- or four-week segments that you can take individually or link together. And then, of course, there are the epic drives – like the Trans-Sahara, Nullarbor Plain and Karakoram Highway – that stand out on their own as great excuses to hit the road, even if it's just for a few days.

> ❛ The road cleaved an arrow path across vast, desiccated plains. Wind pumps pricked the horizon, spinning metal sails from scrawny scaffolds. ❜

ADVENTURE**RATING**

Daring:	⊘⊘○○○
Eco-friendly:	⊘⊘⊘⊘○
Expense:	⊘⊘○○○
Expertise:	⊘○○○○
Fitness:	⊘○○○○

You can often ride on the roof for a panoramic view

ADVENTURE CALLING

The long and winding road

Even if you can't spare a year for 'the big one' (London to Beijing via Kazakhstan and Mongolia, back along the Silk Road to Istanbul, then south to Cape Town), there are still numerous overlanding options available.

THE AMERICAS

Anchorage to Ushuaia

Route: Anchorage → Mexico City → Panama City → fly to Quito → Cusco → Santiago → Ushuaia

Duration: 26 weeks

This all-American odyssey links Alaska with Tierra del Fuego, an extraordinary six-month journey that takes you through a vast range of landscapes and climates, from summer to summer, midnight sun to midnight sun. For much of the way, you follow the Pan-American Highway, a series of interconnecting roads stretching 22,500km (14,000 miles), as the condor flies, from north of the Arctic Circle to the tip of Chile. The only section you'll need to 'cheat' with a flight is between Panama City and Quito. As for highlights, how do the Grand Canyon, Chichén Itzá and Machu Picchu sound for starters?

Anchorage to Mexico City

Route: Anchorage → Whitehorse → Banff → Calgary → Salt Lake City → Las Vegas → Mazatlan → Mexico City

Duration: 7 weeks

Good roads and excellent facilities smooth the way on this overland journey brimming with opportunities for exploring the Great Outdoors of North America. Highlights include spotting bears and wolves in Denali National Park, trekking in the Canadian Rockies, exploring Yellowstone National Park and hiking across the lava flows of Mexico's Paricutin volcano.

Rio to Rio

Route: Rio de Janeiro → Manaus → Caracas → Quito → Cusco → Santiago → Ushuaia → Rio de Janeiro

Duration: 25 weeks

A ring around South America is right up there with Cape–Cairo and the Silk Route when it comes to ultimate overland trips. Not only is there something utterly fulfilling about encircling an entire continent by road, but South America is also undeniably one of the most diverse and fascinating places on earth. From the towering Andes and Altiplano to windswept Patagonia and the sultry Amazon, South America's landscapes provide a head-

Dramatic scenery on the border between Chile and Argentina

spinning backdrop to a kaleido-
scope of wildlife, culture and
adventure activities. See the next
three entries for some highlights.

Caracas to La Paz

Route: Caracas ➤ Cartegena ➤
Quito ➤ Cusco ➤ La Paz
Duration: 8 weeks
Venezuela's Caribbean coastline
and the historic city of Cartegena
contrast with the Ecuadorian
market town of Otavalo and
other Andean hotspots like
Machu Picchu and Lake Titicaca
on this action-packed itinerary.
Most trips feature a trip to
the Amazon, trekking in the
Cordillera Blanca, rafting on the
Urubamba and a flight over the
Nazca Lines.

La Paz to Rio de Janeiro

Route icon: La Paz ➤ Tupiza ➤
Salta ➤ San Ignacio ➤ Bonito ➤
Parati ➤ Rio de Janeiro
Duration: 6 weeks
From the dazzling saltpans of
Bolivia's Altiplano to the crashing
cascades of Iguazu Falls, the route
from La Paz to Rio straddles the
continent and includes activities
ranging from birdwatching in the
Pantanal to sailing on Brazil's
Emerald Coast.

Caracas to Rio de Janeiro

Route: Caracas ➤ Ciudad Bolivar
➤ Manaus ➤ Porto Velho ➤
Brasilia ➤ Rio de Janeiro
Duration: 8 weeks
This challenging route delves into
the Amazon basin, striking south

ACTION 129

Raising a dust cloud: on the road in South Africa

from the Caribbean coast to Angel Falls and the 'Lost World' of Mt Roraima before heading towards the jungle city of Manaus. From there, riverboat travel takes over on the Rio Madeira to Porto Velho – jumping-off point for the onward journey east through the Pantanal to Rio.

Mexico City to Panama City
Route: Mexico City ➤ Tulum ➤ Belize City ➤ Antigua ➤ San Salvador ➤ Roatan ➤ Teguchigalpa ➤ Managua ➤ San José ➤ Panama City
Duration: 8 weeks
From a stroll in Old Panama to a quest for the elusive quetzal, this busy itinerary offers a truckload of experiences. Highlights include Aztec and Mayan ruins in Mexico, the reefs and rainforest of Belize, Monteverde Cloud Forest Reserve and Arenal volcano in Costa Rica and the Mayan citadel of Copán in Honduras.

Carretera Austral, Chile
Suitable for independent overland trips
Route: Puerto Montt ➤ Villa O'Higgins
Duration: 8 days
Fully accessible between January and February and suitable for independent drivers, the 1,240km (770-mile) 'Southern Highway' threads a spectacular route between the mountains, lakes and glaciers of Chilean Patagonia. Although several sections are paved, 4WD is still advisable. You will also have to use three ferries to complete the entire route.

AFRICA
Cairo (or Fes) to Cape Town
Route: Cairo → Khartoum → Addis Ababa → Nairobi → Dar es Salaam → Livingstone → Windhoek → Cape Town; or Fes → Dakar → Accra → Douala → Khartoum, then south as above route

Duration: 30 weeks

The classic African overland journey, Cairo to Cape Town (or vice versa) provides total emersion in the continent's vibrant cultures, landscapes and wildlife (as well as plenty of opportunities to get to know its dust, potholes and protracted border crossings). From Egypt's Valley of the Kings to East Africa's majestic Rift Valley, the route unfolds along the length of Africa, meandering through the safari lands of Kenya, Tanzania and Zambia before notching up the world wonders of Victoria Falls, the Namib Desert and Table Mountain. Several variations are possible, including shifting the starting post to Fes and driving across the Sahara to Senegal before venturing across West and Central Africa to Khartoum, where the 'normal' route continues south. Another natural cross-roads is Victoria Falls, where you can either drive west along the Caprivi Strip and down through Namibia (a must for desert fans) or head east through Zimbabwe, Mozambique and Swaziland. The trans-Africa route also breaks neatly in half, with Nairobi being the start/stop point for most overlanders. See the next two entries for highlights of these routes.

Cairo to Nairobi
Route: Cairo → Luxor → Khartoum → Gondar → Addis Ababa → Nairobi

Duration: 12–15 weeks

In Egypt you will not only see the classic sights, but also veer off the beaten track, hopping between oases in the Western Desert. A boat trip on Lake Nasser takes you to Sudan, where the best part of a week will be spent crossing the Nubian Desert and exploring villages and temples along the Nile Valley. Climbing into the Ethiopian Highlands, you'll explore the ancient capital of Gondar and trek in the Simien Mountains before visiting Lalibela's extraordinary rock-hewn churches. Beyond the Blue Nile (with its spectacular gorge and waterfall) lie remote tracts of arid terrain in southern Ethiopia and northern Kenya, where you will meet the tribal communities of the Omo and Samburu. Rift Valley lakes like Turkana, Baringo and Nakuru provide remarkable wildlife spectacles, particularly for birdwatchers, while Samburu National Reserve promises big game for safari enthusiasts.

Nairobi to Cape Town
Route: Nairobi → Arusha → Zanzibar → Lake Malawi → Livingstone; then either Maun → Etosha → Swakopmund → Fish River Canyon → Cape Town or Maun → Bulawayo → Vilankulos → Swaziland → Lesotho → Cape Town

Duration: 10–15 weeks

Climb Kilimanjaro, roam the Serengeti plains, dive on Zanzibar's coral reefs, kayak on

Lake Malawi, track wildlife on foot in South Luangwa National Park, canoe on the Lower Zambezi and raft the rapids downstream of Victoria Falls. Next, take a breather because you're only half way through this adventure-packed itinerary. Depending on whether you head east or west, the delights of the Okavango Delta, Namib Desert, Mozambique coast and Drakensberg Mountains await.

Trans-Sahara

Suitable for independent overland trips

Route: Tangiers ➤ Dakar

Duration: 4 weeks

A 3,200km (2,000-mile) all-weather road now links Morocco with Senegal, but how long it holds back the constantly shifting sands or flash floods of the Sahara is anyone's guess. Drive your own car via ferry from Europe, or rent one in Tangier. Alternatively, you may want to join a 4WD expedition or go slow on a camel train.

Northern Kenya

Suitable for independent overland trips

Route: Nairobi ➤ Lake Turkana ➤ Nairobi

Duration: 3 weeks

For a self-drive itinerary that bypasses the busy parks of the Masai Mara, Amboseli and Tsavo, head north from Nairobi, lake-hopping between Nakuru, Bogoria, Baringo and Turkana before heading back south to Laikipia and Mt Kenya. Fuel is generally easy to find, but you'll be driving in some remote areas where campsites are basic and offroad driving can be challenging.

Northern Botswana

Suitable for independent overland trips

Route: Maun ➤ Maun

Duration: 3 weeks

One for experienced 4WD users, this circuit through the Kalahari Desert, Makgadikgadi Pans, Okavango Delta and Chobe National Park combines tough conditions with otherworldly landscapes and superb wildlife.

ASIA

Oman

Suitable for independent overland trips

Route: Salalah ➤ Muscat

Duration: 2 weeks

Best driven between October and May when temperatures are less scorching, the route between the coastal resort of Salalah and Oman's capital, Muscat, is easily embellished with camel trekking at Wahiba Sands and a foray into the sandy, sun-baked wilderness of the Empty Quarter, or Rub al-Khali. Although Oman has an excellent road system, the challenging desert driving makes it imperative to hire a local guide.

The Silk Road

Route: Istanbul ➤ Göreme ➤ Malatya ➤ Dogubayazit ➤ Ghazvin ➤ Tehran ➤ Mashhad ➤ Merv ➤ Ashgabat ➤ Khiva ➤ Bukhara ➤ Samarkand ➤ Tashkent ➤ Bishkek ➤ Torugart Pass ➤ Kashgar ➤ Turpan ➤ Dunhuang ➤ Jiayuguan ➤ Lanzhou ➤ Xi'an ➤ Beijing

Duration: 16–24 weeks

Linking Mediterranean to Pacific, crossing no fewer than seven time zones and tracing its ancestry back to the days of the Old Testament, the Silk Road remains one of the world's greatest overland journeys. For much of the way, the 8,000km (5,000-mile) route skirts deserts and mountains, or ploughs straight through them, linking a dazzling succession of fascinating cities.

Kathmandu to Beijing
Route: Kathmandu ➤ Lhasa ➤ Golmud ➤ Xiahe ➤ Xi'an ➤ Beijing
Duration: 7 weeks
Take the high road from Nepal's capital, scaling 5,000m (16,400ft) passes on the Friendship Highway to reach Tingri. Visit the base camp for the north face of Everest before embarking on a breathtaking journey across the Tibetan Plateau to Lhasa and Golmud. Further east lies Xi'an, famous for its Terracotta Warriors. Head north from here, via Inner Mongolia and the Great Wall of China, to reach Beijing.

Kathmandu to Mumbai
Route: Kathmandu ➤ Varanasi ➤ Agra ➤ Jaipur ➤ Delhi ➤ Jaisalmer ➤ Jodphur ➤ Udaipur ➤ Mumbai
Duration: 5 weeks
A classic journey across the Indian subcontinent, this overland route links Nepal's wildlife-rich Chitwan National Park with the cultural treasures of Uttar Pradesh, Rajasthan and Madhya Pradesh.

The open road lies ahead

ADVENTURE BRIEFING
Understanding overlanding

Traversing remote areas and covering huge distances while someone else does the driving, overlanding also takes the hassle out of finding accommodation, reaching places of interest and all the other dilemmas facing independent travellers.

Group dynamics

For some, overlanding promises new friends and shared adventures, while for others, the idea of rattling around inside a truck for several months with a bunch of strangers is not so appealing. Ultimately, an overland trip is a team effort – you will be expected to help the crew pitch tents, prepare meals, wash up and so on. There is usually no maximum age limit, and nowadays a typical trip is just as likely to include 40-year-old career-gappers as pre- or post-university students.

Truck anatomy

Overland trucks are tough, heavy-duty vehicles, but they usually have comfortable seating, along with a few luxuries like a music system and onboard library. Some trucks also boast rooftop seats. Riddled with cunningly designed compartments, overland vehicles swallow a vast range of equipment, from tables, chairs and tents to food, drinking water and personal luggage.

Planning an overland trip

There are dozens of operators offering overland expeditions (see pages 247–8). Remember to budget for 'local payments' – usually cash payable to the driver/guide at the beginning of the trip to cover such expenses as food and day-to-day costs. Certain side-trips and highlights may not be included in the price, so check carefully and compare.

ECOFILE

- Use small locally owned hotels, campsites and restaurants where possible.
- Buy food and other provisions from local markets.
- Employ local guides and support crew.
- For cooking, use gas instead of firewood, especially in areas where nomadic communities depend on scarce supplies of dead wood.
- Buy drinks in returnable bottles and use the truck's large drinking water supply, rather than purchase water in plastic bottles.
- Always ask before photographing people.
- Try not to use non-biodegradable detergents, especially at desert wells.
- Dispose of used motor oil in proper facilities.
- Think carefully about potential erosion before driving offroad.
- Leave campsites as you'd expect to find them.

What to take

Versatility is the key. You're likely to be travelling through several climate zones and experiencing a wide range of travel situations, from city tours to jungle hikes. You'll also need sturdy gear that can withstand the rigours of several weeks on the road.

Opening with a front zip rather like a suitcase, convertible backpacks combine good accessibility with easy carrying. Look for one that has a capacity of around 65 litres (4,000cu in) with an additional 15-litre (915cu in) detachable daypack. Good-quality two-way zips that lock together are an important feature, as is a grab handle, compression straps and comfortable back system. Some packs also boast an integral rain cover, which will keep your gear dry if you get caught in a downpour while loading the truck. Also useful is a cable and padlock for securing your pack to roof racks or bed frames.

For a typical trip in warmer climes, take a two-season sleeping bag along with an easily washable cotton liner for extra comfort and hygiene. A thermal liner can boost your bag's rating by a season. With clothing, a layered approach works best; make sure garments are easily washed and dry quickly.

All good overland companies ensure that their trucks are well equipped for medical emergencies, but as you may be travelling in areas where medical help is more than 24 hours away, make sure you carry essential first-aid equipment with you (see page 47).

ESSENTIAL**GEAR**

• **Sleeping bag and liner** • Lightweight self-inflating mat • **Impregnated mosquito net** • Daypack and convertible backpack • **Versatile clothing** • Padlocks and moneybelt • **Sunglasses, sunhat and sunblock** • Biodegradable soap and 'drywash' • **Lightweight towel** • Insect repellent • **First-aid and sterile kits** • Water purifying kit • **Sewing kit** • Multi-tool • **Head torch (lamp), batteries and bulbs** • Universal plug and clothesline • **Duct tape for emergency repairs**

A stop at the beach, Mauritania

Going solo on the road

Self-drive adventures provide flexibility to decide your own route, pace, detours and overnight stops, but with no guide to help smooth the way, careful planning is crucial.

As well as linking major highlights, the most satisfying do-it-yourself 4WD expeditions involve plenty of minor roads to get you off the beaten track and in touch with local life. Allow plenty of spare days, not only as a contingency in case of breakdown, illness, border closures and so on, but also to allow you the freedom to take advantage of the occasional spontaneous detour.

Choosing the right vehicle
The Land Rover Defender is not only straightforward to drive and maintain, but it is also one of the world's most tried and trusted 4WD vehicles. Other reliable models include the Toyota Land Cruiser and Nissan X-TRAIL, although in some countries, servicing and obtaining parts may be difficult. Older 4WD vehicles are generally easier to maintain than newer versions with complicated electronics systems.

4WD packages
There are specialist operators out there, such as Safari Drive (www.safaridrive.com) for example, who provide a comprehensive

A 4WD will take you places an ordinary car can't reach

self-drive service, including a fully prepared Land Rover with unlimited mileage, all camping equipment, a food starter pack, tailor-made itinerary with maps, reservations service for lodges and camps, national parks booking service, pre-trip safety briefing, full in-country back-up, first-aid kit and enough fuel to get you through your first 1,000km (600 miles).

ESSENTIAL**GEAR**

• **Long-range fuel tanks (120 litres/ 32 gallons)** • Basic spare parts and tool box • **Two spare wheels** • Two batteries • **Tyre pump and pressure gauge** • High-lift jack and block • **Spare oil** • Spade and axe • **Tow rope or strap** • Pair of sand ladders • **Fire extinguisher** • GPS • **Satellite phone** • Rooftop tent • **Bush shower** • Fridge

Tyres will suffer a lot of wear – inspect them regularly

Top 10 tips for 4WD expeditions

1. Plan expenses meticulously, factoring in the costs of fuel, visas, accommodation, food and activities.
2. Plan a route in detail, but allow contingency days for breakdowns, bad weather, poor road conditions and border-crossing problems.
3. Make sure you have adequate mechanical knowledge – it's no good packing a hi-lift jack if you don't know how to use it.
4. Take a 4WD-training course before you depart. Day and weekend courses are widely available.
5. Get as many visas as possible before you leave. You will also need a *carnet de passage* (that allows you to travel in and out of countries without paying import and export taxes), an international driving permit and (at least) third party insurance. Brokers offering travel insurance for overland travel include Campbell Irvine (www.campbellirvine.com).
6. Ensure your vehicle is fitted with long-range fuel tanks and carry more than adequate supplies of drinking water.
7. In remote or challenging areas, plan to travel with another vehicle.
8. Equip your vehicle with an alarm, as well as a safe for valuables.
9. A satellite phone will enable you to keep in touch with contacts at home and let them know where you are headed. Get updates on political situations from websites like the UK Foreign Office (www.fco.gov.uk/travel), and also from local people.
10. Prior to setting off, take a course in wilderness first aid from a specialist like WMT (www.wildernessmedicaltraining.co.uk).

Secrets of the Namib

Pioneered by the Schoeman family in the late 1970s, Skeleton Coast Safaris use a combination of light aircraft and 4WD vehicles to explore Namibia's wild desert shore and its rugged hinterland.

Racing alongside our single-propeller Cessna, five ostriches sprinted across the yellow grasslands of Namibia. Miniature explosions of dust erupted beneath their pounding steps like a trail of machine-gun fire. André Schoeman knew how to fly low. During Namibia's struggle for independence he piloted helicopter gunships along Angola's border at below 15m (50ft) to avoid detection by surface-to-air missiles.

Ahead of us a vivid red gash lanced the horizon. The grasslands became ruffled by long winding ridges of apricot-coloured sand as the land yielded to the Namib — the world's driest and most ancient desert, spawned by the Skeleton Coast over 50 million years ago. André nudged the Cessna on to a wing tip, banking low over a huge dune, the first in a scorched sand sea that led us 100km (60 miles) to the Atlantic.

Landing on a gravel airstrip, I stepped from the aircraft to find jackal tracks weaving down to a beach of purple and grey pebbles. Casualties littered the ground. There were mummified seal carcasses like pieces of

The eerie, bleak landscape of the Skeleton Coast

grotesque driftwood, bleached whale vertebrae and the skeleton of a porpoise. Enormous breakers hissed viciously through the pebbles. Looking north I saw nothing but angry sea and battered shore.

Climbing into a Land Rover (stashed away in a deserted mining shed) we drove into the hostile heart of the sand sea. These were barchan, or wandering, dunes and the constantly shifting sand would soon cover our tracks. But the very wind that obscured all trace of our passing also revealed some secrets of the desert. Microscopic grains of diamonds and garnets winked from the surface of the dunes like trails of glitter. The real magic began when we scooped up the sand and rubbed it between our hands. The desert began to sing.

André beckoned me to the crest of one of the so-called 'roaring dunes' and we slid down in a slow avalanche of sand, the desert resonating around us.

'Let's try it in the Land Rover,' André suggested, pouring the sand out of his boots. The desert-scarred vehicle had a roof seat and from this precarious perch, I began the thrill ride of a lifetime. Gunning the Land Rover along the dip slope of a 100m-high (330ft) dune, André cut the throttle just as the front wheels shot over the crest. Then with wheels locked, we skied down the scarp slope in a tumult of sound, like the deep drone of a squadron of World War II bombers.

A few days later, exploring the Hartmann Valley near the Angolan border, we encountered another spectacular dune field. Hunched like a bear over the steering wheel, André willed the Land Rover through the desert rollercoaster, pallid drifts of sand rearing at every turn. Then, without warning, the sand sea abruptly ended. André swerved on to a curling tongue of sand, beyond which the desert poured into a deep ravine. On the far side, Angola's highlands smouldered in late afternoon sunlight. But it was to the valley floor that my eyes were drawn – to shimmering, flowing water. The Kunene River was a vibrant ribbon of sparkling rapids, calm pools and dense stands of river acacias teeming with birdlife – an emerald vein of life in the desert.

ECO**FILE**

- Safaris are limited to a maximum of eight people to minimize environmental impact.
- Respect ancient Bushman rock art sites and leave all artifacts as you found them.
- Take care not to damage vulnerable desert soils or plant life.
- During meetings with the Himba people in Kaokoland, pay a fair price for handicrafts and ask permission before taking photographs.

FACT**FILE**

Skeleton Coast, Namibia

When to go: Safaris are conducted year-round. Fog can affect the coast, while nights can be chilly.

Need to know: Accommodation is in small private camps with flush toilets and bucket showers. Luggage allowance is restricted to a maximum of 10kg (22 lb) per person, packed in soft, flexible duffel bags. This excludes camera equipment of approximately 2kg (4.5 lb).

Next step: Most safaris start from Windhoek, served by international flights from the UK, Germany and South Africa.

Operators: Skeleton Coast Safaris (www.skeletoncoastsafaris.com) offers trips lasting from four to six days with options to include Luderitz, the Namib Rand and Etosha.

Should I drive offroad?

Personal and vehicle safety obviously rate highly in the minds of most 4WD adventurers, but what about the environmental impacts of driving offroad? Should you even contemplate making tracks in sand dunes or other fragile habitats?

Empowered by the commanding driving position and 4x4 traction, few self-drive enthusiasts are going to restrict themselves to sealed highways. All offroad drivers, however, have a responsibility to choose routes with care. Not only is 4WD access to many national parks and conservation areas controlled by strict regulations, but some particularly fragile habitats, as well as historical and archaeological sites, are best avoided altogether. At the very least, try to keep to tracks approved for 4WD use.

It goes without saying that you should avoid spooking any wildlife or livestock you encounter and resist the urge to give chase for a closer view. Consideration should also be given to other offroad users, like farmers or park rangers, who may well depend on the same tracks for their work. Remember, too, that you should obtain permission before driving on private land.

Which areas are out of bounds?

Avoid vulnerable habitats such as vegetated dunes, alpine meadows, wetlands and seasonal nesting areas, unless on designated routes. Some cryptobiotic soils (which form a living crust of lichen, moss, algae, microfungi and bacteria in some desert and tundra regions) are easily scarred by the tracks of 4WD vehicles and should also be given a wide berth.

How can I drive more responsibly offroad?

The general advice is to drive only as fast as is necessary to negotiate obstacles; the slower you drive the less environmental impact you'll create in the form of erosion, dust and potential damage through accidents.

Engage 4WD and use your low-range gearbox (or select the vehicle's appropriate 'terrain' setting) to maximize control. Take corners slowly, braking smoothly to maintain traction. Similarly, a gradual increase in speed, particularly on ascents or descents, will reduce the risk of the vehicle sliding, skidding or rolling. You will also find that a

Land Rover entering the Valley of 10,000 Dunes on Namibia's Skeleton Coast

well-balanced load and reduced tyre pressure provide extra 'grip' on uneven or soft terrain.

It's a good idea to stop frequently and scout ahead on foot for potential hazards. Where possible try to avoid mud, where wheel spins can cause rutting. Ford rivers and streams at designated points and drive over, not around, obstacles to avoid widening the trail.

An offroad driving course in a controlled setting with an instructor sitting beside you is the best way to learn how to tackle challenging terrain, as well as practise environmentally responsible offroad driving.

What else can I do to safeguard the environment?

Make sure your vehicle is mechanically sound and check regularly for any leaks of oil, fuel or hydraulic fluids. Always wash vehicles well away from water courses (to avoid contamination) and use biodegradable cleaning materials. With the large storage capacity of most 4WD vehicles there is no excuse for not taking away your own rubbish – and maybe that of other people too. Keep the noise and dust down, particularly near campsites or recreation areas, and always yield to hikers, horse riders and mountain bikers.

Mountain-biking

They're environmentally friendly, cost effective and keep you fit. No wonder cycling holidays are so popular. Best of all, they help you blend in and experience destinations on a far more intimate level than if you were in a car, truck or bus.

From its humble beginnings in California, where Joe Breeze devised the first purpose-built mountain bike in 1977, offroad cycling has taken the world by storm. But don't be put off by images of helmet-clad daredevils bouncing off boulders and careering down canyons. There

> 6 One moment we were weaving through rice paddies and fish ponds, the next we were flinching behind trucks on a four-lane highway. 9

are biking adventures suitable for all levels of experience, fitness and ambition, whether you want to dawdle through rural lanes in Europe, stopping each night at a comfortable guest-house, or stuff your panniers with enough gear to keep you going across the Gobi Desert for a month. The recent evolution of the hybrid bike (essentially a mountain bike with added comfort) has opened up a diverse range of destinations to those in search of cycle trips offering a mixture of touring and moderate offroad riding. Numerous adventure operators now offer guided cycling itineraries and many provide full back-up services, such as support vehicles or luggage transfers between each night's stop. Popular places to pedal include the rocky desert of Moab in the US, the blissfully level cycling trails of Denmark and the enticing coastal tracks around the Marlborough Sounds of New Zealand.

ADVENTURE**RATING**

Daring:	✔✔✔
Eco-friendly:	✔✔✔✔✔
Expense:	✔✔
Expertise:	✔✔
Fitness:	✔✔✔

At the watering hole, Mashatu Game Reserve, Botswana

ADVENTURE CALLING

The world's greatest cycle rides

There's a bewildering range of bike tours available, from freewheeling along quiet country lanes in Ireland to pounding the passes on the Karakoram Highway. Get into gear, with 17 of the world's most scenic and rewarding rides.

KEY TO SYMBOLS

Ø **Easy:** Covering 20–50km (12–32 miles) a day over undulating terrain, these trips use sealed and unsealed roads with a support vehicle to carry luggage.
ØØ **Moderate:** You will pedal up to 100km (62 miles) a day, often in hilly areas and using rough tracks. Support vehicles may be provided.
ØØØ **Challenging:** Be prepared for long days in the saddle, tackling rough tracks often at altitude or in remote locations.

Moab, USA ØØ
www.discovermoab.com
Best time to go: April–May, September–October
The world's most famous mountain-biking trail, the 15.5km (9.6-mile) Slickrock pitches and climbs across the rocky desert terrain near Moab, a small Utah town an easy day's drive from either Salt Lake City or Denver. Build up courage on the shorter practice loop before heading out on the ultimate sandstone rollercoaster ride.

Marin County, USA Ø – ØØØ
www.btcmarin.org
Best time to go: Spring or autumn
Take a spin across Golden Gate Bridge to explore the hallowed trails around Mt Tamalpais and the Headlands of California's Marin County, where mountain-biking is said to have had its beginnings in the 1970s. Take your pick of numerous day rides or string them together for a circuit through redwood forests, past lakes and alongside San Francisco Bay.

Icefields Parkway, Canada ØØ
www.icefieldsparkway.ca
Best time to go: Late spring or early autumn
One of the world's most beautiful cycling routes, this 230km (143-mile) highway traces the glacier- and lake-studded backbone of the Canadian Rockies between Lake Louise and Jasper. It's popular with car and motorhome users too, so try to avoid the busier summer months.

Cuba ⌀

www.cubatravel.cu

Best time to go: November–April

Travelling by bike is the perfect way to explore Cuba. Allow around two weeks, cycling 40–50km (25–32 miles) a day, to traverse the length of the island, pedalling along quiet backroads through a mosaic of limestone peaks, jungle, tobacco fields, colonial towns and sandy beaches.

Baños, Ecuador ⌀⌀

www.vivecuador.com

Best time to go: June–September

The spectacular 60km (38-mile) ride along the Río Pastaza canyon from Baños to Puyo descends into the upper reaches of the Amazon Basin, passing the impressive Pailón del Diablo waterfall.

Yungas Highway, Bolivia ⌀⌀⌀

Best time to go: May–October

Dubbed the world's most dangerous road, the 64km (40-mile) stretch of the Yungas Highway between La Paz and Coroico is little more than a narrow gravel track etched into cliffs with sheer 1,000m (3,300ft) drops – a riveting ride for those in search of an adrenaline rush.

Copper Canyon, Mexico ⌀⌀

www.visitmexico.com

Best time to go: October–May

Covering an area four times larger than Arizona's Grand Canyon, the Copper Canyon offers some of the most varied mountain-biking in the world – from exhilarating 1,800m (6,000ft) descents to the slickrock trails of the Sierra Tarahumara.

Danube Trail, Germany, Austria & Slovakia ⌀ – ⌀⌀

Best time to go: Summer

Follow flat, dedicated bike paths alongside Europe's second longest

Moab's sandstone canyons make for great mountain-biking

Fitness is vital for rides in mountainous regions

Top 5 epic rides

You will need several months to complete any of these long-distance cycling odysseys, but the experience could well be life changing.

1. Silk Road from the Middle East to China.
2. Great Rift Valley from Ethiopia to Malawi.
3. Coast to Coast USA along the 6,840km (4,250-mile) TransAmerican Trail.
4. The Pacific Coast Highway from Alaska to Chile.
5. All, or part of, the 25,750km (16,000-mile) Australian coastline.

river. Although the entire route from Passau to Bratislava is a 365km (227-mile) epic, many cyclists opt for a shorter six-day jaunt between Passau and Vienna.

Denmark ∅ – ∅∅

www.trafikken.dk

Best time to go: Summer

With its flourishing bike culture, flattish countryside and excellent network of dedicated trails, Denmark is a superb destination for a cycle touring holiday. Take your pick of ten national routes.

Wales ∅ – ∅∅∅

www.mbwales.com

Best time to go: Summer

North Wales boasts some of Britain's best mountain-biking trails, weaving through Gwydyr and Coed Y Brenin Forest Parks. Base yourself in the local adventure capital of Betws-y-Coed. Farther south, Afan Forest Park, near Swansea, has the downhill Trwch Trail, while the 420km (260-mile) Lôn Las Cymru route across Wales stands out as one of the most challenging on the UK's National Cycle Network.

Tour du Mont Blanc, France ∅∅∅

Best time to go: July–September

A tough alpine route around

Europe's tallest mountain, the 200km (124-mile) Tour du Mont Blanc reaches a highpoint of 3,000m (9,840ft) and is best suited to technically experienced riders.

Jebel Sahro, Morocco ∅∅

www.visitmorocco.org

Best time to go: October–April

Sandwiched between the High Atlas and the Sahara, the Jebel Sahro region is perfect for a mountain bike adventure outside the summer months. Highlights include the Tazarzart Pass, Todra Gorge and Draa Valley where you'll ride between kasbahs on a mixture of gravel and tarmac roads. A typical trip lasts around a week, cycling an average of 60km (37 miles) a day.

Ethiopian Highlands ∅∅ – ∅∅∅

www.tourismethiopia.org

Best time to go: October–May

The dramatic Rift Valley escarpments and plateaux of the Ethiopian Highlands are riddled with epic biking trails, including a thrilling ride down 4,307m (14,127ft) Tullu Deemtu and across the Sanetti Plateau. Head to Bale Mountains National Park for a chance to spot rare wildlife (like Ethiopian wolf and mountain nyala) from the saddle.

Jordan ∅∅

www.visitjordan.com

Best time to go: Spring or autumn

Offering a smoother (and less flatulent!) ride than camels, bikes are ideal for exploring Jordan. Start in Amman and head south, linking top sites like biblical Mt Nebo, the Byzantine mosaics of Madaba, Dana Nature Reserve, the rose-red city of Petra and the wild desert of Wadi Rum. Round your trip off with a soothing dip in the Dead Sea or snorkelling in the Red Sea at Aqaba.

Friendship Highway, Tibet & Nepal ∅∅∅

Best time to go: March–April

Few mountain-biking routes can rival the scenery and sense of achievement offered by the Friendship Highway – a breath-less, 940km (584-mile) route across the Tibetan Plateau between Lhasa and Kathmandu. Allow at least 20 days, including the all-essential detour to the base camp below the north face of Everest.

Vietnam ∅∅

www.vietnamtourism.com

Best time to go: December–April

Two wheels is definitely the way to go in Vietnam, where you'll feel more in touch with local life on a bike. The Mekong Delta is one of the most interesting (and flattest) regions of the country to explore, although you may want to avoid the busy traffic on the highway between Ho Chi Minh City and Cantho.

Queen Charlotte Track, New Zealand ∅ – ∅∅

www.newzealand.com

Best time to go: November–April

Just one of South Island's many fine biking routes, the Queen Charlotte weaves 71km (44 miles) through the beautiful coastal forests of the Malborough Sounds.

ADVENTURE BRIEFING

Preparing for the ride of your life

Numerous operators offer bike tours catering to all levels of skill and fitness. Whatever your experience, however, it's important to have the right gear and prepare well in advance of your cycling adventure.

Choosing the right bike

Whereas racing bikes are designed for speed and road touring, mountain bikes are built for strength and durability. A lightweight but strong frame, low gearing system and wide, knobbly tyres make them well equipped for negotiating obstacles and powering up and down rough tracks. Hybrid bicycles retain these essential features but have modifications for added comfort, such as suspension on the front forks and seat post, as well as a frame designed for a more upright cycling position. Tyres are usually semi-slick on hybrid bikes, making them ideally suited to trips which combine roads and tracks – but don't expect them to offer the same levels of traction as you'd get from a pure-bred mountain bike.

Reputable adventure operators provide well-maintained bikes for their cycling tours, with expert guides on hand to help you make any adjustments to handlebars, gears, brakes and saddles before you set off.

Running repairs, Guilin, China

Travelling in an organized group usually has the added advantage of a support vehicle with supplies, spares and even seats for when you need a break. Hiring bikes is a straightforward option in many countries, but be sure to check your cycle carefully to ensure it's roadworthy. If you decide to take your own bike, contact airlines and airports beforehand for advice on weight limits and handling charges. Box your bike before checking it in. Remember that you may find it difficult to find spares for high-tech models, so take everything you might need with you.

What to wear

Layered clothing is best – peel items off as you warm up; put them back on during rest stops. Your base layer should have good wicking properties, drawing sweat away from your body to keep you dry and comfortable. Your outer layer, meanwhile, should be windproof and waterproof. Padded Lycra cycling shorts prevent chafing, while cycling gloves keep hands warm and protect against jarring and blisters. Don't forget a helmet – it's compulsory in many countries and you would be wise to carry a spare on extended trips.

How to carry gear

Independent cyclists have to carry their own supplies, which can be both liberating and limiting. Bicycle panniers (mounted over the front and back wheels) can swallow large amounts of gear, but a heavy load will restrict you largely to road touring where you're unlikely to need to carry your bike around obstacles. For cycling trips on rougher terrain, opt for a streamlined backpack, which keeps your bike lightweight and unencumbered for shouldering it over streams, boulders and other hazards. Bear in mind, though, that wearing a backpack will reduce your stability. A waist pouch is also useful for carrying a compact camera, sun block and valuables, while a map holder can be mounted on handlebars.

Maintenance and safety

Always carry a bicycle repair kit (see right) and check your bike regularly for signs of worn brakes, buckled wheels and so on. Before you set off learn how to deal with common problems such as punctures and broken chains. It's also crucial to get yourself in good shape before embarking on a cycling adventure. The best pre-trip exercise is cycling, starting a daily programme at least six weeks before you set off. Don't forget to do warm-up exercises before each ride. If you are new to mountain-biking, develop your balance and skills on level tracks before progressing to more hazardous slopes. It's also a good idea to buddy up with other cyclists, as riding solo can leave you vulnerable in the event of an accident or breakdown.

ECOFILE

- Cycle only in permitted areas and avoid muddy trails.
- Keep to the middle of trails to minimize erosion.
- On descents, try to avoid skidding, which can rut the trail.
- Close gates behind you and avoid spooking livestock.
- Keep off sensitive habitats such as meadows and wetlands.
- Carry a trash bag to take away your litter – and that of others.
- Following a ride, wash your bike to reduce the spread of invasive weeds.

ESSENTIAL GEAR

• Helmet • **Eye protection** • High-visibility cycling vest • **Cycling shorts and gloves** • Windproof and water-proof jacket • **Water bottle or hydration backpack** • Bicycle repair kit containing puncture patches, chalk, rubber adhesive, tyre levers, pump, grease, adjustable spanner and spare brake, gear cables and inner tubes • **Bicycle multi-tool with allen keys, crank tool, spoke tool, chain breaker, bottom bracket tool, cone spanner and head tube spanner**

A slow bike through China

There may well be nine million bicycles in Beijing, but the best place in China to share the road with local cyclists is in the south, where a week-long route links Zhaoqing and Yangshuo.

ECO**FILE**

- Keep to tracks, especially when cycling through farmland, where crops could be damaged by careless offroad cycling.
- Support communities by shopping in markets and making use of local services.

FACT**FILE**

Southern China

When to go: Autumn is ideal, with cool nights and daytime temperatures ranging from 15–26°C (59–79°F). Expect local variations and a chance of rain at any time.

Need to know: Organized cycle tours include hotel accommodation, most meals and the use of 21-speed mountain bikes. Only moderate fitness is required since most of the cycling is on easy country roads.

Next step: Numerous airlines serve Hong Kong, from where it's a 4-hour voyage to Zhaoqing. Alternatively, fly to Guangzhou.

Operators: World Expeditions (www.worldexpeditions.co.uk) offers a 12-day fully supported trip cycling between Zhaoqing and Yangshuo.

Heavy clouds slouched over Star Lake, its grey surface fretted by gusts of wind. Typhoon Hagupit had landed and suddenly the hard saddle on my mountain bike seemed the least of my concerns.

We had travelled from Hong Kong the previous day, cleaving the Pearl River on a high-speed catamaran bound for Zhaoqing in Guangdong Province – the starting point for our 600km (375-mile) cycle through southern China. In the lull before the storm, our guide, Stony, had issued detailed copies of the itinerary marked with intriguing instructions like 'Turn left at the roundabout with the big banyan tree'.

As we set off into the sodden clutches of the typhoon, locals were captivated by the strange procession that rolled through their villages. Even buffalo, wandering along the roadside, looked up with bemused expressions as we sloshed past.

Throughout the day, rural tranquillity collided with modern reality. One moment we were weaving through rice paddies and a silver honeycomb of fishponds, the next we were flinching in the wake of trucks on a four-lane highway or cowering beneath a cement factory. I realized that by cycling slowly through China I would get a full picture – sullied and serene – of this fast-changing country.

The following day, we encountered our first stretch of dirt track. Right on cue, Hagupit unleashed a violent squall that transformed the unfinished road into a mud-smeared

You'll be exposed to all weathers in the saddle

battleground. Within minutes, we were wrestling our bikes through a traffic jam of bogged-down buses and wallowing buffaloes.

But it was during the fifth day that we tackled the route's most challenging section – a relentless uphill slog of over an hour, covering 7km (4 miles) on a road chiselled into glaring limestone cliffs. The heat was stupefying, my legs felt like lead and my backside pleaded for mercy.

For the most part, however, the terrain was gently undulating. Daily distances ranged from 20 to 105km (12–65 miles) – and Mr Wong was always at hand if anyone craved a spell of air-con in the support vehicle. At times it felt odd to have this luxury 'life-support system' available in the midst of landscapes where, essentially, farming techniques were still medieval. The greatest culture shock, however, was arriving at Yangshuo – a backpacker's mecca nestled amongst dramatic limestone pinnacles. In the week since leaving Hong Kong we had grown used to being stared at and greeted as novelties in a region where tourists were rarely seen. But in Yangshuo we abruptly found ourselves fair game for tour and curio touts. Bob Marley wafted from pavement cafés offering banana pancakes, steaks and cappuccinos, while market stalls groaned with soapstone Buddhas and bamboo flutes.

On our final cycle to nearby Moon Hill, we followed a rough track that meandered through a mêlée of conical fairytale hills. The sky was milky white, ponds flecked the rice paddies like squares of foil, and thickets of giant bamboo unfurled towering green plumes above our heads. For once, my saddle felt almost comfortable. I felt like nothing could stop me. Not even a typhoon.

Snowmobiling & quad-biking

Riding a snowmobile or quad bike is exhilarating and brings remote tracts of otherwise inaccessible terrain within easy reach, but careful consideration must be given to personal safety and the environment.

ADVENTURE CALLING

Snowmobiling

In many arctic regions, hopping on a snowmobile is more often a case of essential local transport than an excuse for adventure. However, several locations offer snowmobile tours specifically for tourists. In Iceland, for example, daytrips from Reykjavik feature snowmobiling on the 950sq km (370sq mile) Langjökull icecap, while numerous places in Scandinavia, from Stavanger to Svalbard, offer skidoo safaris. One of the best European locations is Lapland, where you can join expeditions high above the Arctic Circle lasting a week or more. Greenland and the Canadian Arctic also offer vast areas of frozen wilderness that are perfect for exploring by snowmobile. In the United States, meanwhile, northern Maine, West Yellowstone (Montana), Eagle River (Wisconsin) and Stanley Basin (Idaho) all have reliable winter snow and excellent trail networks for snowmobiles.

Quad-biking

An increasingly popular adventure sport, quad-biking (or ATV riding) is available in many parts of the world, from Dubai to the Australian outback. Hotspots in Africa include the vast salt flats of

Top: Quad-bikers in the desert in Egypt. Bottom: Snowmobiling in Finland

Botswana's Makgadikgadi Pans and the rocky hills and dune fields of the Namib Rand Reserve in Namibia. Ouarzazate in Morocco is ideally placed for ATV forays into the fringes of the Sahara.

ADVENTURE BRIEFING

On organized snowmobiling or quad-biking adventures you should receive a full safety briefing and usually a few practice runs on gentle terrain before setting off. Travelling single file on designated trails, your guide will take the lead, often with an assistant bringing up the rear.

Snowmobiles and quad bikes are easy to control. Remember to reduce speed and lean into turns with your upper body to avoid sliding or overturning. Allow sufficient braking distance between yourself and the vehicle in front, approach hillcrests with caution and pump brakes when going downhill so you don't skid. Snowmobile riders should take extra care to avoid obstacles hidden beneath the snow. Treat frozen lakes with extreme caution – if in doubt seek local advice or find an alternative route. Similarly, areas prone to avalanches should be given a wide berth.

For independent expeditions, make a realistic plan and stick to it. Always tell someone of your travel plans and, if crossing private property, be sure to ask permission from the landowner. It is a good idea to ride in convoy with two or three riders as going solo can leave you vulnerable if you have an accident or breakdown.

Protective gear is essential for quad-biking and snowmobiling. In addition to helmet, eye protection and high-visibility clothing, take precautions against extreme temperatures in arctic or desert environments.

ECOFILE

- Snowmobiling on trails with inadequate snow cover can damage plants below the surface. Avoid quad-biking in sensitive habitats unless on designated routes.
- Carry a trash bag to take away your litter and any left by others.
- Minimize harmful emissions by keeping your engine properly tuned.
- On quad bikes, drive over, not around, obstacles to avoid widening the trail.
- Never take shortcuts on trails since this can cause erosion.
- Moderate the throttle and use the clutch to maximize traction and reduce wheel spin.

ESSENTIALGEAR

• Helmet • Eye protection • Layered clothing with wind/waterproof outer shell • Small backpack containing emergency items • Tools, spares and a spill kit for trailside repairs

ADVENTURERATING

Daring:	∅∅∅∅∅
Eco-friendly:	∅∅∅∅∅
Expensive:	∅∅∅∅∅
Physical:	∅∅∅∅∅
Technical:	∅∅∅∅∅

To boldly go...

No longer confined to flights of fancy, space tourism is set to become the next great adventure – to gaze down on Planet Earth during a sub-orbital flight or from the International Space Station.

In April 2001, American businessman Dennis Tito rocketed into space (and the history books) as the world's first space tourist. His week spent orbiting Earth on Alpha One, the International Space Station, has since been followed by a handful of others, but with round-trip tickets of around US$30 million, orbital space travel has remained well out of reach of most mere mortals. In recent years, however, the race to launch much cheaper commercial sub-orbital flights has brought the prospect of widely available space tourism a small step closer.

Sub-orbital space travel

Space officially starts 100km (62 miles) above Earth – the kind of altitude that the first generation of commercial passenger spacecraft are designed to reach during a sub-orbital flight. One of the pioneers of sub-orbital space travel, Virgin Galactic (www.virgingalactic.com) plans to commence flights from the Mojave Spaceport in California sometime around 2010. As well as paying US$200,000 for a ticket, would-be astronauts must pass a fitness test and complete three days of pre-flight training to prepare them for the zero-gravity ride. Once

the spacecraft is released from its 'mothership' at an altitude of 15km (9 miles), an onboard rocket will propel the craft to 110km (68 miles) in just 90 seconds, reaching speeds of over 4,000km/h (2,486mph), three times the speed of sound. At the apex of the parabolic flight, the seatbelt lights will go out and passengers will be able to float around the cabin, enjoying extraordinary views of the home planet and deep space. Then the spacecraft feathers its wings in preparation for re-entry to the Earth's atmosphere, gliding back to the spaceport where passengers receive their astronaut wings. Other spaceports are being built in Dubai, Singapore and Kiruna in Swedish Lapland.

Orbital space travel

Blast off from Earth in a Soyuz rocket and ten minutes later you could be docking with the International Space Station for a ten-day stint in space, living, eating and sleeping in zero gravity. During that time, you will orbit Earth around 120 times and travel roughly 5 million km (3 million miles). Prices start at around US$30 million booked through Space Adventures (www.spaceadventures.com), but why stop there? For an extra US$15 million you can include a 90-minute spacewalk.

Moon missions

Commercial lunar flights are still in the research and development phase, but two seats are available (at US$100 million each) for Space Adventures' inaugural DSE-Alpha 'loop around the moon' expedition.

Deep-sea travel

Journeys to the unknown depths of the world's oceans may not match the glamour of space travel, but there's no denying the adventure potential of a submersible ride into the abyss. Available for charter through Deep Ocean Quest (www.deepoceanquest.com), the luxurious MV *Alucia* is equipped with two Deep Rovers, each capable of taking two people to depths of 1,000m (3,300ft).

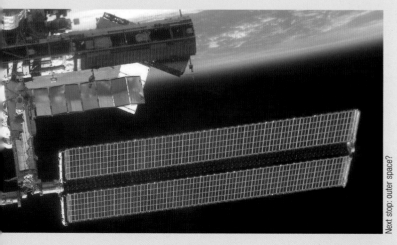

Next stop: outer space?

Water

Rough or smooth, fresh or salty, floating or submerged...however you prefer your water-themed adventure, the world's seas, lakes and rivers are brimming with opportunities. An open-water scuba course can be a springboard into the bewildering range of dive sites around the world, from wrecks and reefs to mysterious blue holes and kelp forests. Activities such as sea-kayaking, canoeing and whitewater rafting require little or no experience – simply pick up a paddle and join a guided group slipping quietly through the wilderness or whooping it up on a wild river like the Tuolumne or Zambezi. Surfing and sailing are equally accessible. Chances are, though, that once hooked you'll soon be pondering Oahu's mighty Pipeline or plotting an island-hopping cruise around the Caribbean. Wherever you take the plunge, remember that all these activities can be unforgiving to those who flaunt safety rules – just as the aquatic environments themselves can be easily damaged by careless adventurers.

Top: Snorkelling in the Indian Ocean. Bottom left: Sea-kayaking in British Columbia. Bottom right: Surfing in Hawaii

Contents

Key

The numbers/letters in circles on this page correspond to the locations marked on the map on pages 158–9.

Water: World Map

Stockholm St Petersburg
Moscow
SAYAN MOUNTAINS
Ulaanbaatar
GOBI
DESERT
Beijing
Istanbul Tehran
Baghdad
Cairo
Karachi Delhi
HIMALAYA
A
Khartoum
Mumbai
Hong Kong
Tokyo
PACIFIC
OCEAN
Bangkok
20
D
nshasa Nairobi
19
A
21
17
22
INDIAN
OCEAN
Cairns
24
10
Harare
8
GREAT DIVIDING RANGE
8
7
6
16
11
Johannesburg
Perth
Sydney
25
Canberra
Auckland
5
10 11
9 12
11

23

Great Barrier Reef

Scuba-diving

Breathing underwater, experiencing weightlessness, riding undersea currents… everything about scuba-diving is exhilarating – not to mention the incredible marine life and seascapes awaiting the underwater adventurer.

One moment you're peering inside a huge barrel sponge filled with tiny blue damselfish flickering like electric sparks; the next you're transfixed by a vast shoal of surgeonfish streaming over-head like silver smoke. Coral reefs are the rainforests of the sea – you can't fail to be captivated by their sheer abundance of creatures.

> I began to make out the shapes of branching corals and sea fans, while the sea began to crackle with the sounds of a myriad fish feeding.

Encompassing the Sulu and Sulawesi Seas in Southeast Asia, the Coral Triangle contains the world's most biodiverse reefs, with 450 species of coral compared to just 60 for the entire Caribbean. But don't be lulled into the false notion that scuba-diving is only worth-while on a coral reef. Ever since Jacques-Yves Cousteau invented the Self-Contained Underwater Breathing Apparatus (SCUBA) in 1943, divers have been able to explore the complete spectrum of marine habitats – and some of the most fascinating lie well beyond the cosy tropics. A Californian kelp forest, for example, is like a giant, swaying underwater citadel, seething with fish and sealions, while for pure adrenaline rush, few things beat cage diving with great white sharks off the coast of South Africa or drift diving on an ocean current past a volcanic cliff in the Galápagos.

ADVENTURE**RATING**	
Daring:	ØØØØØ
Ecofriendly:	ØØØØØ
Expense:	ØØØØØ
Expertise:	ØØØØØ
Fitness:	ØØØØØ

Signalling the boat

ADVENTURE CALLING

The world's great dive sites

It's no surprise that many divers flock to warm-water destinations like the Caribbean, Red Sea and other hotspots of marine biodiversity – but don't overlook equally teeming cold-water destinations like California and New Zealand.

KEY TO SYMBOLS

Ø **Easy:** Good facilities for novice divers or those wishing to learn; plenty of shallow, shore-based dives in generally sheltered conditions.
ØØ **Moderate:** Suitable for confident divers with experience of currents, drop-offs etc. May involve liveaboard cruises to remote locations.
ØØØ **Challenging:** Adventure diving in offbeat locations, often with cold water, strong currents, caves or depths exceeding 30m (100ft).

NORTH AMERICA

Channel Islands, USA
ØØ – ØØØ
www.channelislands.noaa.gov
Best time to go: February–September
Just off the Californian mainland, this cluster of islands is swathed in giant kelp forests that are home to an incredible array of marine life, from bright orange garibaldi fish to migratory grey whales (December–April) and blue whales (spring and summer). Water temperatures hover around a chilly 12–16°C (54–61°F), while visibility can exceed 30m (100ft). Santa Catalina is a good place for spotting lobster, octopus and angel shark, while Santa Barbara is renowned for its California sea lions and harbour seals. Due to exposed conditions on Santa Rosa and San Miguel, these islands are best left to experienced divers.

Vancouver Island, Canada *ØØØ*
www.hellobc.com
Best time to go: June–August
With summer temperatures averaging 10°C (50°F), the seas around Vancouver Island are best suited to divers with plenty of cold-water experience. Liveaboards depart Vancouver for spectacular circumnavigations of the island, were marine highlights include orca, wolf eel and octopus.

Newfoundland, Canada *ØØØ*
www.newfoundlandlabrador.com
Best time to go: May–October
Ranging in depth from 15 to 49m (50–161ft), Newfoundland's

famous World War II shipwrecks in Lance Cove, Bell Island, are easily accessible to divers year-round. Summer witnesses the arrival of vast shoals of capelin, which in turn attract several species of whale, including beluga, humpback and narwhal. For a chance to dive amongst icebergs, time your visit in May or June; for ice diving beneath frozen lakes and sea, visit February to March.

Sea of Cortez, Mexico
Ø – ØØØ
www.visitmexico.com
Best time to go: April–October
Sandwiched between the Mexican mainland and the desert peninsula of Baja California, the Sea of Cortez (or Gulf of California) promises unforgettable diving with legendary marine life, including blue whales (March–April), manta rays (July–November) and whale sharks (May–June). Experienced divers will also relish the challenge of wall and cave dives at Espíritu Santo Island, while novices (or even snorkellers) can enjoy interacting with sealions at Los Islotes.

THE CARIBBEAN
Bahamas Ø – ØØ
www.bahamas.com
Best time to go: Year-round
Diving is one of the major highlights of the Bahamas, with everything from shallow reefs for novices, to drop-offs, wrecks, blue holes and shark diving for the more experienced. You can learn to dive at centres on several islands, while liveaboards operate in the idyllic Exuma Cays.

Turks & Caicos Ø – ØØ
www.turksandcaicostourism.com
Best time to go: Year-round
Renowned for some of the Caribbean's best diving, the Turks & Caicos Islands boast pristine coral reefs, water temperatures ranging from 23 to 29°C (73–84°F) and visibility up to 60m (200ft). The real magnet for divers, however, is the Columbus Passage – a 2,500m-deep

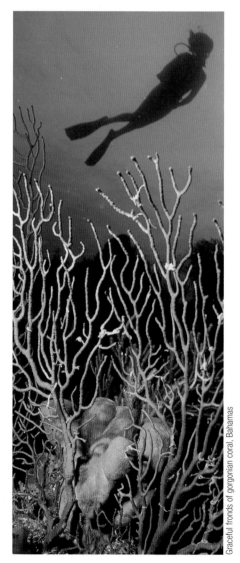

Graceful fronds of gorgonian coral, Bahamas

Caribbean reef sharks, safely on the other side of the bars

(8,200ft) channel frequented by migrating humpback whales, spotted eagle rays, manta rays, dolphins and turtles. Festooned with sponges and sea fans, the sheer walls of this 35km-wide (22-mile) channel provide exhilarating wall diving opportunities.

Dominica Ø – ØØØ
www.dominica.dm
Best time to go: December–June
No fewer than 22 cetacean species are found in the waters around Dominica, earning it the title of 'Whalewatching Capital of the Caribbean'. But even if you're not lucky enough to glimpse one of the resident sperm whales, Dominica's spectacular underwater landscapes promise world-class diving. From bubbling volcanic vents to precipitous drop-offs lying close offshore, divers can discover a wealth of unusual marine life, including seahorses, frogfish and flying gurnards.

Cayman Islands Ø – ØØ
www.caymanislands.ky
Best time to go: Year-round
Dive connoisseurs head to Little Cayman, where, close offshore, the 2,000m (6,560ft) coral cliff of Bloody Bay Wall provides the setting for some of the world's most dramatic wall diving.

CENTRAL & SOUTH AMERICA
Belize Ø – ØØØ
www.travelbelize.org
Best time to go: Year-round
Stretching 300km (186 miles) between Mexico's Yucatán Peninsula and Honduras, the Great Western Barrier Reef (the

second largest in the world) offers visitors to Belize an exotic mixture of shallow reefs, coral cays and mangrove islands. A good option for novice divers and snorkellers, Hol Chan Marine Reserve supports good populations of grouper, barracuda and nurse shark. More experienced divers should consider a live-aboard trip to Lighthouse Reef (one of three atolls to the east of the barrier reef) where a 45m (148ft) descent into the Blue Hole (the flooded remains of a giant cave) is considered one of the world's classic dives. Half Moon Caye, also on Lighthouse Reef, offers good wall diving.

Cocos Island, Costa Rica ∅∅∅
www.visitcostarica.com
Best time to go: January–April
The only way to visit this volcanic outpost, a world heritage site 480km (300 miles) southwest of Costa Rica, is on a 10- to 15-day liveaboard cruise. Expect some of the best shark diving in the world, with vast schools of scalloped hammerheads gathering at prime dive sites like the seamount, Bajo Alcyone. Other frequently sighted pelagic species include sailfish, wahoo, manta ray and whale shark; large shoals of tuna, snapper and jack prowl the rocky drop-offs, while dolphins and humpback whales are frequent visitors. For what is arguably the ultimate dive safari, combine Cocos Island with Malpelo Island, where legendary dive sites like The Fridge and Monster Face provide heart-stopping encounters with schools of silky sharks and eagle rays.

Galápagos Islands, Ecuador ∅∅∅
www.vivecuador.com
Best time to go: December–May
Not for the faint-hearted, diving in the Galápagos involves coping with strong currents, contrasting water temperatures and extreme depths. It is these very factors, however, that nourish the archipelago's extraordinary marine life. On a typical liveaboard cruise, you will encounter marine iguanas, penguins, sealions, manta rays, turtles and a wealth of sharks. The Arch at Darwin Island is a prime spot for whale sharks and scalloped hammerheads.

EUROPE
Scapa Flow, Scotland ∅∅ – ∅∅∅
www.scapaflow.co.uk
Best time to go: Spring–autumn
Scuttled off Orkney in 1919, the remains of the German High Seas Fleet provide Europe's best wreck diving. Lying at depths of 34–45m (112–148ft), three battleships and four cruisers can be explored by experienced divers. The *Markgraf* (43–45m/141–148ft) is the most impressive of the battleships, while the cruisers *Köln* (34–36m/112–118ft) and *Brummer* (36m/118ft) are the two most intact wrecks. Divers not qualified for the depths at Scapa Flow should opt instead for the 12m-deep (40ft) shore dives on the blockship wrecks at Churchill Barriers.

Gozo, Malta ∅ – ∅∅
www.visitmalta.com
Best time to go: April–September
One of the Mediterranean's best dive locations, Malta's twin island

is renowned for its underwater visibility (up to 45m/148ft) and impressive aquascape of drop-offs, tunnels and chimneys. The flourishing marine life ranges from octopus and barracuda to sea-horses and golden-cup coral. Many of the 50-plus dive sites are accessible from shore.

AFRICA
Northern Red Sea, Egypt
∅ – ∅∅∅

www.egypt.travel

Best time to go: April–June, September–November

With courses available in resorts on both the Sinai Peninsula and South Coast, the Red Sea is a perfect place to learn how to dive. Advanced divers, meanwhile, will find dizzying drop-offs and testing currents at more far-flung locations, such as the Brothers – a pair of steep-sided, coral-festooned rocks best visited on a liveaboard from Hurghada. Wherever you choose to dive in the Northern Red Sea, however, the profusion of marine life is extraordinary – from the ubiquitous clouds of golden anthias pulsing in and out of coral heads to chance encounters with reef sharks, lionfish and Napolean wrasse.

South Africa ∅∅ – ∅∅∅

www.southafrica.net

Best time to go: Year-round

Adventure diving at its best, South Africa boasts a sensational range of scuba opportunities and none are more thrilling than cage diving with great white sharks at locations like Gansbaii in the Cape. Heading east towards Durban, the Protea Banks are bristling with copper, dusky, ragged-tooth, thresher, tiger and Zambezi sharks, but with strong currents and depths ranging from 30 to 40m (100–130ft), this is a site for experienced divers only. Nearby Aliwal Shoal hosts con-gregations of up to 150 ragged-tooth sharks between June and November, while Sodwana Bay in the Greater St Lucia Wetlands National Park is an important rookery for leatherback and loggerhead turtles (October–March) as well as a haven for sharks, rays and dolphins. Time your visit to May or June and you might be lucky enough to witness the sardine run – an annual mass migration along the KwaZulu

Natal coastline when millions of the tiny baitfish spark a feeding frenzy as sharks, tuna, sailfish, seals, whales and dolphins drive the shoals to the surface.

Mozambique ∅ – ∅∅

Best time to go: April–November
A rising star in the diving world, Mozambique's pristine, 2,500km (1,550-mile) coastline is fringed with some of the richest coral reefs in East Africa. From sheltered lagoons to current-strafed drop-offs, there's something for all levels of experience. Prime locations include the Bazaruto Archipelago in the south and the lesser-known Quirimbas in the north. Whale sharks are often seen from October to March, while humpback whales migrate along the coast between June and September. For mesmerizing manta rays, head to Tofo, a short distance from the historic port city of Inhambane.

Seychelles ∅ – ∅∅

www.seychelles.travel
Best time to go: February–November
A liberal scattering of luxurious island resorts, combined with wonderful marine life, has established the Seychelles as a leading dive destination. Tear yourself away from your beachfront villa, however, and one of the best ways to experience the archipelago is on a liveaboard vessel – especially one that visits remote Aldabra Island.

MIDDLE EAST

Oman ∅ – ∅∅∅

www.omantourism.gov.om
Best time to go: April–June, September–November
A less-visited alternative to the Red Sea, Oman is the jumping-off point for dive cruises in the Arabian Gulf – a good location for large pelagic species like turtles, dolphins, tuna and whale sharks. In addition to wreck and drift diving, the Gulf has plenty of sites suitable for beginners – particularly around the Musandam Peninsula.

ASIA & MICRONESIA

Maldives ∅ – ∅∅

www.visitmaldives.com
Best time to go: Year-round
With over 100 resorts, excellent dive training facilities and several liveaboard options, the Indian

Teeming underwater life in the Red Sea

Ocean atolls of the Maldives are perhaps the ultimate diver's paradise. Beginners learn the basics in warm, shallow lagoons, while experienced divers ride deep-water currents in the company of manta rays, turtles and sharks. North Malé Atoll is the most popular, while South Malé, Ari and Nilandhoo Atoll will appeal to more adventurous divers.

Thailand ∅ – ∅∅

www.tourismthailand.org
Best time to go: Year-round
Although there is excellent diving around the Phi Phi Islands near Phuket, it's the more remote Similan and Surin archipelagos that appeal to adventurous divers. Combine both on a live-aboard cruise from Phuket and you will visit a succession of diverse dive sites, from tumbled granite boulders to gardens of soft coral. The highpoint, though, is undoubtedly Richelieu Rock, a giant submerged pinnacle smothered in sea fans and swarming with marine life – from tiny seahorses to giant whale sharks. November to May brings the calmest and clearest conditions. At other times of the year, focus instead on Koh Samui and other islands in the Gulf of Thailand.

Northern Sulawesi, Indonesia ∅ – ∅∅

www.north-sulawesi.org
Best time to go: May–September
Lying at the epicentre of the richest, most biodiverse seas on earth, the northern tip of Sulawesi offers incredible diving. Close to Manado, the Bunaken

National Marine Park is renowned for its sponge- and coral-encrusted walls, while Banka Island's seamounts and pinnacles attract rays, sharks and large shoals of barracuda and jacks. Marine connoisseurs, however, will make a beeline for Lembeh Straits, where it's the small wonders – decorator crabs, pygmy seahorses, nudibranchs to name but a few – that steal the show.

Papua New Guinea ∅∅ – ∅∅∅

www.pngtourism.org.pg
Best time to go: Year-round
Like Sulawesi (above), the islands of Papua New Guinea (PNG) are found in the biodiverse honeypot known as the Coral Triangle. Some 900 species of fish and 450 different corals have been identified around PNG, with prime dive sites including Loloata Island and Tufi Harbour. Nip across to the island of New Britain for more underwater gems at Kimbe Bay and Lama Shoals.

Micronesia ∅∅ – ∅∅∅

www.visit-fsm.org
Best time to go: November–June
Off the beaten track and widely scattered across the western Pacific, Micronesia requires at least three weeks if you plan to do justice to its three most popular dive destinations. Palau has everything from wrecks and caves to dazzling drift dives, Yap is famed for its Valley of the Rays (where giant mantas somersault through plankton-rich waters), while Truk Lagoon contains the coral-clad wrecks of a Japanese fleet sunk in 1944.

Stingless jellyfish abound in Jellyfish Lake, Palau

AUSTRALASIA
Great Barrier Reef, Australia
Ø – ØØØ

www.gbrmpa.gov.au

Best time to go: Year-round
Stretching 2,300km (1,430 miles) from Papua New Guinea to the Tropic of Capricorn, the world's largest reef system is a mecca to divers. Coastal towns like Cairns, Port Douglas and Townsville provide excellent dive training facilities, while resorts on coral cays like Heron Island offer superb diving straight off the beach. More adventurous divers opt for liveaboard cruises visiting the famous Cod Hole (home to several large potato cod groupers) before venturing further into the Coral Sea, where Osprey Reef promises exciting diving in the company of grey whaler sharks.

North Island, New Zealand
ØØ – ØØØ

www.newzealand.com

Best time to go: October–May

Regarded as the world's finest subtropical dive site, Poor Knights Marine Reserve off the east coast of Northland has caves, archways, large shoals of fish and several wrecks, including the *Rainbow Warrior*. Further south, adrenaline-charged diving can be found at White Island – an active volcano.

Top 8 snorkelling adventures

1. Manatees, Crystal River Wildlife Refuge, Florida (December–March).
2. Spotted dolphins, North Bimini, Bahamas (year-round).
3. Basking sharks, Isle of Man, England (summer).
4. Orcas, Tysfjord, Norway (winter).
5. Whale sharks, Ningaloo Reef, Western Australia (April–June).
6. Dusky dolphins, Kaikoura, New Zealand (November–April).
7. Jellyfish, Jellyfish Lake, Mercherchar Island, Palau (February–April).
8. Southern stingrays, Stingray City, Grand Cayman (year-round).

ADVENTURE BRIEFING

Taking the plunge

Getting started in scuba-diving may be simpler than you think – there are training centres worldwide – but never let your enthusiasm compromise personal safety or the health of fragile marine habitats.

Land versus liveaboard

One of the first things to consider when preparing for your scuba adventure is whether you want to be based on land or on a boat. Shore-based trips, in which you plan everything through a local dive centre, are particularly well suited to novices or those content with a couple of dives per day. They are also a good option if you are travelling with non-divers (such as young children) or if you simply want the flexibility of interspersing dive days with sightseeing and other activities. Liveaboard dive trips, on the other hand, provide optimum saturation for serious divers. Cruising between a succession of prime dive locations (including those well beyond the reach of daytrips from shore-based centres), you will be able to dive several times a day – and do little else.

ESSENTIAL**GEAR**

• Mask, snorkel and fins • **Wetsuit and booties** • Weight belt • **BCD, gauges & regulator(s)** • Dive watch & compass • **Dive computer** • Dive torch • **Knife and sheath** • Logbook • **Spare straps for fins & mask** • Swimmers' ear medication

Diver training

Several organizations offer training in scuba-diving, from hand-held taster sessions in resort swimming pools to specialist qualifications for advanced divers. The largest is the Professional Association of Diving Instructors (PADI, www.padi.com), although other well-respected groups include the British Sub Aqua Club (BSAC, www.bsac.com), National Association of Underwater Instructors (NAUI, www.naui.com), Scuba Schools International (SSI, www.divessi.com), Sub Aqua Association (SAA, www.saa.org.uk) and World Underwater Federation (CMAS, www.cmas.org). All adhere to strict safety and environmental guidelines, so make sure your dive resort, dive school or liveaboard is affiliated to one of them.

Into the water

A scuba-diving certification is your passport to the underwater world. Each organization offers entry-level courses during which you will learn the fundamental techniques to safely dive in open water. These are variously known as Open Water Diver (PADI), Scuba Diver (NAUI) and Ocean Diver (BSAC). A typical course can be completed in as little as four days and involves three main elements: theory lessons (available online with PADI), diving in a swimming pool or pool-like conditions (learning basic skills like clearing water from your mask without surfacing and how to share air in an emergency) and four open-water dives where instructors will help you develop your technique at a dive site. The minimum age is ten (for Junior Open Water Diver certification) and you will be asked to complete a medical questionnaire before starting.

As a qualified open-water diver, you can progress to higher qualifications, such as PADI's Advanced Open Water Diver, which includes training in underwater navigation, deep diving, wreck diving, drift diving and other activities that will prepare you for the various conditions you might encounter on a diving adventure. PADI's third major tier of training, a Rescue Diver course, teaches essential first aid and life-saving techniques.

ECO**FILE**

- Support Project AWARE (www.projectaware.org), the dive industry's leading non-profit environmental organization, by enrolling on an AWARE speciality course, such as Coral Reef Conservation, and taking part in local beach and underwater cleanups and CoralWatch monitoring.
- Choose operators that use mooring buoys or drift diving techniques whenever possible, rather than anchors, which can cause damage.
- Practise buoyancy control skills in a pool or sandy area before diving near a coral reef or other fragile habitat. Tuck away trailing equipment to avoid accidental contact with the reef, and never touch, stand on, or collect coral.
- Avoid handling, feeding or riding on marine creatures.
- Never purchase marine souvenirs made from endangered species.
- Choose resorts and operators that properly treat sewage and wastewater.
- Support marine protected areas and respect underwater cultural heritage.
- Don't order seafood caught using destructive or unsustainable practices.

PADI Speciality courses
- Altitude Diver
- Boat Diver
- Cavern Diver
- Coral Reef Conservation
- Deep Diver
- Digital Underwater Photographer
- Diver Propulsion Vehicle
- Drift Diver
- Dry Suit Diver
- Enriched Air Diver
- Equipment Specialist
- Ice Diver
- Multi-level Diver
- Night Diver
- Peak Performance Buoyancy
- Project AWARE Fish ID
- Project AWARE Specialist
- Search and Recovery Diver
- Underwater Naturalist
- Underwater Navigator
- Underwater Photographer
- Underwater Videographer
- Wreck Diver

How to...
Choose the right mask:
Hold it to your face, breathe in slightly through your nose and it should stay in place when you take your hand away.
Get neutrally buoyant:
Check that you are carrying the right amount of weights and that they are correctly positioned on your belt; add air in small bursts to your BCD; practise controlled, steady breathing; take a Peak Performance Buoyancy course.
Dive safely in strong currents:
Plan the length and direction of the dive carefully with your buddy, trail a surface marker buoy so the dive boat skipper can track you and streamline your kit so nothing can snag on rocks or coral.

Scuba gear
Diving equipment isn't cheap. However, if you are new to the sport or about to enrol on an entry-level training course you will usually be able rent everything you need from a dive centre. It makes sense, though, to buy basic essentials (mask, snorkel and fins) right from the start. Chances are you will soon become addicted and want to invest in a wetsuit, weight belt, buoyancy control device or BCD (an inflatable jacket that allows you to control your depth or float at the surface), depth gauge (which tells you how deep you are), pressure gauge (which monitors how much air you have left), and regulator (the mouthpiece through which you breathe). Additional accessories range from dive knives and watches to dive computers and flash-lights. You won't need to buy a cylinder and weights – these are normally rented at your destination. And remember that dive knives must be packed in your checked luggage – not carry-on.

Health and safety
As long as you choose reputable opera-tors, get proper training and never dive beyond the limits of your experience, there is no reason why scuba-diving shouldn't be perfectly safe. You do need to discuss with a doctor any health issues that may prevent you from diving, such as asthma, heart conditions and pregnancy, and you should always ensure that your travel insurance provides adequate coverage. See the Divers Alert Network (www.diversalertnetwork.org) for further information.

Many of the health and safety problems associated with scuba-diving can be avoided, including the three most common – sunburn, dehydration and seasickness. Stings from jellyfish can be avoided by wearing a wetsuit or stinger suit, while mastering buoyancy means there is no need for you to touch anything and risk cutting yourself – or damaging corals and other vulnerable marine life. Similarly, proper training will help you to avoid discomfort in your ears by learning how to adjust for pressure changes (although if ear problems persist you need to stop diving and seek medical advice).

The most infamous hazard associated with diving is the bends (or decompression sickness). Again, this is avoidable if you dive with a competent and trustworthy operator that ensures maximum depth, ascent rate and dive frequency never exceed safe levels. Another fear that commonly assails novice divers is running out of air. Keeping a regular check on your pressure gauge will ensure you always return to the surface with a safety reserve remaining. And even if you do run out, you will have learnt how to share air with a fellow diver using their spare mouthpiece. Diving with a competent 'buddy' is perhaps the single most important factor in staying safe underwater.

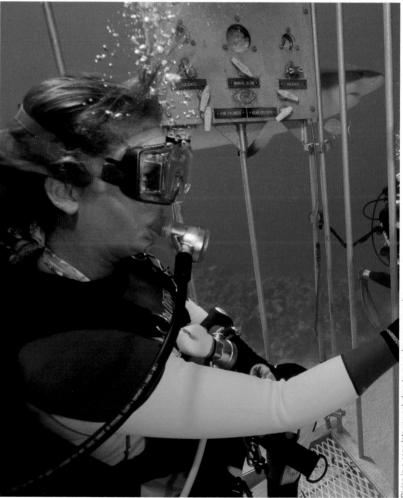

Diving in a cage lets you get close to more dangerous species

Flying with turtles

Rising from the depths of the Celebes Sea off the coast of Borneo and once hailed by Jacques Cousteau as 'an untouched piece of art', tiny Sipadan Island is nothing short of a diving legend.

The transition from turquoise shallows to inky depths was abrupt and slightly unnerving – even before the dive master warned us of potentially strong currents. 'Keep together', he said. 'Follow me.' Then he was gone, somersaulting backwards off the side of the dive boat. I hesitated a moment longer, but already the dive master was fading from view, snatched away by the keen drift. Gravity and adrenaline conspired to topple me in after him. I squeezed the air from my buoyancy jacket and the sky abruptly turned to the silver belly of waves. Chaotic bubbles jostled my mask as I steadied my breathing – and then I felt the irresistible tug of the current. It took a few seconds more before I realized that I was flying.

Like an aquatic Peter Pan I swooped along the plunging wall of the reef. There were turtles everywhere. At least half a dozen were riding the ocean surge; some were feeding amongst branching thickets of coral sprouting from the drop-off, while another was asleep inside a giant sponge shaped like a laundry basket. And there were sharks, too. Not distant, fleeting shadows, but groups of two or three up close – their slender bodies twisting gracefully, mocking the current that held me so powerless.

I gasped away my air supply in 30 minutes. Never before had I witnessed such an explosion of life. Ascending slowly through a vast, shimmering vortex of barracuda, a thousand strong, I tried to fix an image of this extraordinary world in my mind. But I knew

FACT**FILE**

Sipadan Island, Sabah, Eastern Malaysia

When to go: Year-round

Need to know: Following a move to declare Sipadan a world heritage site in 2004, all accommodation was removed from the island – only for a barge heavily laden with building materials to run aground on Sipadan's reef two years later. According to Sabah Parks, the recovery process of the damaged reef was almost complete by early 2008. The nearby resorts of Kapalai and Mabul continue to schedule daily dives to Sipadan.

Next step: Sabah's main international gateway, Kota Kinabalu has good internal links with Tawau (or fly direct from Kuala Lumpur). Buses link Tawau with Semporna, from where speedboats take an hour to reach Kapalai.

Operators: Pulau Sipadan Resort (www.sipadan-kapalai.com).

See *also* Ecofile on page 171

that the moment my head breached the surface, it would seem almost impossible to imagine. Such is the sheer exuberance and diversity of life at Barracuda Point, Sipadan's most famous dive site.

Malaysia's only oceanic island, 20ha (50-acre) Sipadan sits atop a spectacular coral-encrusted volcanic pinnacle. Barely a stone's throw from the beach, its coral reef plunges a giddy 600m (2,000ft) to the seabed, but it's only from nearby resorts that divers can visit the hallowed waters of this uninhabited and off-limits island. The most unusual is the Sipadan-Kapalai Dive Resort – a 'water village' perched on wooden stilts above the sand flats of the Ligitan Reefs.

Whereas Sipadan's appeal lies in its concentration of large pelagic species like sharks, turtles and jacks, Kapalai is renowned for small wonders. One evening, just before sunset, I hovered at a depth of just 7m (23ft) watching jewel-like mandarin fish engage in fin-clasping mating rituals. The shallow reefs and sand flats around Kapalai are also a favoured haunt of technicoloured nudibranchs, flamboyant cuttlefish and quizzical gobies peering from their burrows. Diminutive but deadly, blue-ring octopus stalk areas of storm-tossed coral rubble – a good spot to find exquisitely patterned mantis shrimps with their quick-fire pincers. Grotesque frogfish nestle in clumps of finger sponge, hawkfish stake out branching corals and snowflake moray eels squirm through Kapalai's forest of wooden pylons in search of prey. This is a place to linger and look – a go-slow but equally satisfying alternative to Sipadan's adrenaline-charged drift dives.

Green turtle and bigeye jacks off Sipadan Island, Borneo

Should I swim with wild dolphins

There has long been controversy over whether it's ethical to hold dolphins in captivity in order to interact with them, but is swimming with wild dolphins in the open sea really an acceptable alternative?

Captive dolphins are often caught from populations that are already threatened in the wild, they have lower survival rates than wild dolphins and they have no means of escaping from human swimmers when they do not want to interact with them. These are just some of the objections to swimming with captive dolphins. Yet when it comes to swimming with wild dolphins, some environmental groups are not convinced that this is a desirable option either.

According to the Whale and Dolphin Conservation Society (www.wdcs.org): 'In some locations, dolphins are repeatedly disturbed by boats dropping swimmers in the water next to them. Dolphins have been recorded leaving their usual homes in favour of quieter areas. Disruption to feeding, resting, nursing and other behaviour may have a long-term impact on the health and wellbeing of individual dolphins and populations.'

Reputable operators, on the other hand, insist that wild dolphin swims are entirely on the dolphins' terms. It's up to them if they want to approach and interact with people in the water. As long as strict guidelines are followed, swimming with wild dolphins can not only be an inspiring and educational experience, but it can also benefit

Snorkelling with Atlantic spotted dolphins

local ecotourism projects
and support the
conservation of marine
protected areas.

What should I look for in an operator?

Responsible companies
ensure that their
activities cause minimal
disturbance. Instead of
approaching too closely,
boat operators should
maintain a respectful
distance of at least
50m (55 yards) with
propellers idle to avoid
potential injury. If the
dolphins are resting or

Bottlenose dolphin playing with diver

travelling, move on and leave them in peace. On no account should
they be herded towards swimmers or tempted nearer by food. For a
list of reputable operators in locations ranging from the Azores to
New Zealand, visit www.responsibletravel.com.

How can I minimize stress to the dolphins?

Enter the water in a quiet, relaxed manner. Sound plays a crucial role
in a cetacean's life, so do not add your own noises to the complex
medley of squeaks, clicks and whirrs that dolphins use during hunting
and socializing. Snorkel at the surface, finning slowly and gently with
your arms at your sides. Let the dolphins approach you. Never chase
them or try to reach out and touch them. When free-diving – something that can intrigue wild dolphins – keep your actions smooth,
slow and relaxed to avoid startling them. Remember that dolphins are
powerful creatures and that your own safety relies on you giving them
adequate space.

What about swimming with whales?

Very few countries permit whale swims. The risks to humans are
obvious. Whales are not only massive animals with potentially lethal
flukes and flippers, but they also tend to be found in deep waters with
strong currents and surface chop – conditions that rapidly cause fatigue
in swimmers. Sharks have also been known to attack swimmers, pre-
sumably mistaking them for whale calves. As with dolphins, potential
adverse effects on whales stem from vessels approaching too close or
inappropriate behaviour from swimmers. Swimming with humpback
whales is permitted in Tonga, but opponents claim it can disturb
mothers and calves just when they are most vulnerable.

Sea-kayaking & canoeing

Imagine packing a sea-kayak or canoe with everything you need for a week or two in the wilderness – fresh water, food, camping equipment – and then paddling off to wherever you please.

Sea-kayaks and Canadian-style canoes are quite stable and it doesn't take long to learn how to manoeuvre them. You may be paddling for several hours each day, however, so general fitness is important. One of the great pleasures of a paddling expedition is the ability to silently approach and observe wildlife. If you've ever thrilled at the sight of a whale from a tour boat just imagine what it's like from the perspective of a sea-kayak! In Johnstone Strait off Vancouver Island (see pages 188–9) you may be lucky enough to paddle with orcas, while a canoeing trip on the Zambezi River provides opportunities for viewing elephant, hippo and other wildlife at close quarters. With jaw-dropping scenery, abundant wildlife and a proven pedigree in paddling, New Zealand is hard to beat as an all-round kayaking destination, while the Florida Everglades (see pages 190–1) present one of the world's toughest canoeing challenges – The Wilderness Waterway. For sheer grandeur, Alaska is unforgettable: to be dwarfed by its mountains, glaciers and fjords is a humbling experience. Perhaps the ultimate place to paddle, though, is Antarctica, where some cruises now include this exciting 'optional extra'.

> ❝ When we launched our two-person kayak the sea was so placid that we could hear the sighs from a sealion surfacing 200m (220 yards) away. ❞

ADVENTURE**RATING**

Daring:	◉◉◉○○
Ecofriendly:	◉◉◉◉◉
Expense:	◉◉◉○○
Expertise:	◉◉○○○
Fitness:	◉◉◉◉○

The pace is leisurely enough to take in the scenery

ADVENTURE CALLING: SEA-KAYAKING
Pick of the paddles

Dip into the world of sea-kayaking and you quickly become inundated with likely locations, from the poles to the tropics. Here are 12 top paddling spots that rise above the others.

KEY TO SYMBOLS
∅ **Easy:** Generally sheltered, warm-water locations, with day-trip options or short distances between overnight stops.
∅∅ **Moderate:** Some long days of paddling, often in wilder locations more suited to kayakers with some experience.
∅∅∅ **Challenging:** Remote locations, wilderness camping, long paddling days, often in cold-water locations.

Canadian Arctic ∅∅∅
www.nunavuttourism.com
Best time to go: Summer
Ready for a challenge? Travelling by sea-kayak in the High Arctic enables you to experience one of the world's least visited places and explore a truly wild frontier with minimum impact on the environment. During the brief Arctic summer, when the sun never sets and temperatures creep up to 18°C (64°F), the fjords of Kane Basin, Ellesmere Island, free themselves of enough ice to allow access to kayakers. Paddling between icebergs with a backdrop of high peaks and tidewater glaciers, this extraordinary 'top of the world' experience is embellished by sightings of walrus, muskox and narwhal, as well as fascinating insights into Inuit culture and prehistory.

Alaska, USA ∅∅ – ∅∅∅
www.travelalaska.com
Best time to go: Summer
The jewel in Alaska's kayaking crown has to be Glacier Bay, where you can paddle amongst icebergs, witness calving glaciers (from a safe distance) and probe channels inaccessible to cruise ships. Fly or take a boat from Juneau to Gustavus at the bay's entrance, then allow around 7–10 days to explore Muir Inlet, one of the most popular choices for kayakers. Hemmed in by the Chugach and Kenai Mountains, the sheltered inlets of Prince William Sound are ideal for novice paddlers.

Baja California ∅∅
www.visitmexico.com
Best time to go: January–April
Baja California provides an unrivalled opportunity to paddle

with cetaceans – although close encounters are never guaranteed and you should always respect minimum viewing distances to avoid disturbance. There are two main choices. Between January and April, grey whales visit the Pacific coast of the Baja peninsula to socialize, mate and give birth, often congregating in lagoons like Magdalena Bay. These broad swathes of shallow water, with their mangrove-filled creeks, are ideal for kayaking. As well as whales and dolphins, you'll see plenty of waterbirds, as well as sealions out on the long, sandy beaches. East of Baja, the Sea of Cortez (or Gulf of California) is a wintering ground for blue, fin, humpback, sperm, short-finned pilot, minke and Bryde's whales, as well as several species of dolphin. A multi-day kayaking adventure will also enable you to discover the unique flora and fauna of the Sonoran Desert.

Chilean Patagonia ∅∅
www.visit-chile.org
Best time to go: November–March
The fjords of Chilean Patagonia are crying out for exploration by sea-kayak. A fine spot is the Chiloe Archipelago, sheltered from Pacific gales and endowed with an unspoiled coastline, virgin temperate rainforest and a thriving fishing culture.

Croatia ∅
www.croatia.hr
Best time to go: Spring–autumn
Embark on an Adriatic adventure, paddling from the old town of Dubrovnik through the emerald islands of the Dalmatian coast.

Greek Islands ∅
www.gnto.gr
Best time to go: Spring–autumn
No epic odysseys – just a morning's laid-back paddling in the Ionian Sea followed by lunch in a

Two-person kayaks usually come with a handy sail

Dramatic cliffscapes are often only accessible by sea

taverna and the chance to mingle with locals at the waterfront.

Western Isles, Scotland ∅∅
www.visitthebrides.com
Best time to go: Spring–autumn
The sandy beaches and dazzling blue seas of the Western Isles come as a revelation to many visitors. A good option is west Lewis, where you'll spot seabirds, seals and, with luck, whales.

Skeleton Coast, Namibia ∅∅
www.namibiatourism.com.na
Best time to go: Year-round
From Walvis Bay on the Skeleton Coast it's possible to kayak along a desert shore teeming with seals.

Vietnam ∅∅ – ∅∅
www.vietnamtourism.com
Best time to go: November–April
Kayaking in Vietnam you'll not only witness extraordinary scenery, but also gain an intimate insight into the country's coastal

communities – meeting and dealing with local fishermen who will be only too happy to supply you with your evening meal. The premier sea kayaking location in Vietnam (and perhaps the whole of Asia) is Ha Long Bay, a world heritage site peppered with 1,600 islands – many of which have enticing sea caves, tunnels and mangroves. The Mekong Delta, meanwhile, offers easy paddling through myriad channels and a chance to join the ebb and flow of life at floating markets and fishing villages.

Fiji ∅
www.bulafiji.com
Best time to go: Year-round
Don't be afraid to admit it. If your idea of sea-kayaking is to be able to occasionally flop overboard into warm, azure waters before drying off on a tropical island beach then make for Fiji. A paddle in paradise is a laid-back affair with plenty of time for other

Doubtful Sound, New Zealand

activities like snorkelling, visiting local villages and playing the castaway on remote desert islands. The Yasawas, a chain of 16 volcanic islands to the north-west of Viti Levu, is one of Fiji's most popular kayaking destinations. Allow at least a week for paddling between three or four of the islands.

Australia ∅∅ – ∅∅∅
www.australia.com
Best time to go: Year-round
Boasting a diverse range of coastal scenery, from coral islands and kelp-fringed estuaries to vast bays covered with seagrass meadows, Australia's prime kayaking locations include the Whitsunday Islands, Tasmania and the Ningaloo Reef.

New Zealand ∅∅ – ∅∅∅
www.newzealand.com
Best time to go: Year-round
North Island's watery playground, the Bay of Islands offers

everything from game fishing and scuba-diving to swimming with dolphins. It is also a perfect place for sea-kayaking with some 150 islands to explore and a climate that won't make you shudder at the prospect of getting wet. Nip across Cook Strait and you have a choice of two kayaking hotspots at the northern tip of South Island. Base yourself at Picton or Havelock for forays into the labyrinth of bays and inlets comprising the Malborough Sounds and head to Marahau or Totaranui, gateways to Abel Tasman National Park with its sandy beaches and forest-fringed estuaries. Fiordland is a mecca to sea-kayakers with slightly more challenging paddling in Milford and Doubtful Sounds, while Paterson Inlet on Stewart Island promises hardy souls close encounters with marine life and a chance to visit some of New Zealand's most ancient and intact forests.

ADVENTURE CALLING: CANOEING
Touring on calmer waters

Rivers, lakes, estuaries, sheltered bays…wherever you choose to paddle, a canoeing trip is one of the most practical, tranquil and satisfying ways of exploring wilderness areas – not to mention a great way to spot wildlife.

KEY TO SYMBOLS

Ø **Easy:** Sheltered conditions, with canoes available for short excursions, or with guides paddling.

ØØ **Moderate:** More strenuous paddling, often in wilder locations involving overnight camping.

ØØØ **Challenging:** Remote canoeing locations, long paddling days and wilderness camping.

Boundary Waters, Minnesota, USA *Ø – ØØØ*

www.bwcaw.org

Best time to go: Summer

With over 1,900km (1,180 miles) of canoe routes spread across a million-acre patchwork of lakes and forest, the Boundary Waters Canoe Area Wilderness is a paddler's paradise. Pick and mix from over 1,000 lakes and 2,000 campsites to devise the ultimate backcountry canoe trip.

Kauai, Hawaii *Ø – ØØ*

www.kauai-hawaii.com

Best time to go: May–September

Sea-kayaking in the lee of Na Pali's dramatic cliffs (best from May to September) is world-class, but for an authentic Polynesian experience try paddling an outrigger canoe in Hanalei Bay.

Banff National Park, Canada *Ø – ØØØ*

www.pc.gc.ca

Best time to go: Summer

Novice canoeists can explore a gentle stretch of the Bow River or follow 40 Mile Creek into the Vermilion Lakes – both routes are excellent for spotting wildlife. More experienced paddlers can tackle more challenging sections of the Bow River (Lake Louise to Castle Junction, Castle Junction to Banff or Bow Falls to Canmore) where potential hazards include log jams and summer water temperatures of just 10°C (50°F).

Ontario, Canada *Ø – ØØØ*

www.paddlingontario.com

Best time to go: May–September

From day-trips exploring Algonquin Provincial Park to

week-long expeditions in the remote wilderness areas of Wabakimi or Missinaibi, Ontario has possibly the widest range of canoeing adventures anywhere in the world.

Zambezi River, Zambia
∅∅ – ∅∅∅

www.zambiatourism.com

Best time to go: June–September

A serene contrast to the turmoil of rapids in Batoka Gorge (see page 197), calmer stretches of the Zambezi provide the perfect opportunity for paddling silently past riverside wildlife (from egrets to elephants) and staying overnight in luxury lodges or bush camps. Trips are available on both the Upper and Lower Zambezi, including four-day canoeing safaris covering 60km (37 miles) between the Kafue River confluence and Chakwenga River. Remember that surprised hippos can be dangerous – regularly tapping the side of your canoe usually makes them surface and allows you to steer clear.

Okavango Delta, Botswana ∅

www.botswana-tourism.gov.bw

Best time to go: Year-round

Perhaps the most laidback canoeing experience of them all, exploring the Okavango involves simply reclining in a traditional dugout, or mokoro, while local men from the Bayei tribe punt you expertly through the watery maze of channels and lagoons. It's a peaceful and rewarding way to experience the delta's astonishing wildlife and obtain a snapshot of a way of life that's remained unchanged for centuries. Mokoro tours can last anything from an hour to several days, staying overnight in remote bush camps.

Top: Jungle waterway. Bottom: the wide waters of the Lower Zambezi

ADVENTURE BRIEFING

Steady as she goes

Sea-kayaking and canoeing are about slow exploration, nosing about inlets, drifting with the current and 'rafting up' for a chat, rather than hell-bent blazing paddles.

Packing for an expedition

You will be surprised at how much gear can be packed into a two-person sea-kayak. There is plenty of space for a compact tent, sleeping bags and rollmats, clothing, cooking equipment, food, spare paddles and lifejackets, mast and sail, plus emergency equipment. Canadian-style canoes can hold even more gear, including bulky items like cooler boxes, although you should take care to evenly distribute heavy loads. Remember, too, that there is always a small amount of water inside the hull of kayaks and canoes, so seal everything inside waterproof bags.

Safe mooring

Before setting off, make certain you have a set of tide tables and a navigational chart. These will help you to choose safe moorings for lunch

How to kayak

1. Adjust your seat and foot pedals so that your knees are braced against the inside of the hull. This will help keep the kayak stable.
2. Sit upright with a strong back so that your arms are not taking all the strain.
3. Space your hands on the paddle shaft about 50cm (20in) apart.
4. Grip the paddle lightly to avoid your forearm muscles cramping.
5. Don't dip the paddle too deeply into the water – the top of the paddle should still be just above the surface during each stroke.
6. Rather than pulling the paddle through the water, trying pushing with the opposite arm.
7. Imagine tracing a figure of eight with your hands as you paddle. Keep a smooth steady rhythm (in time with your partner if you are sharing a double kayak).
8. Use the rudder only when necessary – oversteering will slow the kayak and make paddling much harder work.
9. In a light breeze, rig the small sail that usually comes with two-person kayaks, sit back and relax!
10. You can easily get sunburned in a sea-kayak. Always wear sunglasses and a wide-brimmed hat, and apply sunblock at regular intervals.

stops and campsites. In general, avoid areas prone to currents, strong tides or anything that may damage your kayak or canoe, such as large amounts of floating debris. For brief stops, tie up to a tree or other solid shoreline structure, making sure you slacken the rope periodically if the tide is falling. Take care not to allow fully laden craft (particularly with heavy drinking water containers aboard) to ground on submerged rocks. For longer overnight stops it is safer to carry your kayak or canoe well above the high-tide mark.

Beginners and children

Providing you feel confident on the water and can swim, there are plenty of kayaking and canoeing opportunities suitable for beginners and children. Guides will not take novices into rough water so capsize is unlikely. They will also ensure that the group travels at the pace of the slowest paddler. If in doubt, ask to share a two-person kayak or canoe with one of the guides. Choose trips that have a single base, paddling short distances each day.

ECO**FILE**

- Remember that many remote beaches and islands are used by birds, turtles and other species for roosting or nesting. Even minor disturbances may cause them to abandon these refuges.
- Take away all refuse.
- Use biodegradable shampoo and soap if washing in the sea.
- Use biodegradable toilet paper (or burn it) and always use the intertidal zone where daily tides can wash the beach clean.
- Resist the temptation to collect shells or other natural souvenirs.

ESSENTIAL**GEAR**

• Wet-socks or 'all-terrain' sandals with good grip to avoid slipping on rocks when getting in and out of your kayak or canoe • **Waterproof drybags or several plastic bags for storing clothes and gear. Several dustbin liners, one inside the other, are ideal** • Lightweight gloves to prevent hands becoming sore from blisters or exposure to saltwater • **Whistle attached to your lifejacket in case you become lost** • Wide-brimmed hat and sunglasses with side shields to protect your eyes from sun glare on the water • **Sunblock and lip salve to prevent sunburn and cracked skin** • Two waterbottles • **Wind- and water-proof jacket, plus comfortable tops that can be worn in layers and easily removed or added** • Splash-proof binoculars

Realm of the orca

The watery maze of inlets, sounds and islands at the northern end of Johnstone Strait, British Columbia, is not only ideal for sea-kayaking, it's also one of the world's best place to see orcas.

We were paddling through a realm of giants, where towering red cedars grow to 1,000 years old and where bald eagles, black bears and orcas gain mythological stature in the minds and carvings of the local Kwagiulth people.

But it wasn't a wilderness, our guide would remind us. Not any more. There were few hours when we couldn't hear the throb of an approaching tug, hauling barges laden with timber or sawdust. Then there were fishing boats – lured here like the whales and eagles by the summer glut of salmon. Cruise ships also slipped past, bright as slivers of bone against the green flesh of forested hillsides, joining the traffic riding the great coastal highway of the Inside Passage.

In our two-person kayaks we couldn't travel more than 10km (6 miles) a day, but what we lacked in range we made up for in a growing intimacy with our surroundings. We paddled in a tight cluster, nosing about in sheltered inlets where we watched basking harbour seals or grappled with tangled rafts of kelp. Every few hours we landed on deserted beaches strewn with haphazard piles of drift logs that resembled giant versions of pick-up sticks. We began to notice small

Left: Lush coastal forest. Right: Bald eagle

wonders – flocks of dainty phalaropes bobbing at the surface or the distinctive 'plop' of a diving kingfisher. Occasionally we were surrounded by leaping schools of Dall's porpoise – diminutive relatives of the orca.

Venturing deeper into the archipelago, we began to ignore our damp clothes and the hard ground we slept on. Even the bits of seaweed that floated in our coffee from when we last rinsed our mugs seemed perfectly normal. On most days, we caught fresh salmon, which tasted delicious grilled over open fires.

Many of the islands on which we camped were owned by First Nation peoples – the native tribes that settled here thousands of years ago. A few descendants still visit them occasionally to fish or to harvest cedar bark and timber for making baskets and carvings. But in most places, only their spirits remain. We visited one village that had been abandoned in the 1970s. The forest had already reclaimed the wooden buildings, while a century-old totem pole lay cast on its side – the weathered image of a wolf barely visible through layers of moss.

There were real wolves on Hanson Island where we camped on our final night. But still no orcas. The sea's surface remained flawless, like polished ebony. Once, as we crouched on drift logs around the campfire, I thought I heard their distant blows as they surfaced to breathe. But it was probably just a murmur of breeze through the ancient cedars, mingling with the swish of breaking waves as the mist slowly settled over Blackfish Sound.

FACT**FILE**

Johnstone Strait, British Columbia

When to go: Although orcas are resident year-round in this section of the Inside Passage, the best time to see them is during the salmon run, June–August.

Need to know: Kayaking trips operate from Port McNeill, Vancouver Island. No prior experience is required. Expect to paddle 3–5 hours per day.

Next step: Take a ferry from Seattle or Vancouver to Victoria or Nanaimo on Vancouver Island and drive north to Port McNeill. Alternatively, fly to Port Hardy, a 20-minute transfer from Port McNeill.

Operators: Small-group operators include Ecosummer Expeditions (www.ecosummer.com), Pacific Northwest Expeditions (www.seakayakbc.com) and Spirit of the West Adventures (www.kayakingtours.com).

ECO**FILE**

- Abide by all whale-watching guidelines (www.pac.dfo-mpo.gc.ca).
- Practice minimum-impact camping.
- Use biodegradable and phosphate-free dish soaps.
- Store food out of reach of wildlife.
- Respect local heritage sites.

A paddle in the park

Canoeing enthusiasts relish the challenge of the 160km (100-mile) Wilderness Waterway, but there are other more modest paddling adventures available in Everglades National Park, including forays into the Ten Thousand Islands.

Canoeing conditions were perfect as we set off from Everglades City across calm, sun-spangled Chokoloskee Bay. Pelicans belly-flopped in the sea, scooping up fish in their voluminous bills, while ospreys pirouetted overhead.

A chain of marker posts guided us through Indian Key Pass, but we often strayed from the main channel to nose about in the maze of islands. There were occasional sandy beaches strewn with the empty carapaces of horseshoe crabs — bizarre helmet-like structures that could almost have fallen from a ship carrying a consignment for a Star Wars movie.

It only took three hours of gentle paddling to reach our first campsite — a traditional Indian

Top: Brown pelican at sunset. Right: Camping on the beach

dwelling known as a chickee, which resembled a small section of wooden pier that had become marooned in a shallow bay. We moored alongside and pitched our tent on the boardwalk. There was a brisk, insect-ridding breeze and we settled down to our first relaxing afternoon in the Everglades – lulled by the rhythmic slosh of waves against the chickee's oyster-encrusted pillars.

A deep sigh roused us at dusk. A manatee had entered the bay, rising every few minutes to breathe; its stubby, bristled snout just visible above the surface. There are only 2,400 West Indian manatees left and 90 per cent are scarred by boat propellers – their main threat. In the days that followed, however, our encounters with these endangered creatures became more frequent and intimate. On one occasion we were surrounded by a family group of five and, stowing our paddles, we simply let the canoe drift with the herd as it grazed peacefully on seagrass. The manatees, which can reach 4m (13ft) in length and weigh over 1,300kg (2,860 lb), seemed totally unconcerned by our presence – perhaps even curious. When one surfaced directly behind the canoe I found myself face to face with a podgy mermaid figure hanging upright in the water; flippers clasping a beer barrel body and tiny eyes lost in the wrinkled maze of its face.

Gradually, we settled into the natural rhythm of life among the Ten Thousand Islands, trading our wristwatches for the passage of the sun or the tidal mark on exposed mangrove roots. As we paddled from island to island, camping on chickees or deserted sandy beaches, we began to embellish our wilderness clock with subtle cues, marking time by the flock of waders returning to their roost half an hour before dusk; the ospreys calling in the predawn with their anxious, high-pitched chirps; and the racoons always active in the late afternoon.

Inevitably, logistics and schedules eventually intervened. As our backcountry camping permits expired and our water supplies dwindled, we were forced to abandon our castaway existence and head back to Everglades City.

FACT**FILE**

Ten Thousand Islands, Everglades National Park, Florida

When to go: November–April is the driest and coolest period.

Need to know: Wilderness permits must be obtained from the Gulf Coast Visitor Center (www.nps.gov./ever). Take precautions against mosquito bites.

Next step: Numerous airlines serve Miami, 130km (80 miles) east of Everglades City.

Operators: Local outfitters such as North American Canoe Tours (www.evergladesadventures.com) provide canoes, paddles, cooking gear, dry bags, tents, plus food and water containers. Eight-day guided canoeing trips along the Wilderness Waterway are also available.

ECO**FILE**

- Manatees are strictly protected and it is illegal to pursue, feed, touch or disturb them in any way.
- Ensure all food containers are raccoon-proof.
- Do not approach too close to bird nesting and roosting sites.
- Take away all garbage.

Whitewater rafting

Wilderness experience, river journey or pure adrenaline rush…whatever your reason for whitewater rafting, there are few adventures that give such an instant sense of satisfaction.

River rafting has come a long way since the days of the old pioneers who would think nothing of lashing a few logs together and paddling downstream into the great unknown. Not only has rafting equipment become safer and more sophisticated, but the huge popularity of the sport has spawned a whole new generation of expert river guides. You will still need to sign an indemnity waiver (as is the case with any adventure activity involving an element of risk), but the fact that complete novices can join rafting trips on extreme stretches of river like the source of the Nile in Uganda (see pages 200–1) is an indication of just how confident operators are. It goes without saying, however, that you need to be both physically and mentally prepared for whitewater rafting. A one-day dousing on rivers like the Zambezi and Rangitikei in New Zealand is a great way to discover if you are cut out for this fast, furious and foaming sport. Eager beavers and river rats will relish the challenge of longer trips, tuning into the various moods of the river (rough and smooth), spotting wildlife and camping overnight on the riverbanks. Soon they will be adding classic rafting journeys, like the Franklin River in Australia (see page 197) and the Grand Canyon (see pages 194–5), to their lists of must-do adventures.

> Our guide talked of 'flips', 'high-riding' and 'down time'. Each seemed to involve being tossed violently from the raft.

ADVENTURE**RATING**

Daring:	⊘⊘⊘⊘⊘
Eco-friendly:	⊘⊘⊘⊘⊘
Expense:	⊘⊘⊘⊘⊘
Expertise:	⊘⊘⊘⊘⊘
Fitness:	⊘⊘⊘⊘⊘

You will get wet!

ADVENTURE CALLING
Raging rivers worldwide

Brace yourself for a wet 'n' wild rollercoaster ride through some of the greatest rafting locations on earth – from adrenaline-saturated day-trips on the Zambezi to week-long floats through the Grand Canyon.

KEY TO SYMBOLS
Ø **Easy:** Up to grade III rapids, easy access to river.
ØØ **Moderate:** Mostly grade III-IV rapids, remoter locations, overnight options available.
ØØØ **Challenging:** Up to grade V rapids, multi-day expeditons, prior experience recommended.

WHITE WATER GRADES
I Small waves, clear passage, no obstacles.
II Medium waves, some eddies, small drops, few obstacles.
III Irregular waves, strong eddies, moderate drops, obstacles easily avoided.
IV Powerful, usually predictable rapids, big drops, constricted passage.
V Violent, unpredictable rapids, large waves, steep drops, congested chutes.
VI Extreme rapids, severe risk to life. Portage essential.

Grand Canyon, USA
ØØ – ØØØ
www.nps.gov/grca
Best time to go: April–October
Riding the rapids of the Colorado River as it snakes through Arizona's famous natural wonder is an unforgettable adventure that combines breathtaking scenery and heart-stopping action with privileged access to North America's grandest wilderness. Allow 7–21 days to raft the entire canyon, from Lees Ferry to Lake Mead, running 47 rapids rated 5 or above (on the Grand Canyon scale of 1 to 10). How long you take depends on the type of rafting you opt for (see page 198). Major rapids include Hance (8–10), Sockdologer (8–9), Unkar (6–7), House Rock (7–9), Crystal (10), Lava (10), Horn Creek (8–10) and Hermit (8–9), but there are also plenty of calm stretches where you can admire the surroundings or set off on foot to explore side gorges and

waterfalls. If you are short on time, one- to two-day river trips operate between Glen Canyon Dam and Lees Ferry or from Diamond Creek in the western end of the canyon. You can also hike in or out of the canyon at Phantom Ranch at the start or end your whitewater odyssey.

Tuolumne River, USA 𝄌𝄌
www.c-w-r.com
Best time to go: April–August
Tumbling from the High Sierra of Yosemite National Park, the Tuolumne is California's finest whitewater river, with grade V Lavey Falls becoming particularly feisty during the snowmelt season in late May and early June. Most trips put in at Merals Pool for the 30km (19-mile) run to Don Pedro Reservoir.

Gauley River, USA 𝄌𝄌 – 𝄌𝄌𝄌
www.adventuresinwv.com
Best time to go: April–September
West Virginia's wildest river, the grade III–V Gauley gets an extra

rush each September when authorities pull the plug on Summersville Dam, releasing over four million litres (one million gallons) of water per minute over 22 days. Adrenaline addicts combine the Upper and Lower Gauley into a 45km (28-mile), 150-rapid whitewater marathon. Those with little rafting experience, however, should stick to lower reaches of the river, where big rapids like Canyon Doors and Screaming Hell still provide thrills and spills.

Río Pacuare, Costa Rica 𝄌𝄌
www.visitcostarica.com
Best time to go: November–April
With its grade III–IV rapids, the Pacuare is the setting for Costa Rica's longest and most spectacular river trip. Two days are recommended to fully appreciate the 32km (20-mile) jungle-clad river valley, where sightings of monkeys, sloths and birds are possible during calmer stretches.

Few rafting trips can match the Grand Canyon for majestic scenery

Futaleufú River, Chile ⌀⌀⌀

www.exchile.com/guide

Best time to go: December–May

Thundering 50km (30 miles) through a mountain valley in northern Patagonia, the grade III–V+ Futaleufú is not for the faint-hearted. Unforgiving rapids (some over a kilometer in length), lethal undercut walls, re-circulating hydraulics and the sheer volume of water have proved fatal to at least six kayakers and rafters in recent years. Novices should start with the Bridge-to-Bridge section on the Lower Futaleufú, which includes 8km (5 miles) of grade IV rapids. Next, progress to the grade IV+ Más o Menos and grade V Casa de Piedra. Only when you are confident of safety drills and swim techniques should you take on the challenge of the Upper Futaleufú, where the Gates of Infierno unleash a series of grade V drops. Further downstream is Terminator, where even experts opt for a sneak line down the left side rather than risk the raft-swallowing hole in the centre of the rapid.

Çoruh River, Turkey ⌀⌀ – ⌀⌀⌀

www.tourismturkey.org

Best time to go: May–June

Fed by meltwater from the Kaçkar Range in northeastern Turkey, the class III–V Çoruh River churns through spectacular canyons and past ancient ruins on its route to the Black Sea. Day-trips and multi-day river expeditions are available, with the town of Yusufeli lying at the centre of the action.

Omo River, Ethiopia ⌀ – ⌀⌀

www.tourismethiopia.org

Best time to go: November

A superb all-round river, the Omo sweeps through remote parts of Ethiopia where the Bodi, Mursi and Kwegu tribes (renowned for their ornate body decoration) add a fascinating cultural aspect. The best whitewater can be found in the Upper Omo River Canyon, where grade III rapids are abundant.

Zambezi River, Zambia & Zimbabwe ⌀⌀ – ⌀⌀⌀

www.zambiatourism.com

Best time to go: August–January

The Zambezi – one of the world's top rafting rivers

Acclaimed as the world's best one-day, grade V whitewater rafting location, the Batoka Gorge downstream from Victoria Falls is strewn with more than 20 rapids over a 24km (15-mile) stretch of the Zambezi. During high-water season (January–July) only rapids 11–25 are navigable, whereas low water (August–January) enables trips to start near the Boiling Point at the base of the falls. First up are Against the Wall (IV–V), The Bridge (III) and Morning Glory (IV–V), followed by Stairway to Heaven (V) which drops a stomach-lurching 8m (26ft). Next comes the Devil's Toilet Bowl (IV) and Gulliver's Travels (V), a 700m-long (765yd), high-volume rapid featuring the Temple of Doom and Land of the Giants. Midnight Diner (III–V) gives you the option of either the straightforward Chicken Run or the crashing waves of Star Trek and Muncher Run. There's no choice when it comes to Commercial Suicide (VI) – everyone walks around it. Gnashing Jaws of Death (IV) is an easy run before lunch, then it's straight into the Overland Truck Eater (V) with its holes, eddies and whirlpools, and the Three Sisters (III–IV), where kayakers and body-boarders can surf perpetual breakers. Next come four exhilarating wave trains – The Mother (IV–V), Washing Machine (V), Terminator (IV) and Double Trouble (V). But it's Oblivion (V) that really epitomizes the wild spirit of Zambezi rafting. Its third wave flips more rafts than any other rapid in the world.

Nepal Ø – ØØØ

www.welcomenepal.com

Best time to go: October–May

Nepal has several excellent whitewater rafting rivers, catering for all levels of experience. Close to Kathmandu, the Trishuli (mainly grade III) offers one- or two-day trips. Things get wilder on the grade IV Bhote Kosi, while the Karnali involves a grade V, 180km (116-mile) river journey through remote canyons in the west.

Franklin River, Australia ØØØ

www.parks.tas.gov.au

Best time to go: December–March

Forging through the wilderness of southwest Tasmania, the Franklin River provides Australia's ultimate rafting challenge. Allow 8–14 days to complete the 125km (78-mile) epic through the Franklin-Gordon Wild Rivers National Park, where you should be prepared for a mixture of white-knuckle paddling, demanding portages and remote bush camping.

New Zealand Ø – ØØØ

www.nz-rafting.co.nz

Best time to go: November–April

New Zealand has numerous whitewater rafting rivers, from Southland's Kawarau (III–IV) to Northland's Wairoa (V). With 10 grade IV–V rapids on a 12km (7-mile) stretch, North Island's Rangitaiki lays claim to the world's best half-day rafting adventure. On South Island's West Coast, meanwhile, hike the Leslie Track to the Karamea River (V) for one of the world's best trek/raft combos.

ADVENTURE BRIEFING

Taking the rough with the smooth

Apart from minimum age requirements (which vary from place to place), anyone who can swim and is reasonably fit can join an organized rafting trip – even on some of the world's wildest rivers.

To paddle or not to paddle

There are three main types of whitewater rafting styles – and some locations, like the Grand Canyon, offer them all. Motorized inflatable craft provide the quickest, most stable option, but it's far more exciting and peaceful to rely on paddle power. This can take one of two forms. Some rafts are controlled by a guide handling a pair of oars with passengers seated fore and aft, while others involve everyone paddling.

Clothing and equipment

Wetsuits are provided in cold-water locations; otherwise swim shorts with a drawstring waist are fine (anything too skimpy, like a bikini, is liable to have embarrassing consequences in turbulent whitewater!). Wear tennis shoes, water sandals or diving booties – never flip-flops. Remove anything valuable (wedding rings, watches and so on) that you don't want to risk losing. Waterproof sunblock should be applied regularly – though not on the backs of your legs or anywhere else that's likely to transform the raft into a greasy banana. Your rafting operator will provide lifejackets and helmets. Always make sure they are in good condition and fit properly.

Braving the Bujagali Falls on the Nile (grade V)

The calm before the storm

After a safety talk in which you will be briefed on emergency procedures, training begins on a placid stretch of river with expert skippers coaching their crews in basics like paddling technique, positions to adopt when hitting big rapids, what to do if the raft capsizes and how to get back in again.

Going overboard

Despite its popularity and increasing accessibility, whitewater rafting is potentially extremely dangerous – particularly in grade IV–V rapids where rescue opportunities may be limited. If you do fall overboard, try to swim to the upstream side of the raft and hold on until someone can haul you back in by your lifejacket. In the event of a long swim, float on your back, feet first to fend off obstacles. Do not try to stand up – your feet may become trapped between rocks or submerged debris. If you find yourself being swept towards a log or other obstacle try to mount it by throwing both arms and a leg over it. Simply clinging to it with your arms and trying to haul your body up is potentially fatal since the water pressure could easily prove over-powering. Remember that safety kayakers will be waiting downstream to assist you. In major rapids there should also be rescue teams posted on the riverbanks, waiting with throw-ropes.

In some locations, the combination of cold water, chilling winds and strenuous days can lower your core body temperature. Dress appropriately, eat high-energy foods throughout the day and ensure that your supply of spare clothes and sleeping bags remains dry should you need to treat symptoms of hypothermia.

ECOFILE

- On overnight rafting expeditions, avoid damaging fragile riverside habitats by practising minimal impact rafting, camping and travelling in small groups.
- Bury faecal waste 100m (110 yards), or as far as possible, from watercourses.
- Only use biodegradable, phosphate-free soaps.
- Do not feed or disturb wildlife.
- Take away all rubbish.
- Avoid causing erosion or damage to vegetation on approach tracks to put-in and take-out points.

ESSENTIALGEAR

- Wetsuit and/or swimming costume
- **Water sandals or wetsuit booties**
- Life jacket, helmet and paddle •
Sunblock stick attached to wrist-band • High-energy snack bars •
Drybag for spare clothes, camera etc

All aboard the Nile rollercoaster

During most of its infancy, the Nile is calm and well behaved, but like any petulant youth it has its share of tantrums – and nowhere more so than the 31km (19-mile) stretch of rapids below the river's source in Uganda.

The sky was flawless but I could hear thunder. It was coming from directly ahead, where the river seemed to vanish – a fine spray blooming in its place, like steam from boiling water. Our raft suddenly span sideways, teased by a mini whirlpool and the River Nile chuckled beneath us.

'Paddle hard; dig in!' Our skipper's voice became progressively shriller as we approached Bujagali Falls, the first in a series of grade V rapids that turn Mother Nile white a few kilometres downstream from the town of Jinja. I glimpsed the rapid's curling waves – a rollercoaster of perpetual breakers rising from the river like white claws.

'Get down!'

All eight of us slumped from the outer tube into the middle of the raft, fumbling for the safety rope secured to the hull. The raft slid down a smooth, drooling tongue of water before riding high on the first wave. For a second I heard our screams above the raging river, then there was a sickening lurch as we pitched over the crest and rushed headlong into the heart of the rapid. White water exploded in our faces as we collided with the second wave. Someone was snatched overboard, legs cartwheeling into foamy oblivion. The raft bucked and shuddered in the onslaught. Half submerged, it felt like some kind of sadistic Jacuzzi.

Moments later, as the raft spun like an autumn leaf in the aftermath of the rapid, our skipper began leaping up and down, punching the air with his paddle. He was ecstatic. It was a big hit.

The safety kayaker (whose role was to shoot each rapid ahead of the rafts and wait downstream in an eddy to 'mop up the carnage') retrieved our swimmer, and for a few minutes we basked in the warm glow of adrenaline abuse before confronting Total Gunga, the next rapid.

The other rafts went first – drifting serenely through the calm reflections of a wooded islet. One by one they slipped from view only to reappear a second later tossed high on the first breaker, bodies and paddles spinning away like sparks from a Catherine wheel.

The upper reaches of the Nile, Uganda

Hunch-shouldered and forlorn, marabou storks on the banks resembled undertakers as we drifted silently past their roost.

With little hesitation and complete disdain, Total Gunga flipped our raft. The expert advice is to curl up like a ball, conserve air and wait for the rapid to spit you out. But rational thought evaporates when you think you're drowning. Ten seconds (although it felt more like a hundred) passed before I burst to the surface, flailing my arms like a madman. The overturned raft and the rest of the crew were scattered around me, bobbing in the choppy residue of the rapid, like flotsam from a shipwreck. Our guide clambered on to the stricken raft and performed a victory dance.

'Welcome to the Nile!' he shouted. 'I hope you all enjoyed your swim!'

Slowly, through spasms of coughing, I began to laugh. After all, there were only five more rapids to go, including Big Brother and Itanda, The Bad Place.

FACT**FILE**

River Nile, Jinja, Uganda
When to go: Year-round
Need to know: Rafting trips start a few kilometres downstream from Jinja. Minimum age is 16. River-boarding and whitewater kayaking are also available – and if you have any adrenaline left there's also the 44m (144ft) Nile High Bungee.
Next step: The capital Kampala lies 40km (25 miles) from Entebbe International Airport and 80km (50 miles) from Jinja.
Operators: Adrift (www. surfthesource.com) offers one- and two-day rafting trips, plus an option suitable for families. Also try Nile River Explorers (www.raftafrica.com).

See also Ecofile on page 199

Surfing

Where to catch the perfect wave? For serious surf dudes the search for the ultimate break is a never-ending quest, but several destinations have surfaced as top spots to ride on the crest of a wave.

> ### KEY TO SYMBOLS
> Ø **Easy**
> ØØ **Moderate**
> ØØØ **Challenging**

ADVENTURE CALLING

California, USA Ø – ØØØ
www.visitcalifornia.com
Best time to go: Year-round
There is great surf to be enjoyed all along California's coastline, with Highway 1 conveniently providing easy access to kilometres of breaks, including top spots like Huntington Beach, Malibu and Half Moon Bay. Winter generates the biggest swells.

Oahu, Hawaii Ø – ØØØ
www.gohawaii.com
Best time to go: May–September, November–February
With clear waters, constant sunshine and the world's most famous waves, the island of Oahu is entrenched in surfing lore. Take your first surf lesson at Kuhio Beach, Waikiki, then head to the North Shore, where, in winter, the surfing elite take on 6m-high (20ft) waves at Waimea Bay and ride the merciless Banzai Pipeline at Ehukai Beach.

Costa Rica Ø – ØØ
www.visitcostarica.com
Best time to go: Year-round
Warm water, plus good access to

Surfers wade in at Jeffrey's Bay, South Africa

a wide range of surf breaks have established Costa Rica as the 'Hawaii of Latin American surfing'. The northern Pacific coast offers the most consistent waves, particularly from December to April, when breaks like Witches Rock, Playa Grande and Playa Negra are at their best.

Canary Islands Ø – ØØØ

www.turismodecanarias.com
Best time to go: Year-round
Catching the full brunt of the Atlantic swells, the Canaries have some of Europe's best surf – especially on Lanzarote, where the surf school at the resort of Famara is the perfect spot to hone your skills. Waves peak at around 2m (6.5ft) between November and February.

Jeffrey's Bay, South Africa Ø – ØØØ

www.jeffreysbaytourism.org
Best time to go: May–August
Jeffrey's Bay has six main breaks, ranging from Kitchen Window (a good place to learn) to Supertubes – a classic right-hander that's the focus of the Billabong International Surfing Contest each July. Practise first on 'lesser' breaks like Tubes and Magnatubes.

Tahiti, French Polynesia ØØØ

www.tahiti-tourisme.com
Best time to go: November–April
For a pounding in paradise, monster waves like Teahupoo off the southeast coast of Tahiti will punish all but the most experienced board riders. A heavy, left-breaking barrel, it can reach heights of up to 10m (33ft).

Gold Coast, Australia Ø – ØØØ

www.verygc.com
Best time to go: March–June, September–December
The waters may be crowded, but for an all-round surfing resort, Surfers Paradise is hard to beat. The best beach breaks along the Gold Coast include Main Beach, Mermaid Beach, Narrowneck, Palm Beach and The Spit. For point breaks, the revered Superbank, near the Queensland-

ECO**FILE**

- Avoid damaging fragile coastal or marine habitats, such as sand dunes or coral reefs, in order to access a surf break.
- Help keep beaches clean by taking away your rubbish – and that of others.
- Environmental groups campaigning for cleaner seas and beaches include the US-based Surfers' Environmental Alliance (www.seasurfer.org) and the UK charity, Surfers Against Sewage (www.sas.org.uk).

ESSENTIAL**GEAR**

- Surfboard with leash • **Wetsuit and/or rash vest** • Traction pads or surf wax • **Waterproof sunblock**

ADVENTURE**RATING**

Daring:	ØØØØØ
Eco-friendly:	ØØØØØ
Expensive:	ØØØØØ
Physical:	ØØØØØ
Technical:	ØØØØØ

Surf sense
- Seek advice from locals before surfing an unfamiliar spot.
- Regularly apply waterproof sunblock.
- To avoid cramps, perform warm-up exercises before entering the sea.
- For safety reasons never surf alone.
- Only surf waves that you are comfortable with.
- Always be aware of other surfers and water users.
- Wait your turn – the surfer who is closest to the breaking wave has priority.
- Keep to within designated surfing areas on patrolled beaches.
- Be aware of changing surf conditions and your position relative to shore.
- If you get caught in a rip current swim across it, not against it.
- Ensure you are fit enough to swim back to shore if you lose your board.

New South Wales border, generates some of the longest surfing waves on the planet. On a good day, though, it's zealously guarded by local surfers so don't expect to see the inside of a barrel unless you're truly world-class. Other popular breaks include Burleigh Heads and Snapper.

ADVENTURE BRIEFING

As a beginner, surfing can seem rather daunting. Not only is the sport awash with lingo, but there also appears to be an infinite variety of gear to choose from. Joining a surf school will help to smooth the way by teaching you basic techniques. You'll find them at most popular surfing destinations, offering courses ranging from a morning's taster session to a week-long surf camp.

Unless you are fortunate enough to be surfing in tropical waters, a wetsuit is essential for trapping an insulating layer of water against your skin. To prevent chafing (especially under your arms when paddling), you will need to wear a rash vest underneath. Usually these have a high UV protection rating, so it's a good idea to wear them even when a wetsuit is not needed. In cold locations, neoprene boots, gloves and hood will protect extremities. Other essentials include surf wax or traction pads to provide grip when you stand up on your shiny new board, and a leg leash which stops your board ending up on the beach (or in the back of another surfer's head) each time you fall off.

When choosing a board, beginners should aim for one that is roughly 30–60cm (12–24in) taller than they are. Thicker boards float better, while extra width provides more stability. Foam boards are buoyant and forgiving, while foam-fibreglass composites offer better durability and make sense if you are going to be surfing a lot. Surfboards come in a variety of designs. Classic longboards are stable and easy to paddle, allowing skilled riders to 'walk the deck' and 'hang-ten'. Shortboards are highly manoeuverable, so are ideal for late drops and quick turns, while gun boards are suited to fast rides on big waves.

Big surf at Peahi Jaws off Maui, Hawaii

Sailing

From bareboat charters, where you take the helm, to crewed options complete with skipper and chef, sailing can be as adventurous or as laidback as you like.

> KEY TO SYMBOLS
> Ø **Easy**
> ØØ **Moderate**
> ØØØ **Challenging**

ADVENTURE CALLING

Bahamas Ø – ØØ
www.bahamas.com
Best time to go: February–June
Offering everything from uninhabited cays to glitzy resorts, the 700 islands of the Bahamas are a sailor's dream. There are 63 marinas, 3,140 slips, 12 boat repair yards and six bareboat charter companies. Trade winds blow from 5 to 20 knots, seas are usually warm and sheltered, while temperatures languish around 25–31°C (77–88°F). Some of the best cruising in the archipelago can be found around Abaco, where popular anchorages like Hope Town, Green Turtle Cay and Guana Cay are just a one- to two-hour passage from each other. Alternatively, set sail for the 365 Exuma Cays for laidback cruising, great snorkelling and sea-kayaking, plus plenty of Robinson Crusoe moments. Several islands are home to the Bahamian rock iguana – an endangered lizard measuring up to 1.8m (6ft).

British Virgin Islands Ø – ØØ
www.bvitourism.com
Best time to go: November–May
One of the Caribbean's most desirable sailing destinations, the British Virgin Islands boast a superb climate (with trade winds

Sailing in the frozen north, off the coast of Svalbard

offering the most consistent sailing conditions from November to May) and an irresistible range of anchorages, from secluded beaches to low-key resorts. Plot a course that includes deserted Sandy Cay, Jost Van Dyke (with its legendary Foxy's Bar), The Dogs (a cluster of islands renowned for excellent diving) and Salt Island (with its salt-harvesting ponds). Crewed and bareboat charters are available from Tortola.

British Isles Ø – ØØØ
www.visitbritain.com
Best time to go: May–September
From pottering about in sheltered estuaries in Cornwall and Devon to more testing voyages around the Hebrides, the British Isles have a fine sailing heritage – with modern facilities to match. Prime locations include Salcombe, the Isles of Scilly, the Isle of Wight and Oban. In addition to numerous marinas and training schools, crewed and bareboat charters are widely available.

Croatia Ø – ØØ
www.croatia.hr
Best time to go: April–July, September–November
Croatia's island-spattered Adriatic coastline is crying out for exploration by yacht. Dozens of marinas and charter companies make island hopping a breeze. For a sailing trip with a traditional twist, join a cruise on a twin-masted wooden gulet or caique.

Stockholm Archipelago, Sweden Ø – ØØ
www.visitsweden.com
Best time to go: Summer

Popular with the city dwellers, the 24,000 islands of the Stockholm Archipelago are dotted with summer hideaways, sheltered harbours and fishing villages.

Svalbard, Norway Ø
www.svalbard.net
Best time to go: June–August
Barely clinging to the top of a world map, it is only during summer that this remote archipelago struggles from the frigid grip of pack ice – and only then that ships can probe its spectacular wildlife-rich fjords. Shun the bigger cruise ships and opt instead for the *Noorderlicht*, a 50m

ECO**FILE**
- Avoid anchoring on fragile marine habitats like coral reefs.
- Never dump waste or rubbish overboard.
- Dispose of unwanted or tangled fishing line properly.
- Take care not to disturb turtle- or seabird-nesting sites.

ESSENTIAL**GEAR**
• Lifejacket • **Windproof/waterproof jacket, trousers and hat** • Deck shoes • **Sunglasses and sunblock** • Soft luggage for easy stowage

ADVENTURE**RATING**

Daring:	ØØØØØ
Eco-friendly:	ØØØØØ
Expensive:	ØØØØØ
Physical:	ØØØØØ
Technical:	ØØØØØ

(164ft) steel-hulled schooner with a crew of five and berths for just 20 passengers. You'll have to help hoist the sails, but the effort is rewarded by the exquisite silence of sailing in the high Arctic.

Lamu, Kenya ∅

www.magicalkenya.com
Best time to go: July–March
Charter a crewed dhow to explore the historic towns, ruins and mangrove-fringed islets of this fascinating Swahili archipelago. A strong southeasterly trade wind, known as the Kaskasi, blows during January.

Whitsunday Islands, Australia ∅ – ∅∅

www.whitsundaytourism.com
Best time to go: April–November
The Whitsundays are fringed with glorious beaches, including Whitehaven – a sensational swathe of squeaky-clean silica. Bareboat charters are widely available, or you could join a crewed adventure on anything from a square-rigged tallship to an America's Cup racing yacht. With its enviable location as the closest point off the Queensland coast to the Great Barrier Reef, the Whitsunday archipelago is also renowned for its snorkelling and diving. Seven of the 74 islands have resorts, or you could set out from one of the marinas at Airlie Beach on the mainland.

New Zealand ∅ – ∅∅∅

www.newzealand.com
Best time to go: Year-round
In a nation obsessed with sailing, one in four Kiwis has a boat and most families own a beachside holiday house, or bach. Dubbed the 'City of Sails', Auckland offers fine cruising in the Hauraki Gulf, while other sailing hotspots in North Island include the Bay of Islands. For experienced skippers, strong winds in Cook Strait provide some of the country's most exhilarating sailing, while the Marlborough Sounds and Abel Tasman National Park at the northern tip of South Island offer more sheltered conditions, along with immaculate beaches and a rainforest-smothered coastline.

ADVENTURE BRIEFING

With appropriate qualifications and experience you can charter and skipper your own yacht. There are several organizations offering training, including the American Sailing Association (www.american-sailing.com), Royal Yachting Association (www.rya.org.uk) and Yachting Australia (www.yachting.org.au). Alternatively, you can charter a yacht with a skipper and crew who will take control of everything from rigging and navigation to preparing meals – an ideal option for novices who want no more responsibility than taking the helm occasionally. Crewing, meanwhile, offers an exciting opportunity to join more ambitious voyages, where you might find yourself running out the sails on a tall ship or scrubbing the decks on a luxury yacht. Experience is not always required, but don't underestimate the work involved. Useful online sources include Boat Crew (www.boatcrew.net) and SailNet (www.sailnet.com).

New Zealand's Bay of Islands is true to its name

It's a wild world

Wildlife adventures are supercharged with anticipation. They offer privileged opportunities to visit some of the world's last remaining wild places and can provide a lifeline to the creatures themselves.

Wildlife, in any of its myriad forms, is a wonderful excuse for an adventure, inspiring a spectacular array of travel experiences, from diving on a coral reef to scaling a canopy walkway in a tropical rainforest. By supporting ecotourism projects that channel funds back into conservation and benefit local communities, your wildlife adventure can (and should) make a positive contribution. Wildlife increasingly needs to pay its way in order to survive. If visionary, sustainable ecotourism can transform a poacher into a game scout or a dynamite fisherman into a turtle-watching guide, then it's got to be a good thing.

Animal magnetism
There is a bewildering range of wildlife holidays on offer, from African safaris to cruises in the Galapagos Islands. Some revolve around a single charismatic species, while others coincide with a wildlife spectacle, such as the Serengeti-Masai Mara wildebeest migration. For each of the 'mega species' featured below, there are probably dozens of different birds and insects that enthusiasts wouldn't hesitate to travel halfway round the world for a chance to see. A seabird colony, for example, is a must-see – whether it's puffins on the Farne Islands or albatrosses on South Georgia. And when it comes to minibeasts, the mass arrival of monarch butterflies in central Mexico is mesmerizing.

Cats and dogs
Set off early in the morning or late in the afternoon when these predators are more likely to be active. With the exception of cheetahs, most are nocturnal hunters and spend the middle part of the day resting. Their superb camouflage can render them almost invisible, so look for telltale clues, such as fresh tracks or alarm calls from nearby wildlife. On a typical African safari you would be unlucky not to see lions and jackals. The open plains of Kenya and Tanzania offer perfect hunting territory for cheetahs, while Zambia's South Luangwa National Park and South Africa's Sabi Sand Private Game Reserve are renowned for leopards. Nowadays you're fortunate to spot African wild dogs

A field guide will help you identify the species you spot

King of beasts

Top 10 wildlife destinations

1. **Alaska** From tundra to temperate rainforest, Alaska is varied and vast – with wildlife to match. Bears, whales, eagles and wolves can all be found. Visit June–September, focussing on reserves like Denali and Kenai Fjords or cruising the Inside Passage.

2. **The Peruvian Amazon** Tambopata and Manu Reserves protect vast areas of virgin jungle. Visit June–August and venture from your lodge on foot or by canoe in search of giant otters, freshwater dolphins and scarlet macaws.

3. **The Pantanal, Brazil** Huge seasonal wetland (about half the size of France) with superb birdlife, giant anteaters, anacondas, howler monkeys and even jaguars. Visit July–September.

4. **Galápagos Islands, Ecuador** Wildlife bonanza above and below the waves. Seabirds, sealions, giant tortoises and marine iguanas are unfazed by humans. Visit year-round (avoid December–March if you want to see waved albatrosses). Cruises last three to ten days. Some boats offer diving and kayaking.

5. **Costa Rica** Tortuguero and Santa Rosa national parks are two of the western hemisphere's most important turtle hatcheries. Although it's possible to see turtles nesting here year-round, each species has its own season. For example, leatherbacks nest from February to July and green turtles from July to October.

anywhere, but packs still roam the Okavango Delta, Tanzania's Selous Game Reserve and other large wilderness areas. Of the 4,000 or so remaining tigers, over half live in India. Reserves like Ranthambhore and Corbett are the best places to find them. The most elusive of the big cats, jaguars, are rarely sighted. Try your luck at Cockscomb Basin Jaguar Preserve in Belize or Iwokrama Rainforest Reserve, Guyana. For doggy diversions, head to Queensland's Fraser Island for dingoes, to Baja California for coyotes and to Poland's Bieszczady Mountains or Alaska's Denali National Park for wolves.

Whales and dolphins

Although most whale-watching trips are conducted by commercial boat operators, some vessels undertake genuine research to which tourists can contribute valuable sightings. Sea-kayaking, meanwhile, can not only provide heart-stopping encounters from the unique perspective of sea level, but it's also a peaceful way to travel – you may well hear the explosive rush of air as a whale surfaces to breathe.

Whale-watching hotspots range from the Hebrides for diminutive minkes to Monterey Bay for mighty blues. Two of the most enigmatic species, however, are humpbacks and orcas – and the best place to see both is the Inside Passage of Alaska and British Columbia. A voyage by ferry or cruise ship along this tortuous waterway can be rewarded with spectacular sightings of humpbacks breaching and bubble-netting (an awesome display of communal feeding) and pods of orcas a dozen

6. **Poland** The Biebrza Marshes and Białowieża Forest of northeast Poland are primeval sanctuaries for some of Europe's rarest wildlife, including wolf, bison, lynx and no fewer than ten of species of woodpecker. Winter is best for tracking large mammals, while spring and autumn are prime times for observing migratory birds.

7. **Serengeti-Masai Mara, Tanzania & Kenya** Vast plains teeming with big game. Visit August–September for your best chance of witnessing the epic migration of more than a million wildebeest and thousands of zebras and Thomson's gazelles. Take a vulture's-eye view from a hot-air balloon.

8. **Okavango Delta, Botswana** Watery wilderness on the edge of the Kalahari offering an exciting range of game-viewing safaris, by 4WD vehicle, dugout canoe, horse, elephant or on foot. Visit year-round.

9. **India's tiger reserves** Join a big-game safari Asia-style with chances of spotting gazelles, monkeys, sloth bears and tigers. Prime time for big-cat watching is February–April, when vegetation withers at the end of the dry season. However, post-monsoon November is lush, beautiful and bursting with birdlife.

10. **Antarctica and sub-Antarctic islands** Take a peek at life in the freezer during the Austral summer from November to March. Spot whales from the deck of a cruise ship and marvel at crowded seal and penguin colonies.

strong. Other exceptional locations for spotting a variety of whales and dolphins include Iceland, Norway, the Azores, St Lawrence River, Baja California, Valdez Peninsula (Argentina), New Zealand and Antarctica. For landlubbers, South Africa's Cape coast provides a high and dry vantage from which to watch southern right whales close in-shore. Three of the best places to snorkel with wild dolphins are North Bimini (Bahamas), Kaikoura (New Zealand) and the Azores. If taking the plunge doesn't appeal, try paddling in the shallows with bottlenose dolphins at Monkey Mia, Western Australia.

Baby orang-utan

Primates

Few other animals display such a captivating and familiar range of behaviour and expressions. Make brief eye contact with a gorilla or chimp and you are connecting with another mind. It's a sobering and privileged moment that people are more than happy to slog for hours through humid, muddy jungles for a chance to experience. Remember that physical contact is forbidden in order to minimize the risk of passing on human germs.

Prime sites for mountain gorilla-watching are Bwindi and Mgahinga in Uganda and Volcanoes National Park in

How to choose the right trip
- With first-hand knowledge of an area, specialist operators can put together packages that include everything from transport to national park entry fees – and they'll often know where and when to find the best wildlife.
- Check that there enough days allocated to wildlife watching. If you are a keen photographer or interested in animal behaviour, concentrating on one area may prove more satisfying than flitting from one place to another.
- Is the timing right? Bargain deals might conceal unfavourable conditions for viewing wildlife.
- Small groups of half a dozen people are quiet and unobtrusive, boosting your chances of wildlife encounters.
- An expert guide who can communicate with a genuine passion for the natural world will elevate a wildlife holiday to the trip of a lifetime.

Left: Puffin. Right: Hippos

Rwanda, where several families have been habituated. Reserve well in advance for a permit. Chimps can be spotted in forest reserves throughout East and West Africa, including Kibale, Budongo and Semliki in Uganda. Africa is also home to common primates like baboons and vervet monkeys. For a chance to see one of more than 50 varieties of lemur, however, you need to visit Madagascar. The Kabili-Sepilok Forest Reserve in Sabah, Borneo, offers close encounters with orang-utans, while a boat trip on the nearby Kinabatangan River will often reveal proboscis monkeys. New World primates are perhaps more elusive, although you can't fail to miss the cry of a howler monkey.

Bears and pandas

Bears can be extremely dangerous, particularly when surprised or when they've been encouraged to associate humans with food. Hikers in bear country should always take precautions, such as carrying bear bells to warn of their approach and hoisting food out of reach in a tree when camping.

If you want to watch brown bears catching salmon head to Alaska's Katmai National Park between June and September. Another good spot is Admiralty Island, known by local Tlingit Indians as 'the Fortress of the Bears'. Black bears can be glimpsed in forests from Vancouver Island to the Appalachian Mountains, but for polar bears your best option is Churchill on the shores of Hudson Bay, where, during autumn, tundra buggies provide incredible opportunities for viewing these magnificent 600kg (1,320 lb) beasts. Europe also has bears – visit Svalbard for polar bears, Finland and Sweden for brown bears. Pandas are much harder to find. Only 1,000 or so giant pandas survive in reserves dotted through China's Hengduan Mountains. At Wolong reserve visitor trails probe forests of bamboo – the giant panda's exclusive diet. The smaller red panda, meanwhile, can sometimes be glimpsed in forested regions of the Himalayan foothills.

Air

Ever since the first balloon flight in 1873 and the Wright brothers' inaugural powered flight 30 years later, people have been obsessed with airborne adventures. Nowadays, of course, there's nothing particularly adventurous about commercial air travel, which is perhaps the reason why we seek ever more daring and pioneering means of getting aloft. One of the most exhilarating and easily accessible ways of getting off the ground is on a tandem paragliding flight – although adrenaline seekers will get more of a buzz from skydiving (see page 236) or a sub-orbital space flight (see page 154). But don't be put off by these daredevil embellishments. Good old-fashioned hot-air ballooning is still right up there as one of the most moving and memorable forms of airborne adventure – particularly if you happen to be floating over a spectacular landscape like the Serengeti plains or Namib Desert. Light aircraft and helicopters, meanwhile, can whisk you to some of the most remote and inaccessible corners of the world, or provide new perspectives of familiar world wonders.

Left: Wildlife safari by balloon. Right: Tandem paraglide

Contents

Key
The numbers/letters in circles on this page correspond to the locations marked on the map on pages 218–19.

Top: Ultralight over Victoria Falls. Left: Skeleton Coast

ACTION 217

Air: World Map

Stockholm

St Petersburg

Moscow

SAYAN MOUNTAINS

Ulaanbaatar

GOBI DESERT

Istanbul **6** **3**

Baghdad

Tehran

Beijing

Tokyo

Cairo **7**

R A

HIMALAYA

Delhi

Karachi

PACIFIC OCEAN

Khartoum

Mumbai

Bangkok

Hong Kong

Kinshasa **9** Nairobi **8**

INDIAN OCEAN

Cairns

Great Barrier Reef **3**

Harare

12

GREAT DIVIDING RANGE

Johannesburg **10** **11**

5

Perth

Sydney

Canberra

Auckland

Hot-air ballooning

Unless you are preparing for the latest high altitude, around-the-world record attempt, ballooning is usually a gentle adventure where the biggest hardship is a pre-dawn wake-up call.

It might be one of the adventure world's more passive activities, but the anticipation of a ballooning trip is still guaranteed to get your pulse pounding. Arriving at the launch point in the stillness before sunrise, you will find the ground crew busy inflating the voluminous, 30m-high (100ft) envelope. The balloon's gas burners roar in the darkness as the canopy swells under the pressure of eight tons of hot air, straining the anchor ropes and nudging the passenger basket restlessly from side to side. Climbing aboard, you watch your pilot make final checks and then, as the ropes are cast off, you finally float free. Immediately the balloon becomes a calmer creature, no longer fretting at its mooring, but drifting serenely, happily held hostage by whichever way the breeze is blowing.

> To the east: dawn light bathing rocky plains; to the west: apricot-coloured dunes smouldering in the sunrise; and rising above it all, a lone balloon.

ADVENTURE**RATING**

Daring:	⬤⬤◯◯◯
Ecofriendly:	⬤⬤⬤⬤⬤
Expense:	⬤⬤⬤⬤⬤
Expertise:	⬤◯◯◯◯
Fitness:	⬤◯◯◯◯

Bright balloons at Château d'Oex, Switzerland

ADVENTURE CALLING

Up, up and away

From the Nile to the Alps, hot-air balloons can get you on a high above some of the world's most iconic landscapes. Each of the following locations typically offers short morning flights; a few host full-blown ballooning festivals lasting several days.

California, USA

www.visitcalifornia.com
Best time to go: Year-round
Numerous operators offer balloon flights in California, with prime spots including Palm Springs, Santa Rosa, Napa Valley and Temecula Valley.

New Mexico, USA

www.abqballooning.com
Best time to go: Year-round
Thanks to its annual nine-day International Balloon Fiesta held in October, Albuquerque has become known as the world's hot-air balloon capital. There are at least a dozen companies offering balloon flights over the Rio Grande Valley.

Colorado, USA

www.colorado.com
Best time to go: Year-round
One of North America's finest spots for ballooning, the Rockies offer everything from day flights and ballooning festivals to high-altitude expeditions over the Continental Divide. Winter flights are also available, so you can combine a morning's ballooning with an afternoon ski. Get airborne from resorts such as Aspen, Boulder, Colorado Springs, Fort Collins and Vail.

Château d'Oex, Switzerland

www.chateau-doex.ch
Best time to go: Year-round
The European home of hot-air ballooning, Château d'Oex witnessed the lift-off in 1999 of the first non-stop around-the-world balloon flight by Bertrand Piccard and Brian Jones. The Swiss town is also the venue for the annual International Hot Air Balloon Week in January. Visit anytime, though, and (weather permitting) you can get aloft for views of alpine beauties like Mont Blanc, the Matterhorn and the Eiger.

Stockholm, Sweden

www.visit-stockholm.com
Best time to go: Summer
Unusual in that many balloon flights take off at dusk rather than dawn, Stockholm allows safe and spectacular flights during Sweden's long summer evenings — a great chance to gaze down on the lights of the city and the islands of the Stockholm Archipelago.

Balloon reflected in hippo pool, Serengeti

Cappadocia, Turkey

www.tourismturkey.org

Best time to go: April–September
Göreme is the best centre from which to launch a ballooning expedition over Cappadocia – a surreal landscape of plateaux, gullies, stone mushrooms and fairy chimneys riddled with ancient cave dwellings. Small wonder that Star Wars was filmed here.

Nile Valley, Egypt

www.touregypt.net

Best time to go: March–May, September–November
Lift off from Luxor on a dawn flight over the Nile's West Bank, gazing down on the ruins of Medinet Habu and the Ramesseum before drifting on above the elegantly colonnaded Temple of Hatshepsut, which lies at the threshold of the tomb-riddled Valley of the Kings. Ancient wonders aside, ballooning is the best way to appreciate the stark contrast between the verdant banks of the Nile and adjacent stony desert.

Serengeti, Tanzania

www.balloonsafaris.com

Best time to go: Year-round
For a vulture's-eye view of the wildebeest migration (see page 213) aim to go ballooning in the Serengeti between May and August or November to December (or catch the spectacle from an equally exhilarating balloon flight in Kenya's adjacent Masai Mara in September and October). Ultimately, though, a dawn balloon flight over East Africa's wild plains is thrilling at any time of year – wafting over the tawny savannah, the silence broken by the occasional yelp of a zebra stallion or raucous call of a turaco.

Drifting over the Temple of Hatshepsut, Egypt

Kenya

www.magicalkenya.com

Best time to go: Year-round

The most popular location for ballooning in Kenya is the Masai Mara National Reserve, where dawn flights are available from several safari bases, including Governor's Camp, Keekorok Lodge and the Savora Mara Game Camp. Balloon safaris are also possible in the Soysambu Conservancy near Nakuru National Park, while the private 25,000ha (62,000-acre) Loisaba Ranch in northern Kenya provides a dramatic setting for ballooning over the Laikipia Plateau.

Namib Desert, Namibia

www.balloon-safaris.com

Best time to go: Year-round

Drift silently above the heat-shattered mountains and apricot-coloured sand dunes in the Sossusvlei area of the Namib Desert, lifting off from Sesriem or the Namib Rand Nature Reserve. Some of the world's tallest sand dunes, reaching heights of 380m (1,246ft), can be found here, while keen-eyed balloonists may spot mountain zebra, oryx, springbok and ostrich.

South Africa

www.southafrica.net

Best time to go: Year-round

With its superb climate and dramatic landscapes, hot-air ballooning has become increasingly popular in South Africa. Prime year-round locations include Magaliesberg (near Johannesburg), Sabie and Hazyview (Mpumalanga), Oudtshoorn (Karoo) and the Drakensberg and Natal Midlands (KwaZulu Natal). From September to March you can also get airborne above the Cape Winelands.

Australia

www.australia.com

Best time to go: Year-round

Hot-air ballooning is possible at several locations in Australia, from major cities like Brisbane, Melbourne and Adelaide to wine-growing regions such as the Barossa and Hunter valleys. Head into the country's heartland for dramatic sunrise flights over the blood-red MacDonnell Ranges near Alice Springs or get aloft near Cairns for wonderful views of the subtropical Atherton Tablelands.

The surreal landscape of the Göreme Valley, Turkey

ADVENTURE BRIEFING

Hot air and champagne

You need a commercial pilot balloon licence to fly a hot-air balloon, but all that's required as a passenger is a head for heights, some warm clothing and a sense of adventure.

Balloon basics

The physics is simple: hot air rises because it is less dense than the cooler air around it. Heat the air inside a hot-air balloon and it will go up; let it cool and it will go down. Using this basic principle, skilled balloon pilots can fly at anything between grass-skimming height and 18,000m (59,000ft), although a typical flight will undulate between treetop level and around 1,500m (5,000ft). A lot will depend on the wind direction and speed, which often varies at different altitudes; your pilot may need to ascend to 1,000m (3,300ft) simply to pick up a favourable breeze. Strong or gusty winds are not ideal for flights and you may also find your trip cancelled due to rain, which cools the balloon down, makes it heavier, and tends to run straight into the basket.

Pre-flight checklist

Hot-air balloons can carry anything from three to 20 passengers. Typically, there is either a minimum age limit of seven or a minimum height of around 130cm (4ft). It is advisable to book well in advance. In the Serengeti, for example, there are only three balloons operating. Most flights take place early in the morning when not only are winds often at their calmest, but the lower ambient temperature makes it easier to get the balloon aloft. Wrap up warm for the hour or so it takes the ground crew to inflate the balloon and prepare it for boarding. Remember to wear sturdy shoes for clambering in and out of the basket. During the flight, the balloon is carried by the wind so you won't experience any chilling gusts. In any case, the burner serves as such an effective heater you may want to wear a hat to keep your head cool! Finally, make sure all cameras, binoculars and sunglasses are securely attached to straps around your neck.

ESSENTIAL**GEAR**

- **Warm clothing for pre-dawn start**
- Hat and sunglasses • **Sturdy shoes**
- Camera • **Alarm clock**

ECO**FILE**

- Avoid spooking wildlife or livestock.
- Select landing sites with care, particularly when considering access for support vehicles.
- Hot-air balloons can consume around 200 litres (52 gallons) of propane gas per hour.

What goes up…

Flights generally last an hour or two, after which your pilot will start venting hot air from the balloon in preparation for landing. Usually, this is a sedate affair with little more than a gentle bump and a helping hand out of the basket from the ground crew (who will have shadowed your flight in support vehicles). However, if the breeze has picked up during the morning, you may experience a more adrenaline-charged touchdown where the pilot asks you to brace yourself against the basket and flex your knees. Sometimes the basket will be dragged along the ground for a short distance before the balloon finally comes to a flaccid standstill. Then it's simply a case of crawling out of the basket, dusting yourself down and enjoying the balloon aviators' traditional champagne breakfast.

The burner can generate quite a fierce heat

Should I offset my CO2 emissions?

Is carbon offsetting an effective way of tackling climate change, or should we forget about making donations to tree-planting schemes and focus instead on looking for greener ways to travel?

According to the Intergovernmental Panel on Climate Change, 'most of the observed increase in globally averaged temperatures since the mid-20th century is very likely due to the observed increase in anthropogenic greenhouse gas concentrations.' Levels of carbon dioxide (CO_2) – one of the most important greenhouse gases – have increased as a result of human activities, such as deforestation and the burning of fossil fuels. Carbon offsetting schemes offer individuals and businesses an opportunity to compensate for their carbon emissions by donating to various projects, from tree planting to renewable energy schemes. However, some organizations, including conservation groups like Friends of the Earth, are concerned that carbon offsetting is being used as 'a smoke-screen to ward off legislation and delay the urgent action needed to cut emissions and develop alternative low-carbon solutions'.

How does carbon offsetting work?

For every tonne of CO_2 you generate through an activity such as flying, driving or heating a building, you pay for an equivalent tonne to be removed elsewhere through a 'green' initiative.

What initiatives does carbon offsetting support?

To begin with, most funds were ploughed into forestry schemes on the belief that one tree absorbs half a tonne of CO_2 over its lifespan. However, tree planting has now largely been discredited as being based on 'flawed science': using fast-growing species on large monoculture plantations requires high inputs of fertilizer and energy. Carbon offsetting providers have now widened their remit to include climate-friendly technology projects, ranging from the provision of energy-efficient lightbulbs and cookers in the developing world to large-scale renewable energy schemes such as wind farms.

Are they effective in tackling climate change?

Although offsetting is certainly better than doing nothing, it's also important to take long-term action to cut carbon emissions in the first place. An obvious target, travellers are encouraged to use alternatives to flying (the fastest-growing contributor to CO2 emissions) whenever feasible – although it could equally be argued that the social, economic and conservation benefits of responsible travel actually outweigh the effects of carbon emissions.

Some environmentalists claim offsetting gives polluters the 'green light' to continue business as usual, as it is so often easier to pay up rather than make lifestyle changes. However, in the absence of cleaner technologies, there is no denying the fact that it also provides a way of counterbalancing your carbon footprint. In addition to purchasing carbon offsets that support renewable energy projects and contribute to sustainable development, check whether they have been certified by the Gold Standard – the most widely endorsed quality standard for designing and implementing carbon offset projects.

Ready, offset, go!

Carbon Fund:	www.carbonfund.org
Climate Care:	www.climatecare.org
Climate Friendly:	www.climatefriendly.com
CO2 Balance:	www.co2balance.com
Equiclimate:	www.ebico.co.uk/equiclimate
Global Cool:	www.globalcool.org
My Climate:	www.myclimate.org
Native Energy:	www.nativeenergy.com
Pure:	www.puretrust.org.uk
Sustainable Travel International:	www.sustainabletravelinternational.org
Terrapass:	www.terrapass.com

Icebergs off the coast of Greenland – under threat?

Paragliding

Rising on a thermal and a surge of adrenaline, spiralling with birds of prey and swooping across forested mountain slopes, your feet brushing the treetops, paragliding is the ultimate free-spirited, free-flying adventure.

KEY TO SYMBOLS

Ø **Easy**
ØØ **Moderate**
ØØØ **Challenging**

ADVENTURE CALLING

You can take a leap of faith with a paraglider in numerous locations worldwide, from the Sierra Nevada to the Nepalese Himalaya. Tandem flights, in which you are firmly attached to an experienced pilot, are available at the following five top spots.

Iquique, Chile
www.parapenteiquique.cl
Best time to go: October–April
Soar above surf-swept beaches where the Atacama Desert meets the Pacific. Cerro Dragón, a giant dune near the city of Iquique, is the perfect launch pad.

Medellín, Colombia
Best time to go: Year-round
With prevailing northerly winds funnelling up the Bello Valley, Medellín enjoys superb paragliding conditions over the tail end of the Andes.

Flying tandem allows even novices to get aloft

Ölüdeniz, Turkey

www.tourismturkey.org

Best time to go: April–September

Set around an exquisite turquoise lagoon, the resort of Ölüdeniz offers spectacular tandem flights from the 1,900m-high (6,200ft) summit of Baba Dag. Expect to be airborne for up to 45 minutes and, on a clear day, keep an eye out for Rhodes.

Swakopmund, Namibia

www.namibiatourism.com.na

Best time to go: September–April

Early mornings are safest for beginner courses and tandem flights above the towering dunes south of Swakopmund. Later in the day, strong thermals and winds present challenging conditions for paragliding over the Skeleton Coast.

Western Cape, South Africa

www.sahpa.co.za

Best time to go: November–April

Take off from Table Mountain for an incredible flight over Cape Town and the Twelve Apostles before landing at Camps Bay.

ADVENTURE BRIEFING

The best introduction to paragliding is to take a tandem flight where you are strapped into a double harness with a pilot. Take-off usually involves a short, steady run along a gentle slope into the prevailing wind. The canopy of the paraglider fills out as you start to move and suddenly you are aware that your legs are running in air. Most launches are slow and gentle – there is no falling sensation. Similarly, landing is usually calm and controlled. If a tandem flight doesn't put you off, progress to a novice solo-flying course where you will be taught the essentials of launching, turning and landing, as well as the finer points of riding winds and capturing thermals. Although reasonable fitness is required for paragliding (particularly if you need to carry gear to the launch site), alertness and a sensitive touch on the controls are more important than brute strength. Even during a tandem flight, you will be given an opportunity to take control of the paraglider, pulling on left or right brake cords to change speed and direction.

ECO**FILE**

- Powered solely by wind, paragliders are a supremely eco-friendly means of transport. However, you do need to consider the potential impact of reaching launch and landing sites, especially if 4WD vehicles are required.

ESSENTIAL**GEAR**

- **Helmet** • Sunglasses • **Warm clothing, including gloves** • Shoes with good grip

ADVENTURE**RATING**

Daring:	
Eco-friendly:	
Expense:	
Expertise:	
Fitness:	

Aloft in the Alps

Paragliding, or parapenting as it is also known, is a popular summer sport in the Alps, and few locations offer such dramatic flying space as Chamonix, nestled at the foot of Mont Blanc.

The view from the Planpraz gondola was sublime. The snowy summit of Mont Blanc glistened in early morning sunshine, while Chamonix was reduced to a mosaic of rooftops in the valley 1,000m (3,300ft) below. The sky was a flawless cobalt blue; it was warm and there was barely a breeze – the perfect day for leaping off a mountain. Patrice, a paragliding veteran of 3,800 flights, would be with me all the way – thanks to his twin harness with its air-cushioned passenger seat.

Paragliding at Mont Blanc

The paragliding 'runway' (a disturbingly small, grassy slope) was a short walk above the mid-cable-car station on Le Brévent. While Patrice unpacked his paraglider (which was attached to a seemingly irretrievable tangle of multi-coloured cords), I took a lingering look across the Chamonix Valley towards the seven summits of the Mont Blanc massif – each one rising to over 4,000m (13,000ft). But just as I was thinking how perfect they looked with my feet firmly planted on terra firma, Patrice handed me a helmet and clipped me into the harness.

I assumed (or rather prayed) that he was also fastened securely because the next moment I was running down the gentle slope, straining against the resistance of the parachute that unfurled behind me like a giant jellyfish. Abruptly, the slope fell away from under my feet, but instead of the stomach-sliding lurch I'd been expecting, we soared straight out across the valley, the wind roaring in my ears as we picked up speed.

While Patrice waited patiently for me to stop running in thin air and shuffle back into a sitting position, he casually pointed out various land-marks that spiralled a giddy kilometre (half a mile) below us. Then he spotted a pair of buzzards wheeling on a warm updraft. A gentle pull on his right brake cord and we turned gracefully to join them, flirting with the thermal as we pirouetted high above a mountain gully. At other times, we flew much lower over the slopes, our dangling feet barely skimming the treetops. The views were stupendous – but you can get those from cable cars or simply hiking high up. The unique thrill of paragliding was the super-charged sensation of freedom, flying at the whim of the wind, harnessing a subtle shift in the breeze or trying to hitch a ride on a thermal.

Steering a paraglider is as simple as pulling down on the left cord to turn left or on the right cord to turn right. Halfway through our flight, Patrice handed over the controls so I could feel the exuberant tug of the 'chute through my arms and shoulders. But 30 minutes passes quickly when you're pretending to be a buzzard, and soon we were starting our long, spiralling descent towards Chamonix, turning into the wind for a graceful touchdown in a meadow on the town's outskirts. As the parachute collapsed in the grass behind me, I knew the euphoria of the flight would keep me buoyant for the rest of the day.

FACT**FILE**

Chamonix, France

When to go: Good flying conditions last from March to October, when cool nights and hot days create large temperature gradients resulting in strong thermals.

Need to know: Launch between 10am and midday to avoid gusts. In addition to Le Brévent, paragliding is also possible from Les Grands Montets, Aiguille du Midi, Plan de L'Aiguille and Les Houches. Intrepid pilots can fly from Mont Blanc.

Next step: The nearest international airport is Geneva, from where it's a 90-minute drive to Chamonix (www.chamonix.net).

Operators: Tandem paragliding flights are available from various operators, including Evolution 2 (www.evolution2-chamonix.com).

Flying adventures

Whether it's an adventure in itself or simply the means by which you reach the starting point of a remote trek or heli-skiing run, getting airborne in a light aircraft is one of the most exciting ways of exploring far-flung wilderness areas.

ADVENTURE CALLING

Brooks Range, Alaska

www.travelalaska.com

Best time to go: Spring–autumn

Floatplanes are not only the easiest and quickest way of reaching this remote tract of mountains in the arctic Alaska, but they also have minimal environmental impact – particularly when combined with a rafting trip on wild rivers like the Kongakut or Noatak.

ECO**FILE**

- Ensure your operator adheres to strict environmental guidelines.

ESSENTIAL**GEAR**

- Shoes with good grip • Sunglasses

ADVENTURE**RATING**

Daring:	ØØ
Eco-friendly:	ØØ
Expensive:	ØØØØØ
Physical:	Ø
Technical:	Ø

Skeleton Coast, Namibia

www.namibiatourism.com.na

Best time to go: Year-round

One of Africa's harshest environments, the Skeleton Coast (see pages 138–9) is mesmerizing from the air. Flying low across the Namib Desert, the transition to teeming ocean is abrupt. First, there are scattered saltpans, blinding white and so flat you can see the crisp shadow of your Cessna 50m (165ft) below. Then a row of dunes, a beach, waves breaking, water churned to froth, and seals in their hundreds, leaping and twisting from the curling green walls of ocean breakers. Banking on a wing tip, you trace the coastline north, towering dunes to your right, angry sea to your left, all the way to the Angolan border.

Great Barrier Reef, Australia

www.gbrmpa.gov.au

Best time to go: Year-round

You need to get airborne to fully appreciate the vast scale of this 2,300km-long (1,400-mile) chain of coral reefs and islands lying off the Queensland coast. Various operators offer scenic flights over the natural wonder, including helicopters that touch down on pontoons moored on the reef.

South Pole, Antarctica

www.adventure-network.com
Best time to go: December– January

It's a far cry from the relentless overland slogs that faced polar explorers a century ago, but a flying adventure to the South Pole is still an epic undertaking, fraught with the possibilities of delay due to extreme weather. Flying from Punta Arenas in southern Chile by Ilyushin jet aircraft, it takes four to five hours to reach Patriot Hills – the only private camp in Antarctica. From there, you fly a further six hours in a Twin Otter ski plane to cover the 1,076km (669 miles) to the South Pole where, despite average temperatures of –30°C (–22°F), you can tour the facilities of the United States Antarctic Program, pose for a photo at the Geographic South Pole and even buy a souvenir at the small shop.

ADVENTURE BRIEFING

With an experienced pilot at the controls all you need to do is enjoy the ride. Most light aircraft flights have luggage restrictions – usually one soft duffel bag weighing up to 10kg (22 lb). Take care getting in and out. Propellers present one obvious hazard, but your pilot will also show you where it's safe to put your feet to avoid damaging the plane. Taking photographs from aircraft presents special challenges. Fit hoods on lenses to cut out window reflections and set high shutter speeds to reduce camera shake caused by vibrations. Switch to manual focus, turn off your flash and try to pick a seat where the view isn't obscured by propellers, wings, curved glass or heat trails from turboprops.

A ski plane can fly you to the snowy wastes beyond the reach of other transport

Licence to thrill

Several locations vie for the title of 'adventure capital of the world', but whether you opt for Queenstown, Victoria Falls, Chamonix, Cusco or Moab, you're guaranteed an adrenaline-charged cocktail of nerve-twanging experiences.

It all started down under. A New Zealand farmer called Bill Hamilton was having trouble reaching parts of his land that were isolated by shallow rivers, so he invented a jet-powered boat that could travel with incredible manoeuvrability in just a few centimetres of water. In 1970, Hamilton's idea was given the tourist spin when Shotover Jetboat rides were launched in Queenstown. In their wake came whitewater rafting. Then someone had the bright idea of jumping off a bridge on a long elastic rope. Once bungee-jumping took off, there was no looking back. People began leaping off mountains clutching wing-shaped parachutes (see page 232) and cavorting through rapid-strewn canyons.

Nowadays, the former gold rush town offers dozens of daredevil activities, from skydiving to riverboarding. And it's not alone. Several tourist centres around the globe, including Victoria Falls and Moab, have evolved their own portfolio of pulse-pounding pursuits (see page 239).

HOW TO GET THE ADRENALINE FLOWING
BASE jumping & skydiving
Parachuting without a plane, BASE jumping involves leaping from anything tall enough to provide a few seconds of freefall, followed by a gentle landing courtesy of a large, specially adapted parachute. The term is an acronym of the four main types of launch platforms – building, antenna, span (bridge or arch) and earth (cliff or the edge of a sinkhole). Key locations include the 267m tall (875ft) New River Gorge Bridge in West Virginia, USA. Even by the standards of other adrenaline activities featured here, BASE jumping is extremely dangerous and claimed at least 120 lives between 1981 and 2007. A far safer way to experience parachuting, tandem skydives (in which you are harnessed to an expert who controls everything) can involve jumps from up to 4,000m (13,000ft) and freefalls in excess of 30 seconds.

Bore surfing
Powerful waves surging upriver, tidal bores are one of the ultimate challenges for extreme surfers. Racing up Qiantang River in China, the

Queenstown, New Zealand – home of the bungee-jump

world's largest bore reaches a height of 8.9m (29.2ft) and a speed of 40km (25mph) per hour – but no one has managed to surf the so-called Silver Dragon for longer than 11 seconds. Other tidal bores occur on Cook Inlet (Alaska), the Amazon (Brazil), the Severn (UK), the Seine (France) and the Indus (India).

Bungee-jumping

An adaptation of a Vanuatu bravery ritual in which tribesmen from Pentecost Island use forest vines to dive off wooden towers, bungee-jumping has become one of the world's most compelling adrenaline activities. Pioneered in Queenstown, New Zealand, where AJ Hackett opened the world's first commercial bungee site at Kawarau Bridge, other major sites now include Bloukrans River Bridge in South Africa and Verzasca Dam, Switzerland, where James Bond's famous leap of faith at the start of the movie *Golden Eye* was filmed.

Canyoning

Negotiating canyons by scrambling, wading, swimming, abseiling and leaping into deep pools, canyoning (or canyoneering) is popular in numerous places around the world, from the intricate slot canyons of Arizona and Utah to the vast sun-scorched gorge of Wadi Mujib in Jordan. A saltwater variation, coasteering involves climbing, jumping and swimming along sections of rocky coastline.

Jetboating

Careering through canyons, inches from sheer rock faces; spinning through wild 360-degree turns and other G-force-inducing shenanigans are all part of the fun of a jetboat ride. Once the sole preserve of New Zealand's Shotover Canyon, jetboating has spread worldwide, from Sydney Harbour to Niagara Gorge.

Riverboarding

Boogie boarding, whitewater sledging, hydro-speeding, riverboarding… whatever you choose to call it, this is the most intimate way to experience the foaming fury of the world's wild rivers. Basically it involves donning wetsuit, lifejacket, helmet and flippers before confronting rapids at face level clinging to a float or board. A recent embellishment, bungee-tethered riverboarding links you to shore by a long bungee cord attached to a rock, tree or bridge. The current stretches the bungee, which then catapults you back upriver skimming across the surface of the water at speeds of up to 50kph (30mph).

Sandboarding

The hugely addictive winter sport of snowboarding has long had a gritty rival in the form of sandboarding (or duneboarding) – popular in several desert destinations, such as Dubai and the Namib. However, it is only recently that volcano boarding – literally playing with fire – has hit the pumice pistes. One of the first volcanoes to be 'carved' was active Mt Yasur in Vanuatu, but it hasn't taken long for adrenaline addicts to sniff out other potential hotspots in countries like Nicaragua. If only powder snow will do, however, try airboarding, where you ride an inflated 'sled' (with moulded runners on the bottom for excellent turning ability) at speeds of more than 80kph (50mph). Canaan Valley in West Virginia has America's only dedicated airboarding terrain park.

IS IT SAFE?

Reputable operators adhere to stringent safety procedures, employ highly trained guides and use well-maintained equipment. Most activities require you to sign an indemnity-waiver form. Check beforehand which, if any, activities are covered by your travel insurance and, if necessary, top up your premium. Do not even consider one of these activities if you suffer from heart conditions, back problems or are pregnant. If in doubt, consult your doctor. Remember, too, that age restrictions will apply to all activities.

Top 3 adventure capitals
Queenstown, New Zealand
www.queenstown-nz.co.nz
Best time to go: Year-round
Take to the skies above Lake Wakatipu and the Southern Alps by helicopter, hang-glider and parachute; descend river canyons by raft, river board and jetboat; sample four different bungee-jumps, including the 134m (440ft) Nevis Highwire; abseil into gorges and swing across them on the 109m (358ft) Shotover Canyon Swing; delve offroad on a 4WD safari; go canyoning, rock climbing and heli-skiing.

Victoria Falls, Zambia & Zimbabwe
www.zambiatourism.com
Best time to go: Year-round
In addition to the world's best one-day, grade V whitewater rafting (see page 194), the stretch of Zambezi downstream of Victoria Falls offers riverboarding and jetboating. The bungee-jump off the bridge into the 100m-deep (330ft) Batoka Gorge is one of the world's highest, while tandem skydiving and flights in open-cockpit microlights and ultralights provide exhilarating views of the Smoke that Thunders.

Moab, USA
www.discovermoab.com
Best time to go: Spring and autumn
Located between Arches and Canyonlands national parks in the rugged Colorado Plateau, Moab is the home of mountain-biking (see page 142), but it also offers jetboating, whitewater rafting, kayaking, canyoning and skydiving.

Contacts

Contents

Main picture: Mule ride, Grand Canyon. Left, from top: Kayaking, New Zealand; tracking chimps, Uganda; camping at Magdalena Bay, Svalbard; Great Barrier Reef

ADVENTURE PLANNING
ADVENTURE TRAVEL SHOWS
Adventure Travel Expo
www.myadventureexpo.com
Adventure Travel Show
www.adventureshow.co.uk
Adventures in Travel Expo
www.adventureexpo.com

CHARITY FUNDRAISING EXPEDITIONS
Across the Divide Expeditions
www.acrossthedivide.com
Adventure Challenge Events
www.acefundraising.co.uk
Charity Challenge
www.charitychallenge.com

EXPEDITION PLANNING
Expeditions West
www.expeditionswest.com
Explorers Web
www.explorersweb.com
Field Skills Expedition Services
www.fieldskills.com
Royal Geographical Society
www.rgs.org
Young Explorers' Trust
www.theyet.org

FIRST-AID TRAINING
Adventure First Aid
www.adventurefirstaid.co.uk
American Red Cross
www.redcross.org
British Red Cross
www.redcross.org.uk
Medic First Aid International
www.medicfirstaid.us
National Outdoor Leadership School www.nols.edu
Slipstream
www.wildernessfirstaid.ca
St John Ambulance
www.sja.org.uk
Wilderness Medicine Institute
www.wmi.net.au

MEDICAL ADVISORY SERVICES
MASTA
www.masta-travel-health.com
National Travel Health Network and Centre www.nathnac.org
Nomad Travel Clinics
www.nomadtravel.co.uk

WILDERNESS SKILLS
Boreal Wilderness Institute
http://boreal.net
Bushmasters
www.bushmasters.co.uk
Outward Bound Wilderness
www.outwardboundwilderness.org
Ray Mears Bushcraft
www.raymears.com
Survival & Safety School
www.survivalandsafetyschool.co.uk
Wilderness Awareness School
www.wildernessawareness.org
Woodsmoke
www.woodsmoke.uk.com

ADVENTURE EQUIPMENT
GENERAL SUPPLIERS
Berghaus www.berghaus.com
BlackWolf www.blackwolf.com.au
Columbia
www.columbia.com
Craghoppers
www.craghoppers.com
Eiger www.eigeradventure.com
Field & Trek
www.fieldandtrek.com
Helly Hansen
www.hellyhansen.com
Karrimor www.karrimor.com
Lifeventure www.lifeventure.co.uk
Lowe Alpine
www.lowealpine.com
Macpac www.macpac.co.nz
Magellan's http://magellans.com
Marmot www.marmot.com
Millets www.millets.co.uk
Mont Adventure Equipment
www.mont.com.au
Mountain Equipment
www.mountain-equipment.co.uk

MSR www.msrgear.com
Nomad Travel
www.nomadtravel.co.uk
The North Face
www.thenorthface.com
Patagonia www.patagonia.com
REI www.rei.com
Rohan www.rohan.co.uk
Salomon
www.salomonsports.com
Snugpak www.snugpak.com
Vango www.vango.co.uk
Vaude www.vaude.de

SPECIALIST SUPPLIERS
Camping equipment
Terra Nova
www.terra-nova.co.uk
Therm-a-Rest
www.thermarest.com

Clothing
Gondwana
www.gondwanaoutdoor.com.au
Solo Mountain
www.solomountain.com
Tilley Endurables www.tilley.com
TOG 24 www.tog24.com

Cooking
Trangia www.trangia.se
Adventure Food
www.adventurefood.com
Expedition Foods
www.expeditionfoods.com
Fuel for Adventure
www.fuelforadventure.com
Wilderness Dining
www.wildernessdining.com

Footwear
Brasher www.brasher.co.uk
Red Chili www.redchili.de
Scarpa www.scarpa.com
Teva www.teva.com

Knives & tools
Leatherman
www.leatherman.com
Petzl http://en.petzl.com
Silva www.silva.se

Suunto www.suunto.com
Victorinox Swiss Army
www.swissarmy.com

Safety & first-aid
Lifesystems
www.lifesystems.co.uk

Water & food storage
Camelbak www.camelbak.com
Nalgene
www.nalgene-outdoor.com
Sigg www.sigg.ch

ADVENTURE TRAVEL
USEFUL DIRECTORIES
AITO www.aito.co.uk
Active World Adventures
www.adrenalinepages.com
AdvenQuest
www.advenquest.com
Adventure Collection
www.adventurecollection.com
Adventure Sports Online
www.adventuresportsonline.com
Adventure Travel
www.2adventure.com
BootsnAll Travel
www.bootsnall.com
Break Loose
www.breakloose.com.au
Butterfield and Robinson
www.butterfieldandrobinson.com
Find my Adventure
www.findmyadventure.com
Gordon's Guide
www.gordonsguide.com
GORP Travel
http://gorptravel.away.com
iExplore www.iexplore.com
Outer Quest
www.outerquest.com
Out There www.out-there.com
Real Adventures
www.realadventures.com
Responsible Travel
www.responsibletravel.com
Travel-Quest
www.travel-quest.co.uk
Travelroads www.travelroads.com
Wild Things www.wildthings.com

GENERAL OPERATORS: UK

Absolute Arctic
www.absolutearctic.com

The Adventure Company
www.adventurecompany.co.uk

Audley Travel
www.audleytravel.com

Bridge & Wickers
www.bridgeandwickers.co.uk

Discover the World
www.discover-the-world.co.uk

Explore! www.explore.co.uk

Exodus www.exodus.co.uk

Expert Africa
www.expertafrica.com

Footloose www.footloose.com

Full Circle Journeys
www.fullcircle-journeys.com

Gecko's
www.geckosadventures.co.uk

Headwater www.headwater.com

The Imaginative Traveller
www.imaginative-traveller.com

Inntravel www.inntravel.co.uk

Intrepid Travel
www.intrepidtravel.com

Journey Latin America
www.journeylatinamerica.co.uk

KE Adventure Travel
www.keadventure.com

Kumuka Worldwide
www.kumuka.com

Last Frontiers
www.lastfrontiers.com

Neilson Active Holidays
www.neilson.co.uk

On The Go Tours
www.onthegotours.com

Peregrine Adventures
www.peregrineadventures.co.uk

Pioneer Expeditions
www.pioneerexpeditions.com

Regent Holidays
www.regent-holidays.co.uk

Sunvil Latin America
http://latin-america-
holidays.sunvil.co.uk/

Travelmood Adventures
www.travelmoodadventures.com

Tucan Travel
www.tucantravel.com

Wild about Africa
www.wildaboutafrica.com

World Expeditions
www.worldexpeditions.com

GENERAL OPERATORS: USA

Absolute Adventure Travel
www.absoluteadventuretravel.com

Adventure Center
www.adventurecenter.com

The Adventure Travel Company
www.atcadventure.com

Adventure Women
www.adventurewomen.com

Austin-Lehman
www.austinlehman.com

Backroads www.backroads.com

Class Adventure Travel
www.cat-travel.com

Classic Journeys
www.classicjourneys.com

Earthquest
www.earthquestadventure.com

Escape Adventures
www.escapeadventures.com

Journeys International
www.journeys-intl.com

Mountain Travel Sobek
www.mtsobek.com

Ocoee Adventure Travel
www.ocoeeadventuretravel.com

Overseas Adventure Travel
www.oattravel.com

Reef & Rainforest
www.reefrainforest.com

REI Adventures
www.rei.com/adventures

Trek America
www.trekamerica.com

Uncommon Adventures
www.uncommonadventures.com

Wilderness Travel
www.wildernesstravel.com

Wildland Adventures
www.wildland.com

GENERAL OPERATORS: REST OF WORLD

50 Plus Expeditions (CA)
www.50plusexpeditions.com
Active New Zealand (NZ)
www.activenewzealand.com
Active Travel Vietnam (VN)
www.activetravelvietnam.com
The Adventure Travel
Company (AUS)
www.adventure-travel.com.au
Adventure Travel New Zealand
(NZ) www.adventuretravel.co.nz
Adventure World (NZ)
www.adventureworld.co.nz
BikeHike Adventures Inc. (CA)
www.bikehike.com
Eldertreks (CA)
www.eldertreks.com
First Light Travel (NZ)
www.firstlighttravel.com
GAP Adventures (CA)
www.gapadventures.com
Midnight Sun Adventure Travel
(CA) www.midnightsuntravel.com
Quest Travel (CA)
www.questtravel.ca
Wild Frontiers (ZA)
www.wildfrontiers.com

SPECIALIST OPERATORS
4WD expeditions

Africa Unlimited Safaris
www.africansafaris.co.za
Andes Offroad
www.andesoffroad.com.ar
Kudu Expeditions
www.kuduexpeditions.com
Masazane Expeditions
www.masazane.co.za
Pangaea Expeditions
www.pangaea-expeditions.com
Red Centre Adventure Tours
www.redcentre.com.au
Safari Drive www.safaridrive.com
Saharan Exploration
www.saharanexploration.co.uk

Bungee-jumping

A J Hackett www.ajhackett.com
Bungee America
www.bungeeamerica.com
Bungee Experience
www.californiabungee.com
Face Adrenalin
www.faceadrenalin.com
Great Canadian Bungee
www.bungee.ca
Taupo Bungy
www.taupobungy.co.nz

Camel riding

Australian Camel Safaris
www.austcamel.com.au
Camel Company Australia
www.camelcompany.com.au
Crazy Camel Safaris
www.crazy-camel.de
Lewa Wildlife Conservancy
www.lewa.org
Mkuru Camel Safari
www.mkurucamelsafari.com
Off the Beaten Track
www.offthebeatentrack.net
Outback Camel Company
www.camelexpeditions.com

Canoeing

Nature Travels
www.naturetravels.co.uk
Pathways www.canoe-yukon.com
Sunrise Canoe and Kayak
www.sunrisecanoeandkayak.com
Timberwolf Tours
www.timberwolftours.com

Canyoning

Adrenalin Antics
www.adrenalinantics.com
AET Nature
www.aetcanyoning.com
American Canyoneering
Association
www.canyoneering.net
Awol Adventures
www.awoladventures.co.nz
Bushsports
www.bushsports.com.au
Deep Canyon
www.deepcanyon.co.nz

Caving

Avalon Adventure
www.outdoorpursuits.co.uk
Green Mountain Holidays
www.greenmountainholidays.ro
Newmark Adventure Tours
www.newmarkadventure.com
Rocksport Mallorca
www.rocksportmallorca.com

Climbing

Climb France
www.climbfrance.com
Earth Treks
www.earthtreksclimbing.com
Ice & Snow
www.iceandsnow.co.uk
Paragon Climbing
www.paragonclimbing.com
Rock and Ice
www.rockandice.net

Conservation expeditions

Biosphere Expeditions
www.biosphere-expeditions.org
Coral Cay Conservation
www.coralcay.org
Earthwatch www.earthwatch.org
Global Vision International
www.gvi.co.uk
Raleigh International
www.raleighinternational.org
Trekforce Worldwide
www.trekforceworldwide.com

Cross-country skiing

Nordic Challenge
www.nordicchallenge.com
The Telemark Ski Company
www.telemarkskico.com
Waymark Holidays
www.waymarkholidays.com
XCuk www.xcuk.com

Dog sledding

Alaska Dog Sledding
www.alaskadogsledding.com
Arctic Husky Adventures
www.arctichuskyadventures.com
Muktuk Adventures
www.muktuk.com

New England Dogsledding
http://newenglanddogsledding.com
Norrlands Snötroll
Sleddogadventures
www.snoetroll.com
Snowy Owl Sled Dog Tours
www.snowyowltours.com
White Wilderness
www.whitewilderness.com
Winterdance Dogsled Tours
www.winterdance.com
Wintergreen Dogsled Lodge
www.dogsledding.com
Uncommon Journeys
www.uncommonyukon.com

Elephant riding

Abu Camp Elephant Back Safaris
www.elephantbacksafaris.com
Addo Elephant Back Safaris
www.addoelephantbacksafaris.co.za
Pilanesberg Elephant-Back Safaris
www.pilanesbergelephantback.co.za
Zambezi Elephant Trails
www.safpar.com

Family adventure travel

Aardvark Safaris
www.aardvarksafaris.com
The Adventure Company
www.adventurecompany.co.uk
Bushbaby Travel
www.bushbabytravel.com
Cox & Kings
www.coxandkings.co.uk
Exodus www.exodus.co.uk
Explore! www.explore.co.uk
Families Worldwide
www.familiesworldwide.co.uk
The Imaginative Traveller
www.imaginative-traveller.com
KE Adventure Travel
www.keadventure.com
Kumuka www.kumuka.com
Peregrine Adventures
www.peregrineadventures.com
Reef & Rainforest Tours
www.familytours.co.uk
Thomson Family Adventures
www.familyadventures.com

Flying adventures
Brooks Range Aviation
www.brooksrange.com
Coastal Aviation www.coastal.cc
Daintree Air Services
www.daintreeair.com.au
Fly Alaska
www.flyalaska.com
GBR Helicopter Group
www.gbrhelicopters.com.au

Horse riding
American Round-up
www.americanroundup.com
Equine Adventures
www.equineadventures.co.uk
Equitour www.equitour.co.uk
Hidden Trails
www.hiddentrails.com
In the Saddle
www.inthesaddle.co.uk
Last Frontiers
www.lastfrontiers.com
Ranch America
www.ranchamerica.co.uk
Ranch Rider www.ranchrider.com
Ride World Wide
www.rideworldwide.com
Unicorn Trails
www.unicorntrails.com
Wild Frontiers
www.wildfrontiers.co.uk

Hot-air ballooning
Balloon Aloft Australia
www.balloonaloft.com
Balloon Sunrise
www.hotairballooning.com.au
Blastvalve www.blastvalve.com
Hot Air Balloons
www.hotairballoons.com
Life Cycle Balloon School
www.lifecycleballoons.com
Magic Horizon Balloons
www.magic-horizon.com
Namib Sky
www.balloon-safaris.com
Scandinavian Balloons
http://balloons-sweden.se
Unicorn Balloon Company
www.unicornballoon.com

Mountain-biking
Adventure Cycling
www.adventurecycling.co.uk
Adventure South
www.advsouth.co.nz
Adventure Travel Group
www.adventuretravelgroup.com
Alaska Backcountry Bike Tours
www.mountainbikealaska.com
Bike Asia www.bikeasia.com
Bike Greece
www.bikegreece.com
Crossroads
http://crossroadscycling.com
Freewheel Holidays
www.freewheelholidays.com
Guided Cycle Tours New
Zealand www.nzcycletours.com
Northern Trails
www.northerntrails.com
Red Spokes
www.redspokes.co.uk
Roc Tours Australia
www.cycletours.com.au
VeloAsia www.veloasia.com
Western Spirit
www.westernspirit.com

Mountaineering
Adventures International
www.exploreyourplanet.com
Alpine Ascents International
www.alpineascents.com
Asian Trekking
www.astrek.com/asiantrekking
Inka Expediciones
www.inka.com.ar

Overlanding
Absolute Africa
www.absoluteafrica.com
Acacia Africa
www.acacia-africa.com
Africa-in-Focus
www.africa-in-focus.com
Bukima Adventure Tours
www.bukima.com
Dragoman Overland
www.dragoman.com
Economic Expeditions
www.economicexpeditions.com

Guerba www.guerba.co.uk
Karakorum Jeep Treks
International www.kjti.co.uk
Oasis Overland
www.oasisoverland.com
Overland Club
www.overlandclub.com
Overlanding Africa
www.overlandingafrica.com

Paragliding
Namibian Paragliding Adventures
www.paraglidingnam.com
Paraglide SA
www.paraglide-south-africa.com
Skysports Paragliding
www.skysports-turkey.com
Soaring Sports USA
www.soaringsportsusa.com

Quad-biking
Cairns ATV Tours
www.atvtours.com.au
California Motorsport
Adventures www.letsatv.com
Colorado ATV Tours
www.coloradoatvtours.com
Quad Bike Tours
www.quadbiketours.co.uk
Uncharted Africa Safari Co.
www.unchartedafrica.co.za

Sailing
American Sail Training
Association
www.tallships.sailtraining.org
Charter World
www.charterworld.com.au
Minorca Sailing Holidays
www.minorcasailing.co.uk
Nautilus Yachting
www.nautilus-yachting.com
Sail Croatia www.sailcroatia.net
Sailing Holidays
www.sailingholidays.com
Seafarer www.seafarersailing.co.uk
Schooner Sail
www.schoonersail.com
Sunsail www.sunsail.co.uk
Whitsunday Escape
www.whitsundayescape.com

Scuba-diving
Abyss Scuba www.abyss.com.au
Aquatours www.aquatours.com
Barefoot Traveller
www.barefoot-traveller.com
Dive Adventures
www.diveadventures.com.au
Divequest www.divequest.co.uk
Dive Worldwide
www.diveworldwide.com
Explorers www.explorers.co.uk
Goldenjoy Dive
www.goldenjoydive.com
Oonasdivers
www.oonasdivers.com
Planet Dive www.planetdive.co.uk
Pro Dive Americas
www.prodiveamericas.com
Regal Dive
www.regal-diving.co.uk
Scuba Safaris
www.scuba-safaris.com
Snooba Travel
www.snoobatravel.co.uk

Sea-kayaking
Adria Adventure
www.adriatic-sea-kayak.com
Canoe Hebrides
www.canoehebrides.com
Coastal Kayaking Tours
www.acadiafun.com
Coral Sea Kayaking
www.coralseakayaking.com
Crystal Seas Kayaking
www.crystalseas.com
Ecosummer Expeditions
www.ecosummer.com
New Zealand Sea Kayak
Adventures
www.seakayakingadventuresnz.com
Northern Lights Expeditions
www.seakayaking.com
The Northwest Passage
www.nwpassage.com
Sea Quest Expeditions
www.sea-quest-kayak.com
Sea to Sky
www.seatoskyexpeditions.com

Southern Sea Ventures
www.southernseaventures.com
Spirit of the West Adventures
www.kayakingtours.com
Spirit Walker Expeditions
www.seakayakalaska.com
Tofino Expeditions
www.tofino.com

Snowmobiling
Alaska Snow Safaris
www.snowmobile-alaska.com
Arctic Trail www.arctictrail.com
Great Canadian
Snowmobile Tours
www.snowmobilerevelstoke.com
High Country Snowmobile
www.hcsnowmobile.com
Jackson Hole Snowmobile Tours
www.jacksonholesnowmobile.com
Old Faithful Snowmobile Tours
www.snowmobilingtours.com
Rocky Mountain
Snowmobile Tours
http://rockymountainsnow.com
Wyoming Adventures
www.wyoming-adventures.com

Surfing
Alacran Surf Tours
www.alacransurf.com
Kai Nalu Surf Tours
www.mauisurfing.com
New Zealand Surf & Snow Tours
www.newzealandsurftours.com
Panama Surf Tours
www.panamasurftours.com
Partama Surf Tours
www.surfpartama.com
Pure Vacations
www.purevacations.com
Rapture Camps
www.rapturecamps.com
United Surf Camps
www.unitedsurfcamps.com
Wavehunters Surf Travel
www.wavehunters.com

Trekking
Collett's Mountain Holidays
www.colletts.co.uk/
Denali Trekking Co.
www.alaskahiking.com
Everest Trekking Canada
www.everesttrekking.com
High Places www.highplaces.co.uk
Himalayan Kingdoms
www.himalayankingdoms.com
Ramblers Worldwide Holidays
www.ramblersholidays.co.uk
Trekking Britain
www.trekkingbritain.com
Trekking Chile
www.trekkingchile.com
The Trekking Company
www.trekking.com.au
Trekking in India
www.trekkinginindia.com
Walks Worldwide
www.walksworldwide.com

Whitewater rafting
Adrift www.adrift.co.uk
Grand Canyon River Outfitters
Association www.gcroa.org
H2O Patagonia
www.h2opatagonia.com
Rafting America
www.raftingamerica.com
RnR Whitewater Rafting
www.raft.com.au
Safari Par Excellence
http://whitewater.safpar.com
Thunderbow Expeditions
www.thunderbowexpeditions.com
Untamed Path
www.untamedpath.com
West Virginia Whitewater
www.wvwhitewater.com
Wet n Wild Rafting
www.wetnwildrafting.co.nz

Wildlife travel
Discovery Initiatives
www.discoveryinitiatives.co.uk
Reef & Rainforest Tours
www.reefandrainforest.co.uk
Wildlife Worldwide
www.wildlifeworldwide.com
Wildwings www.wildwings.co.uk

Index

Acknowledgements

The Automobile Association would like to thank the following photographers, companies and picture libraries for their assistance in the preparation of this book.

Abbreviations for the picture credits are as follows – (t) top; (b) bottom; (c) centre; (l) left; (r) right; (AA) AA World Travel Library.

2 (clockwise from tl) Corrado Giavara/4Corners Images; Philip Schermeister/National Geographic/Getty Images; William Gray; William Gray; Per Breiehagen/Photographer's Choice/Getty Images; William Gray; Pictures Colour Library; William Gray; 7–18 William Gray; 23 Marcel Mochet/AFP/Getty Images; 25 Hulton Archive/Getty Images; 27–36 William Gray; 37 Photolibrary Group; 39–45 William Gray; 50 AA/R Strange; 52t Marwan Naamani/ AFP/Getty Images; 52tc Jacob Taposchaner/Photographer's Choice/Getty Images; 52bc © Mark A Johnson/ Alamy; 52b Serengeti Balloon Safaris, Tanzania www.balloonsafaris.com; 53 World Expeditions; 54c William Gray; 54b Peter McBride/ Aurora/Getty Images; 54r Phil Chapman/naturepl.com; 58–61 William Gray; 62 AA/M Kipling; 65–72 William Gray; 73 AA/G Marks; 74–9 William Gray; 81 Peter McBride/Aurora/Getty Images; 82 AA/N Hicks; 83 AA/A Mockford & N Bonetti; 85 Photolibrary Group; 86/87 Robbie Shone/Aurora/Getty Images; 88 www.wildernessjourneys.com; 90 Peder Sundstrom/Nordic Photos/Getty Images; 93 William Gray; 94c AA/J Poulsen; 94bl William Gray; 94br Johanna Huber/4Corners Images; 95 William Gray; 98 © Danita Delimont/Alamy; 99 Guido Cozzi/4Corners Images; 101 Massimo Ripani/4Corners Images; 102/103 Lesley Donald; 104/105 © Nick Haslam/ Alamy; 106 William Gray; 107 William Gray; 108 © www.dogsledding.co.uk; 109 William Gray; 110 © www.dogsledding.co.uk; 111 William Gray; 112 William Gray; 115 © www.dogsledding.co.uk; 116–120 William Gray; 122cl AA/A Reisinger & V Meduna; 122cr William Gray; 122b © Catherine Ross/Axiom; 126–7 William Gray; 129 © Ted Levine/zefa/Corbis; 130–133 William Gray; 135 © Oasis Overland; 136–42 William Gray; 143 Pictures Colour Library; 145 Alan Becker/The Image Bank/Getty Images; 146 Giovanni Simeone/4Corners Images; 148–51 William Gray; 152t © Geoff du Feu/Alamy; 152b William Gray; 154 Space Adventures, Ltd., www.spaceadventures.com; 156c William Gray; 156bl William Gray; 156br AA/K L Aeder; 160 Brandon Cole/ naturepl.com; 161 William Gray; 163 Photolibrary Group; 164 Stephen Frink/Photographer's Choice/Getty Images; 166/167 Photolibrary Group; 169 © Bob Krist/Corbis; 170–171 William Gray; 173 Stephen Frink/Photographer's Choice/Getty Images; 175 Doug Perrine/naturepl.com; 176 Doug Perrine/naturepl.com; 177 Jeff Rotman/ naturepl.com; 178–88 William Gray; 189 © Getty Images/Photodisc; 190c © Getty Images/ Photodisc; 190b William Gray; 192 World Expeditions; 193 AA/S Watkins; 195 Photolibrary Group; 196 Guido Cozzi/4Corners Images; 198 © WorldFoto/Alamy; 199 AA/J Gocher; 201 Travel Ink/Gallo Images/Getty Images; 202 © Buzz Pictures/Alamy; 205 © David

Fleetham/Alamy; **206–15** William Gray; **216l** Serengeti Balloon Safaris, Tanzania
www.balloonsafaris.com; **216r** Matthias Pinn/4Corners Images; **217–20** William Gray;
221 Christof Sonderegger/Switzerland Tourism; **223** Serengeti Balloon Safaris, Tanzania
www.balloonsafaris.com; **224** Photolibrary Group; **225** Photolibrary Group;
227–9 William Gray; **230** © Suzy Bennett/Alamy; **232–5** William Gray;
237 AA/A Belcher; **240–1** William Gray.

Every effort has been made to trace the copyright holders, and we apologise in advance for
any accidental errors. We would be happy to apply any corrections in any future edition of
this publication.

Front cover: Alan Becker/The Image Bank/Getty Images
Back cover: (l) Philip Schermeister/National Geographic/Getty Images;
(c) Photolibrary Group; (r) Matthias Pinn/4Corners Images

Extracts
All extracts by William Gray:
p. 59   From 'Going for a Song' in *The Sunday Times*
p. 99   From 'Land of the Long White Cloud' in *Odyssey* magazine
p. 109 From 'The Call of the Arctic Wild' in *The Sunday Telegraph*
p. 127 From 'Floral tribute' in *The Sunday Times*
p. 143 From 'A Slow Bike through China' in *Wanderlust* magazine
p. 161 From 'Playing the Reef Detective' in *The Sunday Times*
p. 179 From 'Wet, wet, wet' in *Wanderlust* magazine
p. 193 From 'Postcard from the edge' in *The Sunday Times*
p. 221 Extract not previously published

The AA would like to thank Climate Care for their help.

About the author

William Gray is an award-winning travel writer,
photographer and TV presenter. In 2006, he presented
family travel pieces for the BBC's flagship *Holiday*
programme (attracting over five million viewers).
AITO Travel Writer of the Year 2002, William is currently
a contributing editor and family travel columnist for
Wanderlust magazine and regularly contributes travel
features to *The Sunday Times* and numerous other
national and international publications. The author and
photographer for several guidebooks, editor of Kenya
Airways' *Msafiri* magazine and patron of Coral Cay
Conservation, William lives in the Oxfordshire Cotswolds
with his wife, Sally, and eight-year-old twins, Joe and Ellie.

Written by
William Gray

Project editor
Cathy Hatley

Design
Catherine Murray

Cover design
Nora Rosansky

Cover photograph
© Lee Cohen/Corbis

Picture research
Lesley Grayson

Internal repro work
Sarah Montgomery

Production
Lyn Kirby

Cartography
Mapping Services Department of AA Publishing.
Mountain High Maps® Copyright© 1993 Digital Wisdom, Inc.

Contributors
Stephanie Smith (copy editor); Rebecca Snelling (proofreader); Marie Lorimer (indexer).

ISBN 978-1-4000-0788-2

FIRST EDITION

Important note
The information contained in this book is for reference only and is believed to be correct at the time of printing. Due to the nature of this information it may change from time to time and cannot be guaranteed to remain accurate. The activities described carry inherent risks and should not be undertaken without adequate training, supervision and safety precautions. All activities are undertaken entirely at the discretion and risk of the participant and responsibility will not be accepted for any damage or injury sustained in this respect. Your statutory rights are not affected.

Special Sales
This book is available for special discounts for bulk purchases for sales promotions or premiums. Special editions, including personalized covers, excerpts of existing books, and corporate imprints, can be created in large quantities for special needs. For more information, write to Special Markets/Premium Sales, 1745 Broadway, MD 6-2, New York, NY 10019 or email specialmarkets@randomhouse.com.

The paper used for this book has been independently certified as coming from well-managed forests and other controlled sources according to the rules of the Forest Stewardship Council.

This book has been printed on GardaMatt Art manufactured by Cartiere del Garda, an environmentally sustainable company, ISO 14001 certified and EMAS registered.

Colour separation MRM Graphics.

Printed and bound in Italy by Printer Trento S.R.L., an FSC certifed company for printing books on FSC mixed paper in compliance with the chain of custody and on-products labelling standards.

FSC
Mixed Sources
Product group from well-managed forests and other controlled sources
Cert no. CQ-COC-000012
www.fsc.org
© 1996 Forest Stewardship Council

WIP A03375   10 9 8 7 6 5 4 3 2 1